How Non-being Haunts Being

The Fairleigh Dickinson University Press Series in Communication Studies

General Editor:
Gary Radford, Department of Communication Studies, Fairleigh Dickinson University, Madison, New Jersey

The Fairleigh Dickinson University Press Series in Communication Studies publishes scholarly works in communication theory, practice, history, and culture.

Recent Publications in Communication Studies

Corey Anton, *How Non-being Haunts Being: On Possibilities, Morality, and Death Acceptance* (2020)
Özüm Üçok-Sayrak, *Aesthetic Ecology of Communication Ethics: Existential Rootedness* (2019)
Jennifer Biedendorf, *Cosmopolitanism and the Development of the International Criminal Court: Non-Governmental Organizations' Advocacy and Transnational Human Rights* (2019)
Kate Dunsmore, *Discourse of Reciprocity* (2019)
Paul Matthew St. Pierre, *Cinematography of Carl Theodor Dreyer: Performative Camerawork, Transgressing the Frame* (2018)
Michelle Scollo and Trudy Milburn (eds.), *Engaging and Transforming Global Communication through Cultural Discourse Analysis: A Tribute to Donal Carbaugh* (2018)
Isaac E. Catt, *Embodiment in the Semiotic Matrix: Communicology in Peirce, Dewey, Bateson, and Bourdieu* (2017)
Craig T. Maier, *Communicating Catholicism: Rhetoric, Ecclesial Leadership, and the Future of the American Roman Catholic Diocese* (2016)
Paul Matthew St. Pierre, *Cinematography in the Weimar Republic: Lola-Lola, Dirty Singles, and the Men Who Shot Them* (2016)
Anastacia Kurylo and Tatyana Dumov (eds.), *Social Networking: Redefining Communication in the Digital Age* (2016)
Phil Rose, *Radiohead and the Global Movement for Change: "Pragmatism Not Idealism"* (2015)
Brent C. Sleasman, *Creating Albert Camus: Foundations and Explorations in His Philosophy of Communication* (2015)
Michael Warren Tumolo, *Just Remembering, Rhetorics of Genocide Remembrance and Sociopolitical Judgment* (2015)
Phil Rose, *Roger Waters and Pink Floyd* (2015)
Ronald C. Arnett and Pat Arneson (eds.), *Philosophy of Communication Ethics: Alterity and the Other* (2014)
Pat Arneson, *Communicative Engagement and Social Liberation: Justice Will Be Made* (2014)

On the Web at http://www.fdu.edu/fdupress

How Non-being Haunts Being

On Possibilities, Morality, and Death Acceptance

Corey Anton

FAIRLEIGH DICKINSON UNIVERSITY PRESS
Vancouver • Madison • Teaneck • Wroxton

Published by Fairleigh Dickinson University Press
Copublished by The Rowman & Littlefield Publishing Group, Inc.
4501 Forbes Boulevard, Suite 200, Lanham, Maryland 20706
www.rowman.com

6 Tinworth Street, London SE11 5AL, United Kingdom

Copyright © 2021 by Corey Anton

All rights reserved. No part of this book may be reproduced in any form or by any electronic or mechanical means, including information storage and retrieval systems, without written permission from the publisher, except by a reviewer who may quote passages in a review.

Fairleigh Dickinson University Press gratefully acknowledges the support received for scholarly publishing from the Friends of FDU Press.

British Library Cataloguing in Publication Information Available

Library of Congress Cataloging-in-Publication Data

ISBN 9781683932840 (cloth)
ISBN 9781683932864 (pbk)
ISBN 9781683932857 (electronic)

For:
Kiki, who understood
more than she could say

Contents

Acknowledgments		vii
Preface		ix
1	Nothing at the Heart of Existence	1
2	Life and Many Modes of Bodily Non-being	41
3	Language, Absence, Negation, and Context	83
4	Death and the Possibilities of Human Morality	123
5	A Mythological/Mathematical Postscript	161
Bibliography		169
Index		175
About the Author		181

Acknowledgments

So many people need to be acknowledged and thanked. First and foremost, I need to thank Grand Valley State University for the kind sabbatical release from teaching duties during Winter 2019. As I did the bulk of the writing during that time, I need to express my deepest gratitude. Without such uninterrupted chunks of time, this book would not have come into existence. I also need to thank GVSU's Center for Scholarly and Creative Excellence and the School of Communications for their generosity in supporting this work. I would also like to thank some of my colleagues at Grand Valley, including Robert Mayberry, Maria Cimitile, Jonathan K. Hodge, Allen Whipps, Judy Whipps, Vandana Pednekar-Magal, Mark Pestana, Stephen C. Rowe, Ivo Soljan, Richard Joanisse, Avis Hewitt, Kathryn Remlinger, and Peter Zhang.

I must acknowledge several academic organizations. The Media Ecology Association (MEA), the National Communication Association, especially the Philosophy of Communication Division and Communication Ethics Division, and the Institute of General Semantics (IGS) have all provided me with space and time to present bits and pieces of these ideas in various locales over the past decade.

I need to thank Lance Strate, Thom Gencarelli, Ed Tywoniak, Paul Lippert, Phil Rose, Teresa Manzella, Dennis Cali, Stephanie Bennett, Paul Soukup, Barry D. Liss, Robert K. Logan, Michael Plugh, Jonathan Slater, and others of the MEA for helping me think about these ideas. I also want to thank and acknowledge Martin H. Levinson, Jacqueline Rudig, and Mary Lahman from the IGS.

I want to recognize and acknowledge a collection of many friends who have talked with me about the book in some form or other. I well know that a few of my friends not only disagree with various views expressed here and would hold counterpositions, but I need to acknowledge the many people who have helped me to think about these issues, often more than they knew. I want to thank Bryan Wehr, Phil Paradowski, Tom Koster, Matt Wass, Kim Helmers, Brian Esparsa, Lynn Brouwer, Robin Andreozzi, Valorie Putnam, Jamie Cross, Rayme Bracken, Brenda "Millie" Payne, Tom McCarthy, Ray Feenstra and Sue Feenstra, Jeremy Czarniak and Polly Czarniak, Toby Moleski, Brent Newville and Marge Newville, Mark Zuidema, Natalie Sydorenko, Laurel Humphreys, Stephen Matchett and Karen Matchett.

I need to express my deepest thanks and appreciation to Valerie V. Peterson for all of her support, encouragement, and detailed assistance in the preparation of this manuscript. She has been there with me through it all. The book, as a whole, has been improved significantly by her many useful suggestions.

For assistance during the final stages I wish to thank and acknowledge Chad Hansen, John Dowd, Jermaine Martinez, Eric S. Jenkins, Leon Cerdena, Joseph Gemin, and Elizabeth Ketcham Kheder.

Finally I need to thank the Josiah Macy Jr. Foundation for their kind permission to reprint the "Diagram for discussion purposes referred to as 'onionskin,'" taken from Bateson's 1955 lecture/group discussion, published in 1956.

Preface

This book attempts to open some room for spirituality amidst thoroughgoing death acceptance. Too commonly, if people say that they do not believe in life after death but that they are not atheists, many Christians (and other religious folks, too) seem confused and doubt that such a position is possible. Or, if it is seen as possible, it is accused of sliding inevitably into nihilism. This work show the contrary: accepting death, and thereby that non-being haunts being, in no way necessitates nihilism. In fact, living a lie—publically claiming to "know" what one privately doubts or even disbelieves—is a subtler, more pervasive and dangerous nihilism in today's world. Nihilism does not come from honest inquiry, humility, and acceptance; rather, it comes from the failures invited by haughty self-importance, wishful thinking, and overdrawn expectations.

The book also carves out a space between two kinds of dogma: on the one hand, scientific dogma that claims agency and choice are epiphenomenal illusions within a fully deterministic universe, and, on the other hand, religious dogma that suggests that "free will" comes from God but only because this world, with all of its hardships and challenges, is an illusory trial, a testing ground for the afterlife. In contrast to those popular views, this work outlines how agency emerges from possibilities provided by the body's sensorimotor powers and its communicative capacities. It furthermore illustrates how agency matters in and for this world. All said, agency reveals its true character only where non-being discloses its relation to being. Were there no non-being in the world, there would be no possibilities, and, were there no possibilities, there would be no moral agency.

The arguments and illustrations advanced throughout seek to defend the reality of this world, which includes phenomena such as agency, choice, meaning, and negation. Agency is not epiphenomenal, and our decisions matter not because life is some kind of cosmic trial, but because there is always something larger than one's own life. At the least, there are always others before one's birth and after one's death, even if we can be conscious of such others only while we are alive. One's death is the end of one's possibilities, but it is not the end of the world. Others have funded our possibilities, at least partly, by the resources they have left in their wake, just as we fund others' possibilities through what we leave in the world that outlives us. It is only here, in this world, where our decisions and actions critically matter. We are part of the cosmos, and agency is one of the possibilities that have come to fruition within it.

People need to wake up to the new millennium. If there is any possibility of individuals wising up, taking better care of each other, seeing to the physical needs of all people, answering the call to lessen social inequality, and becoming better stewards of the planet, it will come by a revolution in self-understanding. The arguments and examples presented here, obviously, are not meant as "the answer" to such massively complex social problems, but, hopefully, they offer the beginning of the kinds of self-examination necessary if people are to grow up and head in the right direction. If people can understand how they fit with the rest of the cosmos and grasp how natural they are to all that is, they might learn the kinds of humility and gratitude that help them become better neighbors and citizens of the world.

We must have acumen of perception, a willingness to think in the largest of possible contexts, a readiness to examine our experiences and to document what shows itself, and, then, we will need to ask ourselves what all of this means and how to respond most fittingly.

This book completes a trilogy of existential thought. Those who have read my earlier works, *Selfhood and Authenticity* and *Sources of Significance*, will easily note many complements and connections to the ideas presented here.

Chapter One

Nothing at the Heart of Existence

PRELUDE TO NON-BEING

A time there was when each of us was not, and now, here we are among the living. And, presumably, there will be a time when each of us no longer exists.[1] Sandwiched between the two receding horizons of birth and death rests the daily reminder where all concerns, differences, and distances vanish from conscious awareness. Night after night, we temporarily undergo the full erasure of consciousness during dreamless sleep.

But "non-being" far surpasses these three limit cases: it haunts waking life and conscious experience through and through. It is a requisite condition for language and symbolic representation; for the experience of meaning and value; and for features of the universe, including "timeless" logical truths, to show themselves as such. Our conscious experience, our sense of past and future, our ability to imagine what could or should be done, and our ability to make choices and decisions, all of these depend upon modes of absence, incompleteness, and negation. Hence, we not only are partly aware of facts of absences and of incompleteness, but, more significantly, modes of absence and of incompleteness are partly what make awareness possible.

We are, as Jean-Paul Sartre would say, ongoing projects of having to be our possibilities.[2] Early adolescence is painfully filled with questions such as "What will I do with my life? How do I fit with everything else? Does my life matter at all?" And mature adults commonly contemplate their death and the meaning of their life, especially as death grows noticeably nearer. But death is not merely a biological event that everyone eventually undergoes. It is also the horizon of intelligibility informing everyone's entire life journey. This is what Martin Heidegger means by "being-toward-death."[3] This is not the death of the deathbed, but the awareness of our "certain-yet-indeterminate death,"[4] an awareness that serves as a "call to conscience" that informs our thoughts and decisions. Alphonso Lingis, in his provocative book, *The Community of Those Who Have Nothing in Common*, illustrates the connection between non-being, thought, and meaning where he writes,

> When I drive distances at night, I, like Simeon Stylites on his pillar in the Egyptian deserts, invariably fall into extremist spiritual exercises revolving around the theme of *Memento mori*, reviewing the meaning or meaninglessness of my life in the cosmic voids ahead.[5]

Death, then, is not simply a future event but an ongoing framework within which the meaning of existence can be contextualized as a whole. The question then arises: can we learn that there is one and only one community—the community of the dying? Look around you. The one true community is not based on race, nationality, age, belief, ideology, and so on. It excludes no one. *We are all dying, and we are dying together.*

The more candidly one thinks about it, the clearer it becomes that being is engulfed and surrounded by nothing at birth and death and then shot through with non-being all along throughout existence. As someone currently existing, you are becoming yourself, aging and growing, and giving birth to new senses of self, as well as casting off earlier beliefs and assumptions. As someone who now "is," you soon enough will be, at least for yourself, somewhat similar to what you were before you were born: in the realm of the "is not." There are admittedly important differences between "never having been" and "no longer existing," as only the dead have the privileges and rights that come with the latter, while the former—those who never have been—are nothing but an imagined possibility of the living! To be dead is to bear the possibility of now existing in the minds and practices of others; it is to have made one's mark in history however massive or miniscule, for good or ill. Indeed, the world remains populated by other people; there were others who predated one's appearance in life and there are others who will live on after one has died. And yet, only those who currently exist can make such distinctions.

Critics of different stripes, both religious and scientific, might maintain that once a human being is conceived, that being, as a soul, exists forever in some form. And some critics might say that souls preexist conception. Others, too, might suggest that reincarnation is a wholly natural phenomenon whereby intangible spirits are recycled across the diversity of life. All such claims amount to deep denial of non-being. Admittedly, no one can say authoritatively that there is no life after death nor can they authoritatively claim that individuals did not exist in some form prior to their current existence. No one knows from direct experience that such claims are false, and, moreover, there are both near-death experiences and psychedelic experiences where people subsequently claim to have been on "the other side of life" as well as reports in depth psychology where some people claim to have knowledge of having lived prior lives. The dubiousness of all such accounts is that they remain hearsay from the living to the living.

In contrast, I take my lead from points of departure that show themselves to everyday experience: (1) the universe did not begin with our birth, and we did not give birth to ourselves, meaning there was a time when each of us was not; (2) we recess night by night into the non-being of consciousness that is dreamless sleep; and, finally, (3) we, each of us, know of others who are no longer with us, others who can be remembered, invoked, and emulated, but who are materially absent from the world and yet intangibly present within it.

The human world is, in fact, filled with absent presences, the deceased but remembered and vicariously present: actors, athletes, artists, authors, celebrities, heroes, musicians, neighbors, pets, playwrights, poets, political figures, relatives, and so on. They are lodged in human memories, carved into statues, printed on money, caught on canvas, captured in text and on film, recorded on tape and vinyl, conveyed by language all along, and they inform and structure people's assumptions, orientations, and life practices. Ancestor worship is part of the fabric of human life everywhere.

What is the "fitting response"[6] to these obvious facts of existence? Could there be any greater ingratitude than the unwillingness to accept our noble yet humble lot? It is humble because we are finite, but it is noble because we are able to meaningfully ask how we relate to everything else that is. We started with absolutely nothing, took on a name, came to self-awareness, had many adventures for good or ill, experienced adversity, hardship, and loss as well as art, laughter, love, and music, and we grew through challenges and struggles of all sorts, but with all of that, we end with nothing. To exist is to know of the profound nothing that bookends our lives; it is to open to the possibility of knowing non-being as a gift, the condition of life's meaningfulness.

If you want a mature laugh that comes from honest self-recognition and acceptance, watch the witty ending of Monty Python's satirical movie *The Life of Brian*. Here, criminals and the wrongly accused are being crucified but still "look on the bright side of life," reminding the audience: "You started with nothing and you end with nothing. What have you lost? Nothing!"

AN OVERVIEW OF THE MAIN ARGUMENT

Absence, incompleteness, negativity, non-being, and nothing all have an undeserved bad reputation. The popular imagination, Kenneth Burke suggests, likes to "avoid the negative and emphasize the positive," and many people assume negativity is undesirable and something we should reject or avoid. On the other hand, many people take "nothing" to be wholly imaginary or unreal, little other than a verbal phantom. They underestimate or simply fail to notice how absence and incompleteness function in everyday life. Also, the idea of nothing is often associated with nihilism, the belief that life is pointless, absurd, and without any real purpose or value. "Nothing" obviously needs some better publicity, a sustained campaign to help people appreciate how "non-being," in fact, is the underlying source of many of those distinguishing characteristics of humanity: temporal openness, the experience of fiction, imaginative thoughts about the future, contemplation of eternal truths, and the experience of meanings, values, and moral choices.

For too long and in countless ways, people have ignored, underestimated, or even denied how non-being undergirds life, especially human life. This isn't all that surprising, for what could be less empirically available, less tangible, and less measurable, than non-being? Part of the difficulty here is that people commonly want to know what nothing or non-being "is" or where it can be found. They seem to believe that "nothing" or non-being must be an extant being, one more piece of the world's furniture, or at least something that fits into the contemporary scientific world picture. Although various mystic religions have incorporated the idea of nothing into their doctrines, some making it a central idea, mainstream Christianity and Western thought more generally, going all the way back to Parmenides, have had an aversion to "nothing" and have traditionally taken the idea to be an aberration, a kind of horror of untruth, an impossibility:

> The concept of Nothing, in Western thought, is a paradox. We simply cannot accept, no less conceive of, the paradoxical concept that "Nothing exists," given that we learn to think and reason in the Western tradition, which is based on Aristotelian logic. The Age of Reason, the Enlightenment, and the scientific method have trained us to think otherwise—rationally, that is. In the material world, which we inhabit, the very words "Nothing exists" are a contradiction in terms, an oxymoron.[7]

Today, most generally stated, popular Western thought tries to deny the "reality" of nothing or non-being because people cannot locate nothing out in nature. "Nothing" does not occur on the periodic chart of the elements, and we do not have any scientific instruments for its discovery.

One can look for nothing, scour the natural world and examine things all day long and never find what is not there. But the very words "look for" and "examine" are already part of the non-being that haunts being; the dimensions of meaning within these words are what we need to attend to if we wish to understand "non-being." They refer back, if only obliquely, to the "non-being" this book is trying to disclose and interrogate. For certainly, we do not look for what is plainly in sight. We only look for what is not yet in view, attained, or fully grasped. We examine only when we know we have incomplete knowledge, when we know that we do not fully comprehend something. Experience, in fact, always unfolds within horizons such that much remains hidden, out of the range of sight or hearing or imagination or comprehension. Moreover, even when in plain sight, objects can be nebulous, multilayered, changing (i.e., including dimensions of the not-yet and no-longer), only partly grasped, and, of course, misidentified or misunderstood.

Hans Jonas nicely captures how our drive for truth is a possibility only because we can be mistaken, in error, deceived. He writes, "the experience of truth, as simultaneous exposure of untruth, includes an element of *negation* . . . the capacity for truth presupposes the capacity to negate, and that therefore only a being that can entertain negativity, that can say 'no,' can entertain truth."[8] Only beings haunted by non-being—only beings who can know that they do not know, only beings who can dwell in the awareness of error as fact, only beings who experience mystery—could seek to know the truth at all, including the obscure, uncertain, and, perhaps, unknowable truth of their ultimate origin and their final destination.

Although the basic argument of this book is fairly simple to state, making it clear and obvious requires walking through a wide range of subarguments, detailed expositions, and carefully considered examples. The basic claim is that "non-being haunts being," and a secondary claim is that "non-being brings possibilities and moral agency." Obviously, much more will need to be said regarding the meaning of the words *non-being*, *possibilities*, and *moral agency*. Explaining those terms, clarifying what they mean individually and when combined, is what this book is all about.

A host of related terms and concepts need to be differentiated and clarified, as *nothing*, most generally defined, is the blanket term and common ancestor for all of the following related distinctions: *non-being, nothingness, nonexistence, negativity, syntactical negation, no, naught, is not, past, future, not yet, no longer, then, later, earlier, absence, incompleteness, zero, the empty set, irony, fiction, illusion, play, pretend, false, errors, accidents, mistakes, otherness, opposition, difference, distinction, don't, prefixes, suffixes, threats, warnings, regrets, revisions, promises, values, meanings, significances*, and so on.

This exploration is needed because of the crisis in thought precipitated by the integration of religious dogma and the dogmas associated with reductive, materialistic, and behavioristic naturalisms into daily life. The challenge is to reconcile the meaning of nature by fully and completely grasping the fact that humans are natural. This means that "nature itself" has already made room for art, imagination, mathematics, music, religion, and many other forms of purpose and intention that, de facto, incorporate and rely upon modes of incompleteness and non-being.

Philosophers traditionally have ruminated over the question, "Why is there something rather than nothing?" In doing so, they have assumed an "either/or" approach where a "both/and" strategy is required. Indeed, why must the situation be framed as "something *rather than* nothing" or "nothing *rather than* something"? Nothing inherently coexists along with something. The universe, and life, too, could not have occurred without non-being, for any delimited "something" always already implies boundaries that would mark whatever is *not* that something. Consider this: if the universe is infinitely expanding, then what is it expanding into and why is that not just more universe? Also, if life could only emerge from the materiality of the physical universe with all of its actual forces and chemical properties, then isn't that, in some important ways, always already partly assumed within what we mean by life? R. D. Laing provocatively writes, "'Is' as no-thing, is that whereby all things are. And the condition of the possibility of anything being at all is that it is in relation to that which it is not."[9] Hence, in contrast to "something *rather than* nothing," what we have is "nothing" ineradicably tagging along on the hither side of being. Perhaps a better question for rumination, then, is: *How, exactly, does non-being haunt being?*

Part of the challenge in attending to forms and operations of non-being is that nothing is not made of anything, nor can it be confined to rigid boundaries of space or time. Non-being, like thought and time, concerns the ongoing delimitations and demarcations by which something is not something else. For example, where are the boundaries that turn the present into the past, or that render the future as now the present? What is it that separates one thought from another? Individual words bear a meaning while utterances accomplish layers of meaning irreducible to the individual words comprising the utterances, but where are the boundaries between words while the words are actively incorporated into a particular utterance? Where, exactly, is the utterance meaning? What separates a person from his or her age, a place from its moment? If not for the intelligibility that thought makes possible, how could such questions occur or be answered?

Thought is that peculiar kind of time that inherently traffics in modes of non-being. Thought deals with an intelligible horizon of *possible* relations, *possible* events, and *possible* facts. Any thought that would deal exclusively in actualities wouldn't be thought at all. Any and all thought, even thought taken to be objectively aligned with the facts, always remains a symbolic representation, an abstraction. Not only does thought handle possibilities per se, but also communication technologies have made such possibilities more salient. Perhaps a few examples will help to clarify what is at stake here.

Consider, as a first example, how boring any sport or game is when reduced to the raw present actions taking place at any given moment. Basically, a bunch of people are standing around, some more active than others, and the focal point, for example, a ball, is simply and only wherever it is at any point. It moves from spot to spot and attention follows it, but anybody really into a sport, whether he or she realizes it or not, is a whirlwind of negativity. The game is so animated and lively, and commands such attention, because of continuous thought about what *might* be the case. What could happen and what might happen, as well as who wants what to happen, are essential parts of any game. Possible pasts, now made more real than ever because of modern communication technologies, exist in televisual form. In a recent football game, two teams battled it out for the playoffs. The home team is trailing behind by only five points with a mere eleven seconds left on the clock; they are in a "do or die" situation. The sports announcers stress that, with over forty yards to the goal line, the underdogs will need a touchdown or they are out of the playoffs. If they make the score, they go on to the next round to play the current leaders of the division. The center snaps the ball and, almost miraculously, the quarterback gets great protection. The wide receiver, faking left and button-hooking right, loses his defender and is out in the clear, absolutely wide-open down field. The quarterback pumps once and then launches the perfect pass directly to his wide receiver, but the wide receiver, noticing that he is fully in the clear, turns his eyes away and accidently lets the ball pass right through his hands. The crowd goes ballistic! Caught on instant replay, millions of people live and live again, over and over, a possible past, one where the athlete successfully caught the ball. During each replay of the segment, the broadcasters groan on how "out in the clear" the receiver was and how the team obviously "would have" won *if* he had caught it and how they *would have been* positioned in the playoffs. Millions of people were dwelling collectively in what "could have been" and what "might have been."

But non-being, obviously, is more than the source of vitality and excitement within games and sporting events. The incorporation of non-being into being is also the basis of the human experience of "fashion." Somewhat similar to the freeze-frame function in film or to an instant replay, photographs, as still shots, accelerate the sense of transience, and they thereby heighten awareness to the sense of fashion.[10] Georg Simmel captures this point quite well where he writes,

> fashion's question is not that of being, but rather it is simultaneously being and non-being; it always stands on the watershed of the past and the future and, as a result, conveys to us, at least while it is at its height, a stronger sense of the present than do other phenomena. . . . If . . . we are convinced that the phenomenon will vanish just as rapidly as it came into existence, then we call it fashion.[11]

If not for the inclusion of non-being into being, the experience of fashion would be impossible.

Something similar could be said, though at a different temporal scale, of antiques, relics, and ancient artifacts. Antiques, relics, and ancient artifacts are haunted by non-being if only because they are here present before us, and yet the particular world into which they originally fit is now absent. And when an antique or artifact goes up for auction, conscious deliberation regarding its final price will attend to its current condition, as well as verbal and other symbolic accounts of its likely (i.e., possible) past and its anticipated (i.e., possible) future value.

As a final initial example, consider how any insurance representative's task is to depict possible futures in such a way that customers will invest money to offset costs in the event of an accident or disaster, whereas the insurance company basically takes money from customers, banking on the chances that the events will not occur. Insurance paperwork admittedly drips with "hard numbers," "facts," and "fine print" regarding optional riders and liability clauses, spells out all of these in exacting specificity, but, despite all of this, the world of insurance is largely a world of what does *not* occur. In fact, insurance providers directly gain from having people pay for what *never* occurs, and the more that people are willing to pay for what never occurs, the more lucrative the company. So, although the company will tell potential customers that they should get coverage because there are chances that something bad could happen, the companies make their money by successfully managing two different stories. For us, the insured, insurance is basically a form of inverse gambling: we pay now hoping to lose less later. But, perhaps obviously, the fact of non-being offers its own obstacles: witness the differences between pharmaceuticals designed to "do things" (e.g., relieve pain or lessen symptoms) and pharmaceuticals designed to "keep things from happening" (e.g., vaccines or preemptive forms of medicine). The latter can be deemed unwarranted by some insurance providers or an unnecessary demand to some patients because, if the drugs work, people may not be sure that it was, in fact, the drugs that prevented what could have happened from happening. "Stay-at-home" and "shelter-in-place" orders issued by state and local governments during the recent COVID-19 outbreak also illustrates this challenge: some people took the absence and slowing of the spread to be proof that social distancing measures were working while others experienced it as evidence that people were overreacting to, or overestimating, the threat. Preventive measures, the "precautionary principle" more generally, and other forms of proactive care, can suffer from this basic asymmetry. More on this issue later and also in chapter 4.

These four simple examples (games, fashion, antiques, and insurance) are a few of countless examples that could have been offered to illustrate how thought, as a mode of non-being, infects the human world. At the least, as I show in detail throughout the rest of this work, "temporality," "thought," "possibility," and "agency," taken together, compose a single phenomenon: a conglomeration of non-being. They are tightly tied knots of existential negation. Hence, species of non-being are inseparable from the operations of conscious thought, the experience of temporality, the sense of possibilities in a meaningful intersubjective world, and, ultimately, the facts of human agency and morality. Without non-being, there would be no thought, no experienced temporality, no possibility, no meaning, no agency, and no morality.

The preliminary task ahead is to show that even if non-being comes to its fullest expression within humanity, it is nevertheless something happening in nature, and, moreover, humans are precisely the part of nature that opens to ever-expanding ranges of possibilities.

A RANGE OF CONSIDERATIONS REGARDING NOTHING

Some critical readers may be skeptical of the above claims regarding "nothing" or "non-being," believing both to be little other than symbolic abstractions, linguistic confusions, or, perhaps, verbal tricks. These critics might furthermore argue that there is only a material reality without gaps in causal connections, however tenuous and distant. If asked about non-being or nothing, they may be inclined to respond along the lines of: "There is no such thing as nothing; non-being does not exist. The nearest we can get to nothing," they might think, "is a vacuum, but even a vacuum is not necessarily empty of certain kinds of unknown particles nor void of the influences of various forces." "The only place where one can unquestionably find nothing or non-being," such critics might continue, "is in language or symbols, or perhaps in the conscious experience of unfulfilled expectations, but not in nature." This position is fair enough, and it seems reasonable, but further scrutiny reveals problematic ambiguities and residual challenges.

An immediate difficulty facing those who would deny the existence of non-being is that they are quickly thrown into what seems to be, at least at some level, a contradictory position. To say that something does not exist is to negate that something, and, in the act of negating it, we find a kind of non-being that cannot be denied. It is, at best, ironic to claim that nothing (or non-being) does not exist, and, at worst, it is self-defeating, as it reflects a flat-out failure to see how non-being infects the human world and thereby nature itself. At this point, critical skeptics of non-being might become irritated, as they began their criticism by suggesting that talk about nothing is just a verbal trick and the response offered here seems to illustrate that fact once again: this discussion still seems highly limited to the domain of language and conscious experience. Perhaps there is something to this concern, and so an initial sticking point is that we cannot deny our ability to talk about what is not the case, nor would it make sense to deny that we can meaningfully employ the concepts of negation or zero. Nevertheless, it will take some more nuanced arguments and examples to show unmistakably how those verbal and cognitive capacities depend on a much more pervasive ground of non-being.

As one simple example, notice that when people speak with one another, any words uttered are uttered in what amounts to a moment of "now," (i.e., uttered words occur within a present situation), and, in that sense, they can appear to be mere organismal sounds occurring within a highly circumscribed there-and-then. But words as words, more than mere sounds, afford people the possibility of transcending the immediate here and now and of opening themselves to situations having variable scope and circumference. People can talk about two weeks earlier, yesterday, tomorrow, or ten years from now. They can talk about their favorite pet or movie from childhood, can bring up a disagreement from years ago, or can outline possible responses to anticipated future threats. In such pedestrian cases, people escape and transcend the immediacy of the moment during which the words are uttered, and, instead, they dwell in expansive meaning-horizons that the words make possible. By way of language, people are somehow "other than" exclusively in the space and time of the words as mere sounds. The speech sounds are thus negated as sounds, denied as organismal exhalations present in the immediate environment; they become vehicles for what they are not, abstract intersubjective representations for distance places and entities. Here, most obviously, non-being haunts being.

We thus need to stress, once again, that the claim "nothing exists" is the most general expression for the fact that non-being lurks within being on many different levels of analysis. And it is, as I try to show in chapter 2, important not to sequester non-being to humanity and the linguistic realm. Moreover, just for the sake of argument, even if it were the case that "nothing" could be reducible to its occurrence within human language and human cognition, these themselves are parts of the universe, something within nature per se. One simple way to clarify this issue is to examine what I will be calling the "A-Naturalist Fallacy," which refers to the imagined separation proposed but then surreptitiously denied between "nature" and "humanity." The recurrent difficulty occurs partly because terms that appear as oppositions (e.g., "nature" versus "humanity," or "body" versus "mind") are in fact dependent hierarchies of different levels, where the former term serves as the environment for the latter.[12]

One way to illustrate the A-Naturalist Fallacy in contemporary thought is to examine how common sense depicts memory and imagination. People commonly treat both memory and imagination as subjective and wholly personal. Memory and imagination are taken to be mental or psychological and hence phenomena to be set in contrast with factually objective "reality itself." In posing such an oppositional contrast, people partly accept the continuities of humanity with the rest of the animal world, via genetics and evolution, but then they also issue a cleft between subject and object in nature, one that omits the former.

People commonly say that memory is "subjective" or something "personal," something other than "objective or factual." To say as much implies that different people have different recollections of events commonly experienced. For example, ten people get together, have a small dinner party, and then, years later, they all get together and talk about the event that took place earlier. Not only do some people initially fail to remember the event, but others fail to remember specific details of the occasion (who wore what, what were the topics of conversations, how late the event ran, and so on). Others wrongly recall what was had for dinner or disagree over who said what to whom, or how much someone drank, and so on. Cast in this way, we attend mainly to the discrepancies between the different accounts: the vague ways that individual memories diverge. We overstress the ways that memory is something "internal," subjective, and outside of "nature itself." But if we recast the account, it becomes apparent that we have under-recognized the processes by which new forms of temporality have emerged in nature; we failed to reckon with memory as one of nature's organs for new species of pasts. We focused on the individual differences between the accounts, whereas, in contrast, we should have registered the miraculousness of the group being able to entertain an event shared a decade earlier. Such brain capacities make memory much more than individual or even human per se. When the ancient Greeks thought of memory under the name *Mnemosyne* and took her to be a god, they were registering that memory is cosmic: our memories are nothing less than the manner by which certain kinds of past have become evolutionarily possible within nature.

The A-Naturalist Fallacy also spontaneously crops up in responses to questions such as "Is there music in nature?"; "Does nature make art?"; and "Does nature have intention within it?" The common reply is: "No. Humans make art and music, but we cannot find nature itself producing either. Nature is without intention." Indeed, many people are inclined to suggest that nature "In Itself" is bereft of such phenomena, to which they might quickly add, "These are aspects of the human realm." The problem with the common reply is that it treats humans and human intentions as other than natural and simultaneously comprehends less than the whole of nature; it assumes that people are not continuous with nature. It is easy to imagine that "humanity" and "nature" are mere opposites, but, as Anthony Wilden suggests, "these imaginary opposites are not of the same level of reality or logical type: the second is the environment of the first: they form a dependent hierarchy."[13] Humans are part of nature and so nature already includes phenomena such as art, music, and intention more generally. Consciousness is natural; it is part of nature, for surely humans are not *not* natural. We might not feel at one with nature, as people today commonly draw a line between themselves and nature; they try to get "back to" nature or to "protect" nature. They have, to evoke a line from Kenneth Burke, "separated themselves from their natural conditions by instruments of their own making."[14] They think somewhat along the lines of "we are over here" and "nature is over there." They also set "the natural" in contrast to "the cultural and sociohistorical." We admittedly can draw such separations and even imagine that these items now form oppositions, but one is part of the other.

Conceptual obstacles await those who assume that if something such as "0" (or any number for that matter) cannot be located within the confines of empirical nature, then it does not exist at all. The A-Naturalist Fallacy occurs whenever people fail to grasp that humans are the part of nature that has intention, creates art and music, calculates with numbers, and lives in a world made moral by countless forms of negativity. Clearly, humans are the parts of nature that "art," the parts of nature that expressly calculate, quantify, group, and reason. The whole of the cosmos includes everything, including humans and all of their creations, and all of those dimensions of imagination and memory made possible in and through the site of nature known as "humanity." The A-Naturalist Fallacy, then, also forces the issue that, at the very least, "nothing" and "non-being" are words, human creations, and, as such, they are already included in all that is.

Non-being is inherent to human life: humans emerge from their progenitors and then fall back to the earth in their ceasing to be alive. Non-being is the very fabric, the warp and woof, of everyday life. We get hungry or thirsty, thus feeling ourselves somehow connected to and driven by what we ourselves are not. Relationships can change so that friendships, neighbors, and jobs are no longer. Someone remembers a building that was demolished and is no longer "there." The non-being of the now-absent building is not wholly reducible to memories of it or our statements about it. They are, to be sure, part of the way that the non-being of the building shows itself, but the non-being of the building is other (and much less) than either statement or memory. When we experience that pain that comes from recalling loved ones who have passed away, the pain is more than merely subjective, as it is registering an objective fact in the world: the others are now gone. Imagine, then, for further illustration, that someone is slightly upset because a friend is overdue for a returned phone call. A critic might claim that there is no non-being here. For a contrasting account, they point to brain states, hormones, cultural expectations within friendship bonds, and other measurable variables, all of which, they claim, collectively can account for the person becoming upset. The critic is correct to point to all of these factors and to other factors, too (e.g., lack of stoic virtues such as equanimity), but a pernicious and subtle fact remains: the *unreturned* call is part of the overall situation. In a similar way, fictions, and dreams too, have their own mode of non-being etched within them, mainly because they are about something that they themselves are not. Perhaps the ultimate fiction, any "path not taken," clearly illustrates how thought, as that time that inherently deals with forms of possibilities, haunts the human world.

The immediate job ahead is to clarify possible objections as well as reveal modes of absence, incompleteness, negation, and non-being that operate *prior to*, *beneath*, and *in conjunction with* various verbal forms. I now offer a brief and highly selective review of five thinkers who have made significant contributions to the topic of nothing: Henri Bergson, Martin Heidegger, Jean-Paul Sartre, Kenneth Burke, and Terrence W. Deacon. This review is not in any way meant to be definitive or exhaustive. Rather, it is meant as a heuristic overview. It is designed to further set the context for the main ideas explored throughout the rest of this book.

I must underscore that the goal ahead is not to winnow out "the" definition of "nothing," but rather it is to show the wide range of interconnected phenomena that relate back to nothing broadly construed, to illustrate the variety of interrelated concepts and terms that deal with species of non-being and negation. The interplay between and among the different thinkers helps to illustrate the varied terrain in which "non-being," most generally and loosely termed, shows itself. If there is a general narrowing point to be gained across the lot, it is that non-being tarries along on the "other side" of being—*is invisibly nestled within being, is intangibly incorporated into being*—and is not a denial of being so much as being's vital complement and counterpart.

Henri Bergson: The Idea of Nothing

Within early modern continental philosophy, a classic work on the "Nought" is Henri Bergson's chapter section titled "The Idea of Nothing," from his book *Creative Evolution*. Bergson seeks to clear up some common misconceptions regarding nothing, the main and pervasive error being the notion that nothing can somehow "be" more than an idea expressed within a negative proposition. Bergson argues that popular sensibilities arise not from empirical encounters with non-being but rather from practical operations in the mind and in experience. "Nought," he thus suggests, is a phantom that comes from memory and imagination; it stems from the ability to mentally substitute one thing for another thing, whereby the former thing pushes the latter thing into the status of "nothing." He writes,

> A being unendowed with memory or prevision would not use the words "void" or "nought"; he would express only what is and what is perceived; now, what is, and what is perceived, is the *presence* of one thing or of another, never the *absence* of anything. There is absence only for a being capable of remembering and expecting.[15]

His point is well taken: we don't stumble across what is not there. But, unfortunately, his account traffics in an overly subjective and psychologically oriented phenomenological analysis. This seems to constrict reality itself to the contents of a subject's consciousness. It also subtly casts memory as that which makes absence a fact per se rather than casting memory as one of the necessary conditions for the experience of an absence—one of the ways that a fact of absence can be registered. Bergson, if ever so lightly, seems to be succumbing to a species of the A-Naturalist Fallacy. Said most simply, we are beings—parts of nature—who have memories and who are capable of expecting. Said with finer nuance: his depiction subtly underestimates the kinds of negativity already at play within thought and language, in particular, words such as *unendowed*. (More on this later in this chapter and in chapter 3).

Bergson usefully critiques the notion that a primordial void could have been filled somehow by creation. He maintains that absolute nothing, *nothing rather than anything at all*, is an absurd idea, one that passes unscrutinized mainly because people can suppose a particular item annihilated, and then another, and because there is no individual object that cannot be so supposed, carried *ad infinitum*, the end result is a vague conception of absolute nothingness. Bergson remains rightfully skeptical of such an approach. It leaves a word without signification, an empty sign. Moreover, there always has to be some remainder, even if only an imagined self who would be conscious of the "all" now annihilated. That is, any account would need to include a particular someone who is judging whether or not *every particular thing* was in fact annihilated. For these reasons, "nothing" forever remains empirically unavailable. Absolute nothingness can never be directly perceived. "I may suppose that I sleep without dreaming or that I have ceased to exist," Bergson writes, "but at the very instant when I make this supposition, I conceive myself, I imagine myself watching over my slumber or surviving my annihilation, and I give up perceiving myself from within only by taking refuge in the perception of myself from without."[16] His example here is both insightful and problematic. The insight comes from his focusing on the fact that consciousness always has some object, whether outer or inward. But he conflates the fact that every day we do dreamlessly sleep—whether we realize it or not, pay attention to the fact or not—with an imagined notion of ceasing to exist. I return to the phenomenon of dreamless sleep near the end of chapter 2, but, for now, we can note that our own dreamless sleep (and our eventual annihilation) need not be something we are directly, immediately, conscious of. The non-being of consciousness and the obliteration of our personal existence can be facts about us without being directly perceivable by us.

Bergson grants that human action naturally moves, as it were, out of desires and wants, and these, by their structure, are experienced as developing from nothing into something, or from a void to a fullness therein. He thus recognizes that, for practical matters, we move toward some end that is yet to be realized, and, in that sense, we go from having nothing to having what we desired. As he states, "if we mean by void an absence of utility and not of things, we may say . . . that we are constantly going from the void to the full."[17] Simply stated, this suggests that the sensibility of "'something' coming from 'nothing'" originates not from some metaphysical source or transcendent ground but from the everyday experience of practical action, from the natural temporal structure of ends to-be-realized as we go about our business.

Finally, Bergson offers insight into "nothing" where he details the conceptual errors entailed whenever affirmation and negation are placed on the same plane or set as equal functions in discourse. Bergson writes, "An affirmative proposition expresses a judgment on an object: a negative proposition expresses a judgment on a judgment."[18] This means that affirmative propositions regarding aspects of the world occur between subject and object directly, where the perceiving and judging are largely psychological or epistemological in nature. In contrast, negative propositions—acts of judging what is *not* the case—intrinsically address other people, or perhaps an imagined future self. They mark the beginning of what has come to be called "theory of mind," the realization that people can have false beliefs.[19] Negative propositions, therefore, are more sociological and rhetorical in nature. As Bergson suggests,

> When we deny, we give a lesson to others, or it may be to ourselves. We take to task an interlocutor, real or possible, whom we find mistaken and whom we put on his guard. . . . There is no longer, then, simply a person and an object; there is, in face of an object, a person speaking to a person, opposing him and aiding him at the same time; there is a beginning of society.[20]

Because negative propositions involve a judgment about judgment, they involve others or a future imagined self. In contrast, affirmative propositions remain relatively confined to the horizons of the individual. Affirmative propositions such as "the ground is dry" specify particular properties or relations of the environment. Negative propositions such as "the ground is not dry" seem to imagine someone, even if only a future self, who might be tempted to believe that the ground is dry, and, although it cautions specifically against those who might *possibly* mistakenly believe it is dry and warns them accordingly, it also leaves unspecified any particular characteristics. "Negation aims at someone," Bergson maintains, "and not only, like a purely intellectual operation, at something."[21]

Bergson further summarizes his thinking: "To deny, therefore, always consists in presenting in an abridged form a system of two affirmations: the one determinate, which applies to a certain *possible*; the other indeterminate, referring to the unknown or indifferent reality that supplants this possibility."²² These are interesting observations and his overall point seems correct, but the examples selected make his arguments rather unconvincing. This is partly because many affirmative statements are evaluative statements regarding aspects of the social world and already have negativity embedded within them. (Notice, for example, the negativity already implied in the words above: *abridged, possible, unknown,* and *indeterminate*). The Nought is already lurking around in there. For example, compare the following three statements: "This argument is not convincing," "This argument is unconvincing," "This argument is convincing." The first expression, "This argument is not convincing," illustrates Bergson's thinking on negative propositions, but the negative lurks in the other two statements as well. For example, the expression, "This argument is unconvincing" is grammatically an affirmative proposition, and yet it seems not really to be so because the word *unconvincing* implies a semantic denial already within the affirmative proposition as a whole. Finally, even the sentence that at its surface appears to be a fully affirmative proposition, "This argument is convincing," is intelligible only by assuming that someone might, in error, think that it is unconvincing. Hence, the word "convincing" does not refer to a palpable material condition like "dryness," something that, properly speaking, is simply between subject and object. It already moves toward horizons of social intelligibility and is by that right a judgment to someone, real or imagined. It is a judgment and an evaluation about some possible judgments or possible expressed propositions. I return to these arguments in chapter 3.

Martin Heidegger: The Metaphysics of Nothing and the Nature of Existence

Another early modern continental philosopher to inquire into "nothing" is Martin Heidegger. Especially relevant is his well-known essay "What Is Metaphysics?" In contrast to Bergson, whose naturalist account of the practical emergence of negative propositions is committed to a phenomenologically grounded scientific empiricism, Heidegger has much loftier aims. He is engaged in metaphysical ruminations, including an extended consideration of "nothing." If "nothing" seems like an odd topic for a lecture on metaphysics, we should note that Heidegger is attempting to rigorously think through the problem of being and what is meant by the "is" when we say that something "is." He spells out how being cannot be grasped adequately without also coming to terms with the fact that nothing exists.

Heidegger's lecture directly confronts the dominant scientific world view where nothing is, by definition, removed from consideration, perhaps relegated to nonsense. Both reviewing and challenging this popular dogma, Heidegger writes,

> "Nothing" is absolutely rejected by science and abandoned as null and void. . . . Nothing—how can it be for science other than a horror and phantom? . . . Even so the fact remains that at the very point where science tries to put its own essence in words it invokes the aid of Nothing. . . . The alleged soberness and superiority of science becomes ridiculous if it fails to take Nothing seriously.[23]

Hard-nosed, no-nonsense scientists can be most unwelcoming to metaphysical speculations regarding nothing. So, then, how exactly does nothing disclose itself, and also, why does putting the essence of science into words necessarily invoke the aid of nothing? Finally, are Heidegger's bold claims about "nothing" coherent and justified?

As his point of entry, Heidegger asks: "Does Nothing 'exist' only because of the Not, i.e. negation? Or is it the other way about? Does negation and the Not exist only because Nothing exists?"[24] Heidegger affirms the latter and seeks to clarify what that would mean, writing,

> Nothing occurs neither by itself nor "apart from" what-is, as a sort of adjunct. Nothing is that which makes the revelation of what-is as such possible for our human existence. Nothing not merely provides the conceptual opposite of what-is but is also an original part of essence. . . . It is in the Being of what-is that the nihilation of Nothing occurs.[25]

Before advancing on to an examination of Heidegger's metaphysical claims here, we might slow down and begin by at least granting the ubiquity of negation within human existence and recognize some of its different forms: We negate something when we find it undesirable and turn away from it or when we withdraw from the scene. We negate when we rebuke what someone has done or when we reprimand someone for what they have failed to do. We negate when we gainsay what someone has said or as we tune out what we don't want to hear. We negate on a micro-scale as we skeptically question a belief and on a macro-scale as we renounce an entire world view. We negate wherever we entertain ideas of what is not the case or imagine what could never be. We negate when we tell lies. We negate negation when we correct an error or forgive a wrongdoing. And we negate what "is not," giving birth to what now "is," whenever we create anything at all. So when Heidegger asks, "What could provide more telling evidence of the perpetual, far-reaching and yet ever-dissimulated overtness of Nothing in our existence, than negation?"[26] we might allow a wide variety of negations and also accept practical notions of a void being filled with something, and yet we still might need more evidence for metaphysical claims regarding nothing. Again: how does the "Nothing" that Heidegger has in mind show itself?

Normally, routinely, we are lost, dispersed amidst the things of the world, caught up in practical affairs whereby items are disclosed as relevant (or not) according to various dealing and engagements. It is only when an all-pervasive mood such as profound boredom overcomes us that "what-is-in-totality" is disclosed. Heidegger writes, "Because of these moods in which, as we say, we 'are' this or that (i.e. bored, happy, etc.) we find ourselves in the midst of what-is-in-totality, wholly pervaded by it."[27] The boredom under consideration here does not refer to occasional moments of being bored with one item or another, but a profound and pervasive boredom with everything, the *whole* as such. Here, instead of being lost in daily affairs, attending to this particular thing and then another, the whole of our dealings become infused with the mood that discloses what-is-in-totality. Now Heidegger asks, "Does there ever occur in human existence a mood of this kind through which we are brought face to face with Nothing itself?"[28] Evidently so, for the key mood, according to Heidegger, is *dread*. It alone brings us face to face with nothing; it authentically discloses nothing. Although dread is always "dread of," it, unlike fear or anxiety, is not a dread of this or that. As Heidegger suggests, "The indefiniteness of *what* we dread is not just a lack of definition: It represents the essential impossibility of defining the 'what.'"[29] In dread, the what-is-in-totality slips away, becomes something to which we experience total indifference, and later, when the moment of dread has passed, we, returning to the practical world of what-is, can rightfully say, "It was nothing."

Some critics and those struggling to follow his logic might take umbrage with Heidegger's placing so much weight on moods, and they might claim that his project is thereby more psychological or perhaps anthropological than ontological or metaphysical. They might ask, how is any of this more than psychology or feelings? I grant that Heidegger does seem to be drifting into more of a poetic stance than a metaphysical one. His account, especially in this lecture, lacks clarity and requires charitable readings. Nevertheless, it is much more than psychology and humanist anthropology. Heidegger consistently cuts against the A-Naturalist Fallacy, and moods or "feelings" are more than something occurring within a subject—more than a psychological happening. They are sociocultural articulations of the places and moments in which people find themselves. They are disclosive not only for individuals in their current situations, but, when examined metaphysically, they reveal something about what it means to exist at all. They tell us something about the *whole* of what-is.

The intimate connection between thought, being, and non-being appears clearly in Immanuel Kant, who is well known for suggesting that there is no difference between thinking a thing and thinking of that thing as existent in some manner. We cannot think about something without giving some kind of reality to it. It bears some kind of ontological status. For example, people say that Santa Claus does not exist. I think we adults all know what they mean. There is no such magical man who knows all and keeps a list; it is all just a story told to children during the holidays. Fair enough, but the human world seems more complex than this as there are different kinds of truth. For, even though we can all agree that there is no Santa, if I try to claim that Santa Claus wears a black and green jumpsuit and that he rides in a Chevy pulled by flying penguins, anyone who knows of Santa will say that I am incorrect. To which they will add that Santa, who does not exist, wears a red and white robe and rides in a sleigh pulled by flying reindeer, one of which has a glowing red nose. This example attempts to illustrate how thought ranges over all that "is," and it reveals much that "is" but which is *not* merely "extant." Even if we think of unicorns, those unicorns we are thinking about have some sort of reality. We might say that unicorns are products of the imagination or unicorns are fictional beings existing only in fables and stories. But they're still objects of thought and exist if only as such, meaning also that they are *not* living beings subject to touch, and so on.

Thought is inseparable from being insofar as being necessarily includes a nothing that nihilates itself, as Heidegger might say, "a nothing that *noths*." Thought is inseparable from the Being of beings, if only insofar as thought inherently handles and operates with nothing. As Heidegger says elsewhere, "The nihilating in Being is the essence of what I call nothing. Hence, because it thinks Being, thinking thinks the nothing."[30] Thought cannot think about what-is without opening to the possibilities of what-is. And, although the moment of dread is brief and brings humans face to face with nothing, nothing operates in tandem with thought, serving as the underbelly to delimit and articulate the essence of what-is. Heidegger writes, "Nothing 'nihilates' unceasingly.... Nothing ... reveals itself as integral to the Being of what-is. ... This, the purely 'Other' than everything that 'is,' is that-which-is-not.... Yet this 'Nothing' functions as Being."[31] As Heidegger's metaphysical claims may still seem somewhat confusing, I try to supplement and complement his thinking by offering a wider range of homelier examples and considerations throughout the rest of the book, especially in chapters 3 and 5. For the present, I turn briefly to Heidegger's early thinking on the word *existence*, and this will hopefully clear up some residual ambiguities.

For the young Heidegger, the main task was to get clear on the range of *possible* meanings for the word *being*. Although Heidegger's later work abandoned this project (moving from the "meaning of being" to the "truth of being"), there remains in his early writings useful resources for grasping how nothing and non-being relate to existence.

The word *being*, or *is*, most often remains ambiguous and without adequate specificity. Hence, when people say that something "is" (or "is not"), they may not be exactly sure what they mean by that "is." Moreover, qualitative differences occur across many different kinds of being such that we need to avoid conceptual confusion. At the very least, we can say that *being*, the most general and inclusive term, ambiguously slides around between and among the following three sub-differentiations: *extants*, *lives*, and *exists*.

A rock or chair, or any physical object for that matter, is as an extant. It has physical properties, mass, qualities, and other aspects. As an object, it occupies space but is limited to the boundaries of its own surfaces; it can be subject to compositional analysis for an understanding of what it is. Heidegger struggled to keep this all straight, as his project had to deal with the many ways that objects are, or can be, tools "ready-to-hand" rather than merely objects "present-at-hand."[32] He realized that even though some objects can seem to be, in some ways, subject to compositional analysis and defined by their properties, other objects (e.g., tools and utensils and human artifacts) are also connected to other tools and items within a constellation of relations that disclose the object as *being* what it *is* within a larger context of equipment more generally, and a *for-the-sake-of-which*, however vague. For example, hammers are more than objects per se, as their being implies nails, boards, buildings, and other objects that need fastening and also implies people who want objects fastened this way and not another. Moreover, Heidegger found that works of art *are*, and they are objects too, but their mode of being is other than either object or tool per se.

In addition to "extants," we can note the kind of being exhibited by the "living." Living organisms, Heidegger stresses, are much more than objects within space-time. They naturally transcend the surfaces of their bodies. Even plants, with their highly limited motility, show openness to their environments. They find their environments more or less nutritive, more or less conducive to growth and development. Without any sentience or emotion, plants exhibit a mode of being that is qualitatively different than what is merely extant. The being of animals, with their sensory capacities, appetites, and needs to move through space for their own sustenance, development, and reproduction, also is quite distinct from the being of mere extant materials and much more complex than the being of plants. Animals, especially mammals, can be subject to social needs, have complex internal representations, experience a range of emotions, engage in playful interaction, and bear some degree of self-relation.

Finally, the word *existence* incorporates but moves beyond the kinds of being already discussed. Existence includes historical and future dimensions, capacities for language and symbolic representation, and capacities for novel expression, as well as, fundamentally, awareness of death. Heidegger, stressing the importance of dread and death awareness, writes, "Without the original manifest character of Nothing there is no selfhood and no freedom."[33] The word *existence* thus includes various possibilities of freedom and truth. In a word, only beings who exist can be open to their own non-being.

Jean-Paul Sartre: Nothingness and the Freedom of Having to Be Possibilities

Jean-Paul Sartre's classic philosophical treatise *Being and Nothingness* stands as essential reading on the topic of nothing. Sartre provides an incredibly rich and extensive ontology of being and nothingness, and he, like Heidegger, finds "nothing" to be a central philosophical issue. But Sartre advances his ontological claims more directly and more clearly, partly because of the wide range of detailed examples he employs and the degree to which he postulates the problem of non-being within a series of quandaries that amount to forms of metaphysical logic and an entire metaphysical system. That is, unlike Heidegger, who either roughly asserts his claims regarding nothing or poetically alludes to them but in either case leaves a good deal of work to the reader, Sartre offers highly intricate descriptions of nothing and non-being within the whole system he outlines.

All consciousness is consciousness *of* something, and consciousness wholly considered seems to be *nothing but* its intended objects. It is a lack that exists only to be its possibilities. This means, as Sartre would say, "consciousness is not what it is and is what it is not." His point is that *being-in-itself* could introduce the possibility of *being-for-itself* only by somehow infecting itself with the otherness of nothing. The plenum of being, or being-in-itself, in order to upsurge into experienced and knowable reality, had to include lacks, cracks, or fissures in being, all so that being might be *for-itself* as well as *for-others*, rather than merely *in-itself*. It is as if being-in-itself, wholly and completely in self-same identity—without gaps or absences—suffers from an unending (and basically *logical* rather than merely *temporal*) attempt to gain some distance from itself so that it might possibly return to itself, found itself, and remove contingency from its being. Perpetually failing in this attempt to serve as its own ground of self-relation, *being-in-itself* degenerates into localized pockets—places and moments—of room-making nothingness. *Being-in-itself*, in its ongoing failed attempt to serve as its own foundation, produces within itself countless forms of non-being. In this way, nothing does not predate being, nor is nothing on par with being, as if it were simply the opposite of being. On the contrary, nothing remains parasitical upon being. As Sartre suggests, "*nothingness haunts being* . . . nothingness, *which is not*, can have only a borrowed existence . . . the total disappearance of being would not be the advent of the reign of non-being, but on the contrary the concomitant disappearance of nothingness."[34]

Non-being, for Sartre, is not merely subjective nor is it reducible to verbal judgments regarding what is not the case. It is inseparable from humanity and human reality: what separates any figure from its background? Nothing. What separates past from present from future? Nothing. The human being is that being whose own nothingness is in question; nothingness comes to the world through that being who is "made to be" and who can negate non-being. Sartre's point here is that even if we agree with Heidegger and wish to accept some claim to a metaphysical, extra-mundane Nothingness, we need to make sure not to sever it from the everyday negations within human life. In this regard, Sartre's phenomenological descriptions are even more powerful than Heidegger's in defending against the A-Naturalist Fallacy.

As an invaluable resource to this study, *Being and Nothingness* will be drawn upon liberally throughout chapters 2 and 3. For now, I briefly review four of Sartre's phenomenological exemplars regarding nothing: first, his account of questioning; second, the case of the "destruction" of something in the world; third, looking for someone somewhere only to find that that someone is "not there"; and finally, his account of the anguish that comes from being condemned to freedom—the anguish that derives from having to be one's possibilities.

First, only a being already capable of releasing nothingness into being could ask a question. To question, at all, is to negate; it is to halt, if only momentarily, one's ongoing involvements and engagements. Human questioning, properly understood, is not "caused" by any material items or forces. Questions are not within being-in-itself, but rather, they emerge from being-for-itself or being-for-others. Questions thus move beyond the world of what-is in its immediacy; we do not produce questions in the same ways that weather patterns occur. The possibility of asking a question is a testimony to nothingness already coiled within being:

> It is essential therefore that the questioner have the permanent possibility of dissociating himself from the causal series which constitutes being and which can produce only being. If we admitted that the question is determined in the questioner by universal determinism, the question would thereby become unintelligible and even inconceivable. . . . Thus in posing a question, a certain negative element is introduced into the world.[35]

Actual questioning always already implies some kind of break in being, a looking beyond perception, a consideration of possibilities, an interrogative attitude that bears the expectation of some kind of reply, though not necessarily verbal, from either the person questioned or the state of affairs at issue. In the attitude of expectant interrogation, in recognizing that I do not know something, I expect that the unknown something could be known, could be disclosed—if only I could find the right way to approach it, perhaps a way not yet considered. To expect is to project possibilities; it is to negate the non-being of uncertainty. It is to delimit the horizon of intelligibility in terms of what is not yet known or not yet present or not yet in existence. When I question, Sartre writes, "I expect from this being a revelation of its being or its way of being. The reply will be a 'yes' or 'no.'"[36] This is not to suggest that all questions can be intelligibly responded to with either a "yes" or "no," but, more generally, that "the question is a bridge set up between two non-beings: the non-being of knowing in man, the possibility of non-being of being in transcendent being. Finally the question implies the existence of truth."[37] Beings who can question being open beyond what shows itself as evident at first appearance in whatever is; questions enable us to reveal truths out of our clouds of unknowing. Where, then, do questions come from if not from what is? From what is possible. But what does that mean? Without possibilities—themselves grounded in non-being—there would be no questions, and without questions there literally are no answers. Answers are possibilities that come into being by way of that being who inherently dwells in nothing.

Second, something quite similar can be found in the case of "destruction," where non-being shows itself as part of the world, but not as something "there" without a witness to it. Note here, as Sartre suggests, "destruction although coming into being through man, is an *objective fact* and not a thought."[38] Clarifying this issue further, Sartre writes,

> "Destruction" presents the same structure as "the question." In a sense, certainly, man is the only being by whom a destruction can be accomplished. A geological plication, a storm do not destroy—or at least they do not destroy *directly*; they merely modify the distribution of masses of beings. There is no less after the storm than before. There is only something else.[39]

Consider another example: someone is at a woodshop and they accidently place their hand too near an active saw. Their hand moves and the blade slices off a couple of fingers. As far as the realm of physics is concerned, no matter was created or destroyed; there is simply the valueless moving of things from one place to another, all in accord with the "law" of entropy. But for that person, something significant and horrifying has happened: they just lost vital parts of their hand! But without a human consciousness, without someone "there" to perceive what has happened, there is little other than redistribution of mass.

Growing up entails learning that much of the world is populated with fragile items and fragile relationships. The very concept of *fragility* is a register of the possibility of non-being within being. Addressing the facts of destruction and fragility, Sartre suggests that people strike two different stances toward these highly interrelated phenomena. We must "either take the necessary measures to realize it (destruction proper) or, by a negation of non-being, to maintain it always on the level of a simple possibility (by preventive measures)."[40] Although destruction is fairly easy to recognize and easy to experience as negative or undesirable, preventive measures, as modes of negating possibilities, are not only more elusive, they easily cover themselves over. For example: if someone learns that candles are the number one cause of all household fires and therefore never buys a candle and his or her house never burns down, passersby are most unlikely to suddenly attend to this fact. As nobody's attention is abruptly grabbed by houses holding steady and standing in peace, that is, houses "*not* burning down," so, too, active engagements in negating possibilities can remain underappreciated, ignored, or even neglected. I return to the issue of preventive measures in chapter 4.

Third, in documenting how the appearance of non-being is not reducible to analytic judgments, Sartre considers the case of arriving a little late for a lunch date. He is scheduled to meet Pierre at the café. When finally arriving there, he looks around and, knowing how punctual Pierre is, tries to see if Pierre is in the café. To look for Pierre is to imaginatively project an image of him in the visual field, expecting to see him, hoping that he is about to appear in concrete perception, all the while making that image vanish before those others who are recognized as *not* Pierre. As Sartre says, "This figure which slips constantly between my look and the solid, real objects of the café is precisely a perpetual disappearance."[41] The total visual field is assembled and organized for precisely this task. Attention scans the room item by item, person by person, with each figure released out and momentarily isolated from an amorphous, naturally self-negating ground, but the projected image of Pierre is just as quickly nihilated as each figure is revealed as *not* Pierre. This is a direct experience of the fact that Pierre, although somewhere that remains currently unknown, is *not* in the café. Only when Pierre is seen as present in the café does the image become filled rather than self-liquidate and vanish. And when that does occur, the entire ground—that is this café as a whole—becomes reassembled around Pierre now as its central figure. But, alas, Pierre is not there.

Sartre contrasts this experience of a concretely discovered absence with the analytic judgment of the countless other people, some of whom are deceased, who also are not present in the café. His point here is that the full range of negation provides something quite more than mere thought about what is not. Sartre suggests, "This example is sufficient to show that non-being does not come to things by a negative judgment; it is the negative judgment, on the contrary, which is conditioned and supported by non-being."[42]

Fourth and finally, Sartre maintains that "anguish," highly similar to Heidegger's notion of "dread," is not only a key to grasping how nothing infects being—basically secreting itself between the past and the future—but furthermore discloses the freedom that humans suffer. We can best begin to elucidate the character of anguish by contrasting it with fear. As Sartre puts it:

> [F]ear is fear of beings in the world whereas anguish is anguish before myself. . . . A situation provokes fear if there is a possibility of my life being

changed from without; my being provokes anguish to the extent that I distrust myself and my own reactions in that situation."[43]

When we are afraid, we are afraid of something in the environment. Our object of fear might be a stranger, an unfamiliar location, a wild animal, a high cliff, or some other perceived danger. In the experience of anguish, our concern regards our own capacities to meet and handle such challenges, past, present, or future. People can distrust themselves and their capacities to react in the situations they face, and they also may anticipate or recollect their failure to manage situations. They realize the continuities but also the existential "gaps" between past self, present self, and possible future selves. Fundamentally posed toward the future, *always having projected possibilities still outstanding and always moving however dimly toward that certain-yet-indeterminate not-yet, my death*, I can be conscious of the distance between my present self today, with its promises and resolves, and any future self who will face those promises and resolves as possibilities which "I" will either carry out, *or not*. "Thus the self which I am depends on the self of which I am not yet to the exact extent that the self which I am not yet does not depend on the self which I am."[44] People do not merely encounter entities in the world, they also bear self-relation, which means that past self, present self, and future self are all separated by nothing. As Sartre suggests, "Freedom is the human being putting his past out of play by secreting his own nothingness."[45] Any past self and any future self cannot be within consciousness per se, for they can only be something we are conscious *of* in a mode of self-relation. This also means that we, in anguish, cannot rely upon prior decisions, prior acts of courage to carry us through current challenges, nor can our possible future selves rely upon the resolve and bravery we have today. Hence, Ludwig Wittgenstein's pithy insight: "Courage is always original."

The feeling that comes from looking to oneself rather than to external circumstances—from attending to my ability to act or not—this is anguish, and it is a register of our experience of freedom. As Sartre writes, "[A]nguish has not appeared to us as a *proof* of human freedom. . . . We wished only to show that there exists a specific consciousness of freedom, and we wished to show that this consciousness is anguish."[46] People are free only insofar as they must continually make themselves out of their possibilities. Some of the struggle in any undertaking is facing and living in the possibility of it not coming to completion, of nursing a flower that never comes to bloom. One could, for example, get hit by a bus or maybe just give up midway through a project, or perhaps get thwarted by others. These are possibilities that haunt any project.

To say that people are free does not imply that they have control over all the circumstances that bear upon their lives, nor does it suggest that people control the eventual outcomes of their engagements. It simply acknowledges, as did ancient Stoic schools, that reality is such that some aspects of it remain under our control while some aspects are simply beyond our control. Concrete freedom is the experienced need to act in response to circumstances, not to have control over results.

Both fear and anguish are powerful experiences. People suffer fear or anguish according to the way their situations are arranged and organized, the way that they are contextualized. For example, when a threatening situation is framed in terms of "things that happen to people," we think of the exterior world and dwell in a sense of fear. Inversely, when that situation is framed in terms of what "people are doing to respond," we think of self-relation and introduce some degree of anguish. Fear is direct and unreflective, whereas anguish is indirect and reflective, bearing the encumbrance of self-relation. Some people seem to realize their freedom, and accordingly, they try, in good faith, to be courageous, moment by moment, situation by situation, knowing that yesterday's courage comes one day too late for today's encounters. Others try to hide from the fact of having to be their possibilities by subscribing to some form of determinism. Depicting the motives for people to downplay, ignore, or outright deny their experience of freedom, Sartre writes,

> Psychological determinism, before being a theoretical conception, is first an attitude of excuse, or if you prefer, the basis of all attitudes of excuse. . . . [D]eterminism, a reflective defense against anguish[,] . . . is given as a faith to take refuge in, as the ideal end toward which we can flee to escape anguish.[47]

Humans, as Sartre famously writes, "are condemned to freedom."[48] People literally need to make something out of themselves because they are not yet fully themselves, and inversely, they are nothing more than what they have made of themselves. If they have been cowards, it is not because they had cowardice as a pregiven essence in their nature. Cowardice is not, and cannot be, an extant property of a person. People cannot be cowards in the way that an inkwell is an inkwell. It is because people exist, haunted through and through with many forms of non-being, that people cannot escape their freedom, cannot avoid having to be their possibilities.

Kenneth Burke: Ambiguity, Action, and "the Hortatory Don't"

Another scholar to take "nothing" seriously, making "the negative" a central feature of his overall thinking, is the rhetorical critic and literary theorist Kenneth Burke. One thing that makes Burke's account so interesting is how ambiguous it is. On the one hand, Burke asserts that "the negative" comes through symbol use, language in particular, and that it is a main means by which humans transcend sheer "bodily motion" and become capable of "symbolic action." He critiques existential thinkers such as Heidegger and Sartre who seem to turn nothing into something metaphysical. And yet, on the other hand, careful examination of Burke's writings reveals that his position remains fairly undecided regarding any metaphysics of nothing. Whereas Heidegger famously distanced himself from Sartre's characterization of existentialism as atheistic humanism, Burke's agnosticism subtly insinuates itself where Burke himself suggests, in speaking more generally as a rhetorical critic and theorist, "What we want is not terms that avoid the ambiguity, but terms that clearly reveal the strategic spots at which ambiguities necessarily arise."[49] I return in a moment to the places of ambiguity in Burke's position, but, for now, I briefly review just a few of Burke's main claims regarding the negative.

Burke routinely argues that "the negative" is one of the essential "marvels" of language and that *"negation is of the very essence of language."*[50] Not only must one know, as Alfred Korzybski routinely stressed, that "the word is not the thing," but one must be able to discount much of what is literally said if one is to understand irony, jest, metaphor, and other forms of word play. Also, the negativity within language is intricately woven into the experience of expectations so that what does *not* occur (or is *not* happening) can be directly registered and talked about. One of Burke's repeated examples is that someone can ask you if it is fifty-four degrees outside today, and, if it is any other temperature, you can truthfully say, "No; it is not fifty-four degrees."[51] But, strictly speaking, there is no such thing as being *"not fifty-four degrees."* The temperature simply is whatever temperature it happens to be at any given moment (e.g., forty-nine degrees or thirty-eight degrees or whatever).

Deriving from resources of language, the negative passes well beyond the domain of language, which means that Burke's interest in the negative is not simply with language, poetry, drama, fiction, and so on. On the contrary, the more significant point is that without the negative, humans would neither experience time the way that they do nor could the world blaze with the moral light that it does. Negativity, which is the essence of language, casts its shadow over all things that language would behold, and, without the negative, people would not be the moral agents that they are. These ideas are fleshed out within Burke's most concentrated discussions of the negative, which occur within early and later parts of two of his final books: *The Rhetoric of Religion* and *Language as Symbolic Action*. The latter book begins with his well-known "Definition of Man," where Burke offers, as one of his five clauses, the idea that humans are *"the inventor of the negative (moralized by the negative)."* Given this double locution, "inventor of" and "moralized by," we might analytically consider each side of the clause. First, to say that humans are the inventor of the negative is to acknowledge that nothing, the negative, the square-root of negative one, and so on, cannot be found or discovered out in nature, and therefore the negative is a peculiar kind of idea that comes to the world through people. Here Burke seems close to inadvertently courting the A-Naturalist Fallacy. Moreover, in identifying Bergson's chapter "The Idea of Nothing" as an "an eye-opener," Burke agrees that "*the negative is an idea*; there can be no image of it . . . *in imagery there is no negative*. . . . An idea, insofar as it is a 'principle,' is intrinsically *beyond* image. From the standpoint of image, it is as 'nothing.'"[52] But this half of the clause remains ambiguous and problematic—and Burke admits as much and seems to be staving off the A-Naturalist Fallacy—because, as he recognizes, we cannot say that people invented the negative anymore than we can say that people "invented" language.

Regarding the second part of the clause, "moralized by the negative," we should underscore how selves and societies develop their moral sensibilities out of various forms of negation—ranging from personal threats to legally sanctioned property rights. Language issues a deep-seated transformation; it takes flesh and blood organisms and transforms them into reasoning moral agents. Burke thus strategically appropriates Bergson's insight about social admonishment nestled within negative propositions to: (1) more globally show how negative admonishments and commands are precursors to negative propositions, and (2) examine the kinds of communicative processes that act back upon human beings to transform them into *persons* (i.e., moral agents). This partly means that Burke considerably advances the insights of Bergson, but he radically revises Bergson's orientation to a more explicitly communicative, less "scientific" one. He maintains that philosophers commonly start with the "is not," whereas they should begin with the "shall not" or the "hortatory don't." A child's experience with the "don't" must be strong enough and pervasive enough for the "is not" to be taken seriously.

Here, roughly, is how things go down in Burke's account: each of us, a body who learns language, is subject to a flurry of "tribal thou-shalt-nots." Note that the Ten Commandments, what Burke calls the "Decalogue," are almost exclusively negative in character. Not only are moral injunctions negative, but also the commands are issued at one time while the possible acts of obedience to the commands are set for another time. This is one of the interesting features of language more generally but it becomes particularly salient when considering how the negative bears upon the development of moral character. In much of nature, broadly construed anyway, "command" and "obedience" occur simultaneously, whether it is an object moving to the pull of gravity or the salivation of Pavlov's dogs; forces and relations are continuous and contiguous. In the human realm, an existential gap opens up between the command and its obedience, and persons, as moral agents, come to dwell in that gap, sometimes agonizingly so. Notice, too, that children are taught "thou shalt not commit adultery" well before they are in a position to heed such commands. Here Burke's discussion of the form of the command

and obedience owes much to Aristotle's notions of formal causality and final causality. By the purely formal structure of such an arrangement, people can either say "Yes" or "No" to their tribal thou-shalt-nots. Burke, citing himself, writes:

> *Action* involves *character*, which involves *choice*—and the *form* of choice attains its perfection in the distinction between Yes and No (Shall and shall-not, will and will-not). Though the concept of sheer motion is non-ethical, action implies the ethical, the human personality. Hence the obvious close connection between the ethical and negativity, as indicated in the Decalogue.[53]

We are not born as the ethical agents that we eventually experience ourselves to be. As we grow and increasingly internalize our culture's thou-shalt-nots, we develop a sense of conscience such that we will feel good when we say "Yes" to the "thou-shalt-nots," and we feel bad when we say "No" to them. This also means that moral agency is not reducible to simply doing what one is told to do or merely avoiding what one is told to avoid. The ability to say "Yes" *or* "No" to any tribal "thou shalt not" thus implies an ability to deliberate and to choose; morality, entailed by choice, is quite other than blindly falling into line.[54]

Further underscoring the intimate connection between negativity and morality, Burke argues that moral terms are "polar" rather than "positive,"[55] meaning that words employed for the moral realm are already partly defined by not-being their opposite. Hence, a word such as *chair* is differentiated in meaning from other items such as *desk, couch, table*, and so on, but there is no anti-chair, unchair, de-chair. In contrast, moral words, all words geared for moral action, have a tangle of negativity implied within them. Words such as *pious, kind,* or *just* are by their very definition set in contrast with their polar opposites: words such as *impious, unkind,* and *unjust*. They thus do not refer to material reality per se but to ideas regarding moral order. Even the word *order*, morally speaking, makes sense only in contrast to *disorder*.

In his chapter, "A Dramatistic View of the Origins of Language and Postscript on the Negative," Burke writes in two places, both in italic: *"The essential distinction between the verbal and the nonverbal is in the fact that language adds the peculiar possibility of the Negative."*[56] For Burke, "the negative" within language originates naturally out of practical affairs. It is aligned with desires and preferences, so that what is "negative" is not so much negated or nihilated as ignored or avoided or abandoned. In its initial, preverbal stage, the negative is experienced wherever something seems undesirable. He thus traces the development of the negative naturalistically, beginning with preverbal positives such as simple animal preferences, and preverbal negatives such as capacities to withdraw or turn away. He follows these through to commands such as "No!" or "Don't!," which, it should be noted, lie at that interesting intersection that makes it possible for humans to communicate with some kinds of animals, especially dogs. All said, Burke argues that only humans can go on to speak of universalized "Thou-Shalt-Nots" as well as the propositional "It is not."

Philosophers who begin with the metaphysical "is not" rather than the "hortatory don't," Burke suggests, easily become subject to psychoanalytic debunking. For example, Burke argues that Heidegger's views could very well be correct. Nonetheless, there still might be other motivations that drive him to his orientations and conclusions. As Burke writes,

> Even if we agree with Heidegger's views, we could still note strands of motivation here that should first be considered without reference to a supernatural realm. For instance, if you agree that, in terms of natural experience, the negative *Command* is prior to the purely *Propositional* negative, and may be glimpsed "beyond" it or about its edges, you see a possibility that the metaphysician could be rediscovering, through the labyrinthine virtuosity of his dialectic, the respect and awe of the original no, communicated to him as a child by parents who represented the principle of personal authority.[57]

Indeed, Burke routinely criticizes existentialists for making "nothing" more than a verbal device. Yet he himself begrudgingly admits, in more than one place, that the negative is more than verbal, or at least other than something expressed by language, either as command or proposition. Some of this is slippery, as Burke seems to court the A-Naturalist Fallacy in his eagerness to critique the ontological accounts offered by Heidegger and Sartre. Said most simply, in stressing that the negative comes through language and human beings, he downplays how humans and language are, from a different scenic placement or a different frame of consideration, events occurring within the universe.

The remaining ambiguity within these issues persists in three different places: First, Burke agrees that, in principle, there are strictly logical reasons for postulating that negation, at least as far as language is concerned, is prior to affirmation. For example, he suggests that,

> ...I personally would treat the negative as in principle prior, for this reason: (1) Yes and No imply each other; (2) in their role as opposites, they *limit* each other; (3) but limitation itself is the 'negation of part of a divisible quantum.'[58]

Although his discussion here still moves within the realm of the verbal, he is not discussing any expressed negativity per se (e.g. "don't" or "is not"). Rather, he is talking about the logical underbelly of expressions, something more akin to extra-verbal rules embedded within language use and logical structure. More on these issue in Chapter 3.

Second, an extended consideration of the metaphysical implications of "nothing" occurs in Burke's *The Rhetoric of Religion*. I quote him at length:

> Existentialists such as Heidegger and Sartre should certainly be examined quizzically for their tendency to "reify" the negative, by starting from the quasi-substantive "nothing" rather than from the moralistic "no." Consider, for instance, Heidegger's "meonic" notion that, if "Being" can "be," then *Nichts* can *nichten*, the symbolic negativity here being given quasi-positive substantiality by the suggestion that *Angst* is the evidence of non-being's validity as the metaphysical ground of being....
> An uncompromising naturalistic view of such linguistic maneuvers would simply dismiss them as sheer nonsense. But Logology would admonish us to take Heidegger's comedy seriously. For there is always the possibility that, if language does lead ultimately to this generalized use of the negative, the *implications* of such an end are present in even our ordinary thoughts, though in themselves these thoughts possess no such thoroughness. That is, though they are far from taking us "to the end of the line," they may *imply* this end, if we were but minded to follow them through persistently enough. So such an end may be lurking in them, an implied end that we cannot avoid by merely being trivial. For if man is the symbol-using animal, and if the ultimate test of symbolicity is an intuitive feeling for the principle of the negative, then such "transcendental" operations as the Heideggerian idea of "Nothing" may reveal in their purity a kind of *Weltanschauung* that is imperfectly but inescapably operating in all of us.[59]

Here Burke admits how his own project of Logology, where theology offers ideal resources for studying the thoroughness of motivations within language, aligns with Heidegger's observations. "Nothing" appears to anyone who is willing to chase language and its forms of transcendence down "to the end of the line." Burke, too, is most explicit where he writes, "[T]here is nothing in our position requiring us to deny the possibility that language, with its basic No, is grounded in a transcendent ground."[60]

Third, and finally, we find a most subtle and profound ambiguity between being and non-being in Burke's "Epilogue: Prologue in Heaven" in *The Rhetoric of Religion*. There he poses an imaginary dialogue between The Lord and Satan regarding the "word animal" (i.e., humans). In the dialogue Burke places the negative outside of the human realm, entertaining a metaphysical place for it. At one point, Satan asks God why it matters what people think about Him given that He is so far beyond all speech and thought. Humans are mortal animals using a language that grows naturalistically out of practical affairs, and all theological talk—even negative theology—seems to fall considerably short of reaching the divine. Why, then, should God care about human ideas of God, given that human words are hopelessly inadequate to touch the infinite and eternal? The Lord's response to Satan is as follows:

And in any case, you will agree that, even if their ideas of divine perfection were reducible to little more than a language-using animals' ultimate perception of its own linguistic forms, this could be a true inkling of the divine insofar as language itself happened to be made in the image of divinity.[61]

Obviously, then, in significant ways Burke shows himself as undecided on the question of whether or not "the negative" has a metaphysical status. The main difficulty is that Burke does not sufficiently buttress himself against the A-Naturalist Fallacy in ways that Heidegger's and Sartre's ontologies do. This means that even if Burke is roughly correct in tracing the negative's humble roots out of organismal desire, we can admit different scenic placements for that fact. Whereas Burke mainly emphasizes the operation of "division," we would, from the other angle, emphasize the operation of "merger": The negative is something that is occurring in language, and that is happening in life, and that is happening in the cosmos itself, if only broadly construed. The negative is part of the cosmos, and we happen to be places and moments of its flourishing.

Terrence W. Deacon: Life, Value, and Incompleteness

Few people, if any, have more powerfully and rigorously examined the ranges of non-being nestled within life than Terrence W. Deacon in his masterful book *Incomplete Nature: How Mind Emerged from Matter*. But this transition to my fifth and final thinker to have seriously explored the topic of nothing involves a significant change of venue, a big leap in conceptual space and a jump across disciplinary boundaries. Deacon, an evolutionary biologist, anthropologist and neuroscientist, opens new vistas within science for considering the role and operations of nothing, showing how forms of incompleteness are the very essence of life. Moreover, Deacon's work on various forms of emergence moves his naturalism well beyond the human realm, as it demonstrates how forms of non-being and absence are integral to the emergence and sustenance of life itself, not merely human thought and language.

Deacon does not reference any of the four thinkers already reviewed here, but he brings an enormous amount of synergistic insight into the areas already covered. One can only imagine how each of the four thinkers just reviewed would respond to Deacon's project. His considerations keep him, on the one hand, committed to a naturalist or nonsupernatural account of life's origins, but, on the other hand, open him to the continuities between human sentience, life generally considered, and the dynamics of physics and biochemistry that make life possible. Moreover, to the extent that the emergence of life and mind was one of matter's possibilities, Deacon does weigh in on metaphysical concerns. In particular, his "emergentist" position—which becomes plausible only if forms of non-being exist—enables him to deny panpsychism on the one hand, and also to reject the claim that conscious agency is an illusion or merely epiphenomenal on the other. Conscious human thought, with all its implied claims to agency and value, is real and must be adequately taken into account. But to do so, we need not subscribe to religious or spiritualist dogmas asserting either Intelligent Design by God or that everything is alive or everything is conscious in some way or other. Deacon's work offers a fine rounding out of some of the main ideas discussed so far as well as an excellent set-up for ideas to come. For this present section, I very briefly underscore a few of his insights and contributions regarding the dynamics of absence and incompleteness.

As a scientist breaking ranks with those colleagues who see agency, choice, and meaning to be illusory or epiphenomenal, Deacon accounts for mind, purpose, and value without either ascribing to them supernatural origins or treating them as something soon enough adequately handled by quantum mechanics. Within contemporary mainstream Western science, phenomena such as goals and purposes may be granted as subjective mental states tightly aligned with brain activity, but they appear fundamentally disconnected from the world of material forces and causality. Deacon acknowledges the difficulties that such facts of mind pose for the contemporary view where he writes, "[T]he idea of allowing the potentially achievable consequence characterizing a function, a reference, or an intended goal to play a causal role in our explanations of physical change has become an anathema for science."[62] Everyday phenomena such as ideas or meanings or values, when accepted by science as real, are quickly bracketed as "outside" the domain of science. Or they are understood as something that eventually will be captured by more fundamental laws of physics and, so the story goes, will reveal the full truth of absolute determinism or quantum indeterminacy, neither of which is compatible with the sense we have of ourselves as conscious moral agents.[63]

Consider one of the most familiar aspects of human life: the everyday use of language. Showing the challenges posed to science by this ordinary phenomenon, Deacon writes,

> The meaning of a sentence is not the squiggles used to represent letters on a piece of paper or a screen. It is not the sounds these squiggles might prompt you to utter. It is not even the buzz of neuronal events that take place in your brain as you read them. . . . The information conveyed by this sentence has no mass, no momentum, no electric charge, no solidity and no clear extension in the space within you, around you, or anywhere. . . . [T]he content of this, or any sentence—a something-that-is-not-a-thing—has physical consequences. But how?[64]

Not only is there a qualitative difference between the physical materiality of words and the intangibility of meanings, but, furthermore, as Deacon points out, "*Such concepts as information, function, purpose, meaning, intention, significance, consciousness, and value are intrinsically defined by their fundamental incompleteness. They exist only in relation to something that they are not.*"[65] This basically means that they all pose significant problems for any inclusive "Theory of Everything," for such a theory would need to account for nature in its totality (i.e., nature including humans and all of their cultural, artistic, and moral achievements).

Focusing on key differences between the inanimate world and realms of life and mind, Deacon writes, "What needs explaining is not how brains are like the weather, but how and why they are so different, despite the fact they both are highly complex physical processes."[66] The weather unfolds through highly complex relations between atmospheric pressure, temperature, humidity, sunlight, and various gasses, all of which undergo continuous and contiguous interaction. One might be tempted to suggest that brains are no different. They are connections of neurons, neurotransmitters, electrical storms of neurophysiological connectivity. The problem with such obviously reductive accounts is that minds emerge from brains (and from their larger surroundings), and, much more significantly, minds inherently deal with countless forms of non-being: intentions, not-yet realized achievements, abstractions, meanings, values, experienced absences, and so on. As Deacon states,

> This paradoxical intrinsic quality of existing with respect to something missing, separate, and possibly nonexistent is irrelevant when it comes to inanimate things, but *it is a defining property of life and mind*. A complete theory of the world that includes us, and our experiences of the world, must make sense of the way that we are shaped by and emerge from such specific absences.[67]

The vital dynamics here in view range from those functions that operate through absence within biological systems (e.g., a hemoglobin molecule or an autogen) to those dimensions of meaning, significance, and value that align with human mentality per se. Furthermore, to handle the challenge of absence playing a vital role across such a variety of contexts, Deacon coins the term *ententional phenomena*, which attempts to capture the "generic sense of something existing with-respect-to, for-the-sake-of, or in-order-to-generate something that is absent that also includes function at one extreme and value at the other."[68] From this perspective, non-being occurs within multiple levels of life, including mind per se, not merely in commands of "Don't!" or within negative propositions.

To get a better sense of his point, consider one of Deacon's many thought-provoking examples. Imagine the case of a stone found along the beach. Now, stones can be moved around in different ways. We might first consider the processes that led a particular stone to a particular beach. Here the forces and dynamics described by physics and geology (gravity, water pressure and momentum, rip currents, stone size and density) can account fully for how the stone formed, moved, and eventually landed on the beach without anything like volition or intention. But now a boy finds the stone upon the beach and he tries to skip it along the surface of the water. A stone skipping across water is a highly improbable occurrence, and yet the probability of such an occurrence becomes much higher when we include a person's conscious intention to make a stone skip. In this case, the stone does not escape or evade any of the physical forces just mentioned, but some very different properties and dynamics are involved. The boy has an intention to throw it in such a way as to see how many times he can make it skip. Three? Four? The boy's body is subject to describable physical laws, and chemical processes within his body can account for the distance of the throw. But no amount of reductionist scientific method or description will be able to grab hold of the whole account, for the boy's intention to throw the rock does not fit within the bulk of modern reductionist science. How could we say the intended outcome was the cause of the toss? This readmits teleology back into nature after science had worked so hard to remove it. Some will argue that the boy's intention to throw came before the actual toss. But how so? What "caused" the intention? Imagine now that we discover that the boy, a year earlier at a different beach, had witnessed someone skipping stones and had learned that such an activity was possible with certain kinds of stones. How did he come to believe that this particular stone on this particular beach on this particular day could be brought to such purposes? Scientifically speaking, there seem to be significant gaps. Deacon suggests that this kind of "multiple realizablity" depends on the existence of general types. General types must have some kind of reality or purposive activities would be impossible. There must be the right "kind" of stone for the purpose and a general "stillness" of the water. As such, any particular stone selected for skipping across water is already haunted by absence in both directions; the stone is recognized as similar to previous stones that have been skipped, and the stone itself is part of a project that can fail to be realized, meaning that the skip may not exist despite the boy's best intentions.

In this example, a mind deems a stone to be a certain "type" based roughly on shape and size, perhaps under the makeshift concept of "skipableness." Also, a memory from the past is evoked so that any present situation opens to possible futures. We find here endless discounting of particulars and connections, including gaps within the continuous and contiguous relations that brought the stone to the beach. Where the stone lands after the boy throws it cannot be fully understood without incorporating the role played by possible futures, which also means repeatable possibilities represented by the boy's mind. Haunted by absence, general types operate within life, ranging from biological functions of eating and drinking to people making reference with language. "So, accepting that ententional phenomena are causally important in the world appears to require that types of things have real physical consequences independent of any specific embodiment."[69] The occurrence of types or general kinds of things is more than merely subjective. Not only do autogens (and other forms of rudimentary life functions) operate with types (e.g., hemoglobin is perfectly "formed" to carry oxygen), but, within human cognition, Deacon's argument for the existence of types can be appropriated as one more strategy for defending against the A-Naturalist Fallacy. Said most simply, even if conceptual types are abstractions—concepts formed by discounting empirical particulars—these are, in their own right, something occurring within nature. We happen to be the site of their occurrence.

Part of the difficulty for a scientific account of mind is that representations can be of *possibilities*, meaning that there is nothing to *re-present*, especially in those cases where the possibility is never actualized. As Deacon suggests,

> [T]hought is about a possibility, and a possibility is something that doesn't yet exist and may never exist. It is as though a possible future is somehow including the present. . . . It seems we must explain the uncaused appearance of phenomena whose causal powers derive from something nonexistent.[70]

He furthermore asks, "How can something not there be the cause of anything?"[71] One of the ways to illustrate the kinds of impasse within the contemporary reductionist scientific world-picture is to point to the peculiar problem posed by possibilities per se. Where, exactly, are possibilities located? If all reality is reducible to physical and chemical causal chains, and if everything is suspended within concatenated connections of both cause and effect, then what causes possibilities? And, assuming that something can cause possibilities, what would it mean to say that possibilities could be the cause of something? Whereas perception can only open to what is happening, thought can recognize what could possibly "not happen." Consider a mundane example that moves non-being well beyond the phenomenon of unfulfilled expectations: if we watch a dog's tail swing side to side and can see the clear possibility of its tail knocking over a glass of wine on a table, we may move the wine to a different location, thus preventing any chance of the dog spilling it. In this case, we never see such "not spilling" occur; the glass is moved from one spot to another. We thus were not representing an actual occurrence here and now, and, in fact, quite the contrary: we made something "not happen" by intentionally moving against an imagined possibility. We are able to represent something that has not yet happened and then act to make sure that it, in fact, does not happen.

Thought thus entertains possibilities but then covers over its own acts by ensuring that those possibilities do not happen. When they do not happen, all is as if the thought of non-being were not there at all. Much of the world around us is as it is only because people have been able to imagine accidents and then have strategically headed them off. This simple example, one of an infinite range of preventive measures that could have been offered, illustrates that much of life takes its order from people purposefully avoiding imagined possibilities.

When a predator attempts to hunt down an elusive prey or when a prey seeks to elude a stalking predator, the slightest misstep means the difference between life and death. From such lowly beginnings, organisms not only thrive and flourish by entertaining what is not yet the case, but increasing possibilities grow and bloom out of such facts: by learning what is not to be brought together, (what not to touch, what not to drink or eat, where not to go, what not to do), we bring order and meaning to our lives and our world.

As all organisms are fundamentally *incomplete* beings, humans are the supreme exemplar of incompleteness. We can imagine and hunger for senses of completeness on multiple levels of experience (perceptual, conceptual, aesthetic, historical, logical, etc.). People can feel the need to know how they fit in with and relate to everything else; their incompleteness drives them to seek identification with their pasts and futures. People can feel incomplete if they don't know the origins of their ancestors. People can feel the need to connect themselves to the creation of the universe (whether by religion with its origin and destination narratives, or by science with its theories of how it all began and will likely end).

TAKING INVENTORY SO FAR

Much can be gleaned from this brief survey of scholarly insights on nothing. Non-being haunts being and appears to have some ontological origin even if it remains nebulous and mysterious. At the least, we have found, in addition to any stated propositional negations, a social-moral order (and the phenomenon of conscience too) precipitated by the commands "No" and "Don't." When people consider the phenomenon on nothing, they too commonly begin with the "is not," and they routinely underestimate the significance of the verbal commands "Don't" and "No." Hence, we ought to attend to the ways negativity plays out in language in different modes and at multiple levels, not simply propositional negations.

The phenomena of absence, incompleteness, negativity, and non-being shoot through life and mind, and they can be seen most clearly in the activities of thought. Thought, as inherently handling possibilities, is drenched in non-being and absence.

We also have seen that the natural world provides ample evidence for modes of absence and incompleteness, and that non-being makes both life and mind possible. Here we find the clearest cases for non-being somehow *above*, *below*, and *beyond* language. *Nothing* is much more than a word, more than an idea; it is an ontological problem, one caught in the origins of life and the nature of mind.

All five of the thinkers discussed in this chapter, in various ways, contribute to an overall understanding of the dynamic role of "nothing." A little bit more will be made of them, and many others too, throughout the remaining four chapters of this book. The important point at this juncture is that, as different as these thinkers are, all of them lead us toward the phenomenon of human morality, agency, and action. All of these thinkers have recognized human action and agency as natural facts. They have sought to counter reductionist, mechanistic, and devitalized nature. They have argued that agency, action, choice, and values are not mere illusions. We live our lives in *possible* worlds, moving through existential situations that have no exactly specifiable coordinates.

What I wish to do over the next four chapters of this book is as follows: first, I show how the body itself, in countless ways, is marked by modes of absence, incompleteness, and non-being. I also show how the body, as a network of different sensory capacities, provides the foundational ground for agency and possibilities. Second, I devote concerted space to the myriad ways that language and communication are infused with negativity in different ways on many different levels of analysis. Third, I work out and present a few of the social and ethical implications that this orientation entails, focusing mainly on death acceptance. I explore how death acceptance—denial of any personal life postmortem—can invigorate ethical possibilities and motivate certain forms of social justice. Finally, in chapter 5, I offer a very brief speculation, an imaginative exercise, on the possible origins of all that is. I explore a possible ontological ground for nothing.

NOTES

1. Do you remember when you first discovered that you existed? Do you recall how miraculous was the sheer fact of the discovery?

2. Jean-Paul Sartre, *Being and Nothingness*, trans. Hazel Barnes (NJ: Gramercy, 1956).

3. Martin Heidegger, *Being and Time*, trans. Joan Stambaugh (Albany, NY: State University of New York Press, 1997).

4. Martin Heidegger, *The Concept of Time*, trans. William McNeill (Cambridge, MA: Blackwell, 1992).

5. Alphonso Lingis, *The Community of Those Who Have Nothing in Common* (Bloomington: Indiana University Press, 1994), 96.

6. For more on the notion of "fitting response," see Calvin O. Schrag, *The Self after Postmodernity* (New Haven, CT: Yale University Press, 1997).

7. Joan Konner, *You Don't Have to Be Buddhist to Know Nothing* (Amherst, NY: Prometheus, 2009), 15.

8. Has Jonas, *The Phenomenon of Life* (Chicago: The University of Chicago Press, 1966), 175.

9. Ronald David Laing, *The Politics of Experience* (New York: Pantheon, 1976), 41.
10. See Marshall McLuhan, where he writes, "If we open a 1938 copy of *Life*, the pictures or postures seen then as normal now give a sharper sense of remote time than do objects of real antiquity," *Understanding Media* (Corte Madera, CA: Gingko, 2003), 266.
11. Georg Simmel, "Fashion, Adornment, and Style," in *Simmel on Culture*, ed. David Frisby and Mike Featherstone (Thousand Oaks, CA: Sage, 2000), 192–93.
12. Anthony Wilden, *Man and Woman, War and Peace: The Strategist's Companion* (New York: Routledge and Kegan Paul), 61–66.
13. Wilden, *Man and Woman, War and Peace*, 63.
14. Kenneth Burke, *Language as Symbolic Action: Essays on Life, Literature and Method* (Berkeley: University of California Press, 1966), 13–15.
15. Henri Bergson, *Creative Evolution*, trans. Arthur Mitchell (New York: Random House, 1944), 306.
16. Bergson, *Creative Evolution*, 307; also see Corey Anton, "Dreamless Sleep and the Whole of Human Life: An Ontological Exposition," *Human Studies: A Journal for Philosophy and the Social Sciences* 29, no. 2, (2006): 181–202.
17. Bergson, *Creative Evolution*, 323.
18. Bergson, *Creative Evolution*, 313.
19. See Robin Dunbar, *Grooming, Gossip, and the Evolution of Language* (Cambridge, MA: Harvard University Press, 1997).
20. Bergson, *Creative Evolution*, 313–14.
21. Bergson, *Creative Evolution*, 314.
22. Bergson, *Creative Evolution*, 319.
23. Martin Heidegger, *Existence and Being*, trans. R. F. C. Hull and Alan Crick (Chicago: Henry Regnery Co, 1967), 328, 329,; 347.
24. Heidegger, *Existence and Being*, 331.
25. Heidegger, *Existence and Being*, 340.
26. Heidegger, *Existence and Being*, 341.
27. Heidegger, *Existence and Being*, 334.
28. Heidegger, *Existence and Being*, 335.
29. Heidegger, *Existence and Being*, 335.
30. Martin Heidegger, *Basic Writings*, trans. David Farrell Krell (San Francisco: Harper Collins, 1993), 261.
31. Heidegger, *Existence and Being*, 341, 346, 353.
32. See Heidegger, *Existence and Being*.
33. Heidegger, *Existence and Being*, 339–40.
34. Sartre, *Being and Nothingness*, 16.
35. Sartre, *Being and Nothingness*, 23.
36. Sartre, *Being and Nothingness*, 4–5. We also can note that Burke agrees. He writes, "[Q]uestions imply a feeling for the negative, since the 'perfect question' is so phrased as to permit of a yes-no answer," in *Language as Symbolic Action*, 459.
37. Sartre, *Being and Nothingness*, 5.
38. Sartre, *Being and Nothingness*, 9.
39. Sartre, *Being and Nothingness*, 8.
40. Sartre, *Being and Nothingness*, 8.
41. Sartre, *Being and Nothingness*, 10.
42. Sartre, *Being and Nothingness*, 10–11.
43. Sartre, *Being and Nothingness*, 29.
44. Sartre, *Being and Nothingness*, 32.
45. Sartre, *Being and Nothingness*, 28. Vilém Flusser writes, "We are free because we are able to say no to everything and commit suicide. It is not suicide itself that is freedom, however, but its availability as an option at any moment—not constant rejection, but the constant possibility of rejecting," in *Into the Universe of Technical Images*, trans. Nancy A. Roth (Minneapolis: University of Minnesota Press, 2011), 122.
46. Sartre, *Being and Nothingness*, 33.
47. Sartre, *Being and Nothingness*, 40.

48. See Jean-Paul Sartre, "Existentialism Is a Humanism," trans. Philip Mairet (New York: Double Day, 1971).
49. Kenneth Burke, *A Grammar of Motives and a Rhetoric of Motives* (New York: The World, 1962), xx–xxi.
50. Burke, *Language as Symbolic Action*, 457.
51. See Burke, *Language as Symbolic Action* and *The Rhetoric of Religion*.
52. Burke, *Language as Symbolic Action*, 430, 440.
53. Burke, *Language as Symbolic Action*, 11.
54. Georg Gusdorf offers a nice complement to this line of thought where he writes, "In fact, the life of the mind ordinarily begins not with the acquisition of language, but with the revolt against language once it is acquired," in *Speaking (La Parole)*, trans. Paul T. Brockelman (Evanston, IL: Northwestern University Press, 1965), 40.
55. Burke, *Language as Symbolic Action*, 11.
56. Burke, *Language as Symbolic Action*, 420, 453–454.
57. Burke, *Language as Symbolic Action*, 454.
58. Burke, *Language as Symbolic Action*, 12.
59. Kenneth Burke, *The Rhetoric of Religion: Studies in Logology* (Berkeley: University of California Press, 1970) 20–21.
60. Burke, *Language as Symbolic Action*, 455.
61. Burke, *The Rhetoric of Religion*, 298–99.
62. Terrence Deacon, *Incomplete Nature: How Mind Emerged from Matter* (New York: W. W. Norton and Co., 2012), 10.
63. People commonly are misled by mechanistic and reductionist accounts of human beings within popular science, where humans, and all organisms really, are depicted as some sort of informational–representational machine, a squishy computer, one that simulates agency and decision-making but is, all said and done, fully determined or random all the way down: there is only the illusion of agency and the delusion of decision-making. Second-tier sciences such as chemistry and biology and third-tier "sciences" such as anthropology, economics, and psychology will simply have to wait it out until the particle physicists eventually tell us how everything really works. The obvious difficulty with this latter view is that people are denied teleological experiences, intentions, and the like, while simultaneously being metaphorically compared with something that clearly was built and designed with intention and ends in view. It is strange, indeed, and not without significant contradiction, to suggest that humans are special forms of computers. Given that modern science abhors teleology and has been successful only by ousting it from their explanations, computers, obviously built with intent and designed to serve prespecified ends, seem a pretty poor metaphor for humans. A bit harshly stated, there seems not to be any human of the human left or life in the life remaining after scientific explanations have reduced them to blind chemical processes and mindless physical forces.
64. Deacon, *Incomplete Nature*, 2. Erving Goffman well captures some of this logic where he writes, "Of all of the things of this world, information is the hardest to guard, because it can be stolen without removing it," in *Strategic Interaction* (Philadelphia: University of Philadelphia Press, 1967), 78–79.
65. Deacon, *Incomplete Nature*, 23.
66. Deacon, *Incomplete Nature*, 41.
67. Deacon, *Incomplete Nature*, 3.
68. Deacon, *Incomplete Nature*, 26. Anthony Wilden, a fellow Bateson scholar, writes, "[G]oal seeking within constraints, is an informational relationship defined by the future. . . . Causality here is negative: it is the result of the absence of the goal, the result of something not yet happening," in *The Rules Are No Game: The Strategy of Communication* (New York: Routledge and Kegan Paul, 1987), 78.
69. Deacon, *Incomplete Nature*, 29.
70. Deacon, *Incomplete Nature*, 21, 39.
71. Deacon, *Incomplete Nature*, 45.

Chapter Two

Life and Many Modes of Bodily Non-being

THE HUMAN BODY AND THE REALITY OF RELATIONS

No matter how much religious or scientific inquiries may have led people into somewhat simplified or trivialized notions of selves and spirituality, people are, quite fortunately, as Joseph Campbell would say, "riding atop a whale while fishing for minnows." Many people, said differently, may have yet to learn that they are much older and other than they commonly think they are. They may have yet to grasp the many different ways that nothing infects being for the sake of beings. They may have yet to come to terms with the fact that relations, though no thing, are just as real as things are.

We, each of us, are an actualization of the universe's capacity to enable parts of itself to relate to other parts, as if each part were an other. Each of us is a place and moment of the "self-aware cosmos," an emptiness through which "whatever is" comes to presence. To suggest that the cosmos is self-aware is not at all to propose panpsychism, the belief that consciousness is everywhere and hence precedes the emergence of life and humanity. On the contrary, it is simply a buttress against the A-Naturalist Fallacy. It is to recognize that we are both self-aware and part of the cosmos. We happen to be that part of the cosmos that is able to consciously reflect upon "what is" and differentiate it from what only "seems to be" and what "is not." The cosmos is self-aware in that we who are not *not* the cosmos bear various forms of awareness regarding ourselves as aspects of the universe.

Life thus emerges by way of a lack, a gap, a crack in being. The fissures of non-being into the inorganic realm make way for highly complex relations in both space and time. One of the most important kinds of relations for the human body are *possibilities*, often concretely experienced as "needs" and "desires." Laing and Cooper write, "Need detotalizes the full, indifferent, persisting totality of the inorganic. This detotalization, the injection of nothing into the world, is a univocal, non-reciprocal relation."[1] This partly means that *all* desire: for food, water, sleep, sex, yearnings for success or fame or fortune. and especially desires for the unattainable (e.g., return of a deceased loved one, perpetual youth, control over what others think of us, the dissolve of all mystery, etc.), come from the incompleteness at the heart of life. Because we live, we have needs, and needs are exemplars of non-being haunting being. More concretely considered: how, exactly, is the experience of thirst possible?[2] How is hunger possible? If these questions seem obtuse, ask how the body, which is always a fully positive set of conditions, an actual state-of-affairs, can experience the *absence* of food or water. Someone can feel hunger, a need for something not yet eaten, even though the body itself is exclusively a set of actual physiological conditions. Isn't this a simple and powerful illustration of a ubiquitous mode of non-being in the cells of the living?

Metabolism is a very special mediation: it allows elements of the environment to become us while also allowing parts of us to become waste in the environment. When we look at a body, it is easy to see it as a complete whole, as if it were fully present to itself and self-sufficient. But that overlooks the fact that human bodies have holes on both ends, top and bottom. Regarding anyone whom you ever can see, you can be sure that they ate some food earlier and they will need to eliminate waste soon enough. Hence, when we look at organisms available to the naked eye and see whole, complete beings, our eyes are basically deceiving us, oversimplifying matters quite a bit. "You are what you eat" is more than a metaphor. It expresses a profound truth about the amorphous boundaries between body and environment. Clearly we are not our food, but we are not not it either. We commonly treat food with a self-serving mismatched attitude: we act as if the food is not itself alive (or did not demand a sacrifice earlier). We also act as if we "are who we are" without food. We maintain both of these beliefs despite that fact that we grew our very materiality out of the foods we have digested. (Note, too, that food itself is demarcated by non-being on both sides of its temporal journey: it goes from being "inedible" [e.g., raw] to being "edible" [e.g., cooked] but soon enough becomes "inedible" again [e.g.. spoiled]; it *is not* food then *is* food and then *is not* food once more.) To be deprived of food is to deny one's body of life itself. That such deprivation is possible at all reveals the body as an incomplete being, an environment-dependent being.

It should be obvious that we come from others, in the plural, and that single human beings are incomplete, haunted by absences. This is apparent in sex and marriage. Not only do many people spend oodles of time and effort in their mate selection, but in their minds and practices we find many enactments of the expression "you complete me." In Plato's *Symposium*, Aristophanes tells the story of the four-legged, four-armed, cart-wheeling humans, who, after being cut in half by Zeus, were turned into two separate creatures, each now needing the other for completion. Also, consider the ugly fact of genitalia.[3] Is it not profound and fascinating that people have genitalia? Focusing upon the discrete and individuated body, no amount of analytic study reveals the deeply social nature of genitalia. The question is not: "How do genitals relate to the body's overall functioning?" This is a worthy question, but, no, the more interesting question in this context is: "How do one's genitals relate to the genitals of another's body?" We have organs that evolved to physically interact with the organs of others, meaning that we can comprehend genitalia only by appreciating how one's private parts relate to others' private parts. We speak of genitalia as "private parts" despite the fact that sex organs, in fact the most inherently "social" of all organs, are something that we *withhold* from those with whom we are *not* intimate. R. D. Laing nicely addresses genitalia, incompleteness, and interpersonal relationships where he writes, "Nipple and mouth, vagina and penis, are the separate ends of a connection. It is the sense of connection, or the absence of any connection, established between us, through them, which seems to be the key concern."[4] What could be a clearer example of the body's incompleteness: separate individuals not only originate from the sexual actions of others but each person is ontologically precast for possible fecund interactions with others.

All living organisms are incomplete by their very nature. They are not fully self-contained. Arthur Koestler, in his book, *The Ghost in the Machine*, writes of the need to

> get away from the concept of the individual as a monolithic structure, and to replace it by the concept of the individual as an open hierarchy whose apex is forever receding, striving towards a state of complete integration which is never achieved.[5]

We are alimentary canals flowing through the river of life. Not only are we always in contact with something that we are not, we are in need of food and water, air to breathe and space to rove through. We need somewhere to go, something to do, and we need others, too. The body's sensory capacities traffic in absence and incompleteness; they furnish horizons of possibilities and open domains for meaningful action. As Deacon suggests, "Because organisms are constituted by specially organized, persistent, far-from-equilibrium processes, they are intrinsically incomplete. In this regard, they are processes organized around absence."[6] As absences that make room for contexts of care, we are projects ever-on-the-way. We live our lives such that a meal from two days ago fails to satisfy today's hungry belly. Like food already digested, goals once achieved lose their meaning; our current goals—

the ones to which we are actively committed—feed our lives with significance. We are futural through and through; we dwell within what is still outstanding, what still remains to be done. Only the dead are complete.

Non-being, I have been trying to show, pervades human life on many different levels. The solitary visible organism is not only bound for its survival upon countless modes of commerce and exchange with others and its environment, but it also relies upon innumerable symbiotic relationships with other microbiotic organisms. Hence, before considering the modes of possibilities offered by the human body in much greater detail, I take a brief detour to address the ancient and the tiny, the world unseeable to the naked eye and upon which the body vitally depends. Here we find that the body is not what common sense takes it to be.

THE EUKARYOTE INVASION AS THE GREATEST STORY EVER TOLD

Human individuals are incomplete in both space and time; they are a link within the chain of being, a node in the multileveled network of life.

Somewhere in the past, particular individuals had a relationship, connected in a certain way, and one of the possibilities of that connection came to fruition: here we are. Because we see life all around us with its sequence of birth, aging, reproduction, and death, it is easy to get the impression that sex and death are intrinsic to life. Sex and death seem synonymous with life, at least as far as the eye can see; the cycle of life seems everywhere and universally true. But, in fact, such an account would be an oversimplification; it tells only part of the story.

The strange world discovered by the microscope first entered popular understanding under the expression "germs" and even that was initially quite a hard sell. People tend to trust what they see; they find it hard to believe in living beings so small that they remain unseen. Who could imagine organisms so tiny that they can float through the air without appearing at all! Although "germ theory" eventually did make its way into popular thought around the time of the American Civil War, its initial effect resulted in people trying to kill germs. Soon enough and in due course, it led to the overuse of antibiotics. Now, well over a century later, more and more people grasp our need for certain kinds of bacteria, realize the importance of probiotics, and understand how we, in fact, owe our very lives to certain kinds of microbes.

Within the human body itself, microbe cells significantly outnumber human cells, and, by some estimates "more bacteria inhabit your mouth right now, even if you've just brushed your teeth, than there are people in New York City."[7] Scientists today are learning more about the gut-brain connection, and many people are now aware that babies birthed through the birth canal, as opposed to those birthed by cesarean section, gain some health and immunity benefits from the mother's microbiome. Two hundred years ago, no one would have predicted the procedure currently known as "fecal microbiota transplantation." At the least, increasing numbers of scholars in the field of microbiology are recognizing the many ways that a human being is more a colony and a complex system within other systems than it is a single being per se.

Some of the most provocative research on the diversity of microbiotic life comes from Lynn Margulis and her son Dorion Sagan. In their fascinating books *What Is Life?*, *Acquiring Genomes*, and *Microcosmos*, among others, they account for the forms and modes of life present on Earth since its inception. They explain how, for a couple of billion years on this planet and before the eukaryote invasion, life initially consisted of single-celled organisms: archaea, bacteria, viruses. These organisms had no life cycles as we experience them today, and they did not pass off genetic material by offspring. Single-celled organisms had some kind of genetic information, a kind of RNA/proto DNA located as ciliates on their bodies, but two of the Darwinian paradigm's key players, sex and death, were not yet in the game. That is to say, for the first two billion years of evolution, there was no evolution in the Darwinian sense of genetic material having survival value passed on to offspring.

According to Margulis and Sagan, "symbiogenesis" signifies something quite different than Darwinian notions of evolution (i.e., "descent with modification"). Life began on Earth—and in fact persisted for billions of years—with bacteria that did not experience life as a journey from "birth to death." These tiny single-celled organisms had no offspring. Their mode of life included kinds of metabolism and particular means of relating to their immediate environment, including growth and division. Of course, a given organism could be nutrient deprived or ingested by a neighbor, but neither death nor sex were inherently stitched into life the way that these phenomena are for multicellular organisms such as ourselves.

For a very long time, eating and "mating" were inseparable affairs. Both processes involved sharing genetic information; ingesting included acquiring genetic material. A basic revolution happened as one of the organisms attempted to devour another and was unable to digest it, while, simultaneously, the organism that had been swallowed found its new environment preferable to its previous one, and it also fortuitously produced waste material that benefited the ingesting organism. So began the nucleated cell. The emergence of eukaryotic cells (i.e., nucleated cells) marks some of the first forms of symbiogenesis, and it led the way for protocist colonies which, in turn, paved the way for forms of multicellularity. This led to most of the life we see all around us.[8]

Margulis and Sagan describe the symbiogenesis that led to the nucleated cell by suggesting that "[v]ery different bacteria—one type that oxidized sulfide to sulfur, and another that reduced it back to sulfide—became fused. The two became one by symbiogenetic merger, and this chimera was the ancestor of us all."[9] It is worth making the side comment that just as people commonly think of sex and death as an inherent part of life, so too they think of oxygen as hospitable to life. Oxygen, in fact, is a highly reactive and corrosive gas. While some forms of bacteria produced it as waste and over millions of years created the vast resources that later animals would use for respiration, many other early bacterial forms of life found it intolerable, especially in direct sunlight. Interestingly, we still have within our bodies—in addition to our aerobic metabolism, which burns sugars by using oxygen drawn from the air—an anaerobic metabolism where muscles ferment sugars in the same ways as did early bacteria, and, hence, our bodies still retain some connection to the oxygen-deprived biosphere as it was billions of years ago.

Accounting for the symbiogenetic origin of protocists, Margulis writes, "Four once entirely independent and physically separate ancestors merged in a specific order to become the green algal cell. All four were bacteria."[10] Moreover, sex, in this account, began as kind of "truce," a stalemate born out of "abortive cannibalism."[11] Notice here that life somehow figured out a way to incorporate modes of non-being into itself, by way of sex and death, with the general consequence being increased complexity and expanded horizons for experience and development.

It is hard for many people to believe that all life visible to the naked eye grew *symbiotically* out of a long, slow evolutionary accomplishment where tiny creatures incorporated each other and which then branched into the world of animals, fungi, and plants.[12] Reviewing and summarizing the previous discussion, I quote Margulis and Sagan at length:

> Although of course, like all life, bacteria can be killed by starvation, heat, salt, desiccation, these microbes do not normally die. As long as the ambience permits, bacteria grow and divide, free of aging. Unlike the mammalian body which matures and dies, a bacterial body has no limits. . . . These new cells were the first protocists, and their coming brought the kinds of individuality and cell organization, the kind of sex, and even the kind of mortality (programmed death of the individual) familiar even to us animals. . . . The first new kind of cell—the nucleated cell—evolved by acquisition, not of inherited characteristics but of inherited bacterial symbionts. . . . Each animal body is a sort of diploid husk, morbidly discarded by those haploid sex cells that manage to produce each generation a fresh new body and thus continue beyond the death of the "individual.". . . Perhaps originally cannibals in distress, chromosomally doubled protists are our ancestors. Humans and all animals inherited death from these early eukaryotes. . . . Strange to say, death itself evolved.

Indeed, it was the first—and is still the most serious—sexually transmitted "disease."[13]

Elsewhere, Margulis writes:

> Evolution of the protoctist ancestors to plant and animal bodies required sacrifice and loss: multicellularity and complexification ushered in the aging and death of individual bodies. . . . More than one billion years ago, when protoctists evolved by integration of bacterial symbionts into permanent and stable communities that became protoctist individuals, the kind of scheduled death that disturbs us today first appeared. . . . In animals, plants, and even fungi, sex is no dispensable option for staying in the evolutionary game. . . . Mortality is the price they pay for fancy tissues and complex life histories.[14]

The non-being of death and the modes of absence that characterize sexuality were integrated into multicellular life. The consequence was greater orders of complexity and wider fields of possibilities. For multicellular organisms such as ourselves (organisms with complex nervous systems and sensory capacities and all the possibilities included therein), sex and death are necessities. They are two modes of incompleteness that make possible the lives we experience: not only is each person the product of sex, and each person sentenced to die as the price paid for having been born, but, if humans wish to stay in the unfolding of evolution, they will need to procreate.[15]

Death is built in, folded over into the processes of life for the sake of increased specialization within the development of the organism: sperm and ovum merge into a single fertilized egg that divides by mitosis to form a blastula. As cell division continues, the fertilized egg becomes an embryo. In the usual course of animal development, the cells of the blastula continue to divide, move, and die, much of that death making way for the gastrula, the beginning of the digestive tract, with openings at mouth and anus. "The vast majority of blastulas in the thirty million animal species 'gastrulate' and end up with a distinctive tube-within-a-tube digestive system."[16] Life's designing-in of strategically timed death, of programmed death, was essential for its more complex features to become possible. Note also that during the "intrauterine development of the mammal brain more than 90 percent of the cells that develop die before the fetus becomes an infant. These brain cells stop growing and disintegrate, are sacrificed in the process of growing a healthy infant."[17]

The challenges in appreciating our long and complicated evolutionary history are significant: theories of symbiogenesis are so bizarre and odd, so beyond people's wildest imagination, that, comparatively, myths and origin stories from religious texts seem easier to believe.[18] It is just too difficult for many people to accept that "we people are really walking assemblages, beings who have integrated various other kinds of organisms."[19] Indeed, if people found Darwin's claim that humans evolved from earlier species of primates to be heretical and beyond belief, what can they possibly make of the notion that humans evolved from immortal cannibalistic bacteria?

Before leaving this brief detour, it should be underscored that the eye, the organ sometimes offered by creationists as proof of intelligent design or of an "irreducible complexity" that could not have been formed by evolutionary processes, has as its ancestor a species of light-sensitive bacteria. Margulis and Sagan write, "Vision was anticipated in light-sensitive bacteria. . . . Retinal, the absorber of light in the retina of the mammalian eye, has a 3,500-million-year history."[20]

To be human is to be "walking talking minerals," chemistry afoot, a mobile zoo.[21] Sometimes people speak of death pessimistically and egocentrically. They say, "I'll tell you the purpose of life: we are little other than worm food!" How untrue, for, *at the very least and if only for countless tiny others*, we are edible homes all the way along! We are not simply beings who are alive; each of us is a massive multileveled site of life feeding upon itself. We are not who common sense takes us to be; we are much older, other, and more dependent upon others, even nonhuman others, than we commonly recognize.[22]

DISTANCE, ACTUAL AND POSSIBLE

Bodies, colonies of life, are thickly through and through *of* the world, not merely discrete things *on* the planet. They are something the larger environment is doing, one of the Earth's possibilities. All human bodies come into the world by literally coming out of another body, who has come out of another body, and so on. Again: one's body is *of* space not merely *in* space, and it has always already made room for itself. Yet, despite these facts, the world somehow remains at a distance.

Seriously, what is distance and how is it both actual and possible? It has no materiality and cannot be weighed or reduced to material components. It is a fine exemplar of a relationship that obtains between organisms and other points. Clearly, distances are not "not real." They can be measured precisely. But because of the room making measuring that interjects, there also must be nihilating gaps at both points outside any measured distance. That is, measured distances posit a nothing "before" the measuring, so that the measuring may commence, and also a nothing "after" the measuring, so that the measurement can be specified; all distances presuppose some kind of delimitation, a selective and limited releasement and appropriation.[23]

Without bodies, there are no singled-out, particular, and specified distances whatsoever, and also, there are certainly no *possible* distances. Moreover, a human body is a multimodal nexus of different sensory-motor capacities, meaning that it seamlessly integrates the different space-time horizons offered by each sensory capacity. Because one sensory horizon can be the environment for the others and vice versa, we experience different kinds of distances as both actual and possible.

Someone carries a pencil into a room. What, exactly, has been added to the room? It seems like a simple question but so much is involved, for the person has not simply added the mass of the pencil and the mass of their body to the room; they have not merely increased the overall occupancy of the room by measurements reducible to the space of their body and the pencil. The pencil is a mere extant and as such it brings with it no distances, no perspective, no representations, no concerns about the overall size or roominess of the room. It does not dwell in such phenomena. A living person, fundamentally more than the mass of their body, is the very clearing by which the room can show itself from certain vantages, with walls and objects being at specific delimited distances. And this includes, but is fundamentally more than, representation. Both pencil and body are at measurable distances from the room's walls, but bodily modes of representing those distances also include, as their ground, a capacity to move and spontaneously change what those distances are. The directionality, positionality, and motility of the body, its forward orientation and its built-in perspective, add "nothing" to the room, but a new constellation of relations, that of *possibilities*, is born and amounts to a rendering of distances (touchable distances, seeable distances, hearable distances, etc.) that otherwise remain without specific delimitation.

Organisms occupy space-time differently than things do, and, for organisms such as us, the space-time of the hand is different than the space-time of the eye, both of which are different than the space-time of the ear, and so on. A person is a clearing, an opening and integrating, of the world from various vantage points. As a multisensory network with a range of motor and tactile capacities, the body opens to different configurations of space-time that are integrated, organized, and synthesized by the nervous system. We mostly experience the synthesis rather than attend to the contributions of each sense in isolation. Our experience commonly intermingles inputs from the different senses and we only analytically and reflectively parcel out the contributions each makes. This means that we routinely prereflectively dwell in their net product. Nevertheless, through reflection and analysis, we can identify some key differences between and among the five senses, and, hopefully, we can reveal how each sense relates to the experience of distances both actual and possible.

When we stand on the ground, our feet occupy an actual, exclusive space.[24] Of course, we can see many other possible places to stand, but our standing per se is without any unactualized possibilities. We always are standing (or sitting) wherever we currently are. Touch is a realm of actuality, one of constitution. But to say as much is to imply that touch is also that sense most capable of reaching into the future and leaving items for the past—through material artifacts, handicrafts, and the like. Said from the inverse angle, eyes and ears leave no footprints, nor can they change objects. Touch is so much pure actuality—with its sense of possibilities funded from the other senses—that the bulk of the human world was built by hands. Hands (and even feet) can do much more than represent the world: they can change parts of it as well as spontaneously alter our distances from things, bringing us nearer to particular items or removing us from the scene.

What are we to make of the fact that four of our main senses (sight, hearing, smell, and taste) operate through openings? Does this not reveal something significant about our porous commerce with the environment, something about the way that absence relates to the world and to possibilities? Now, if our only sense organ were some bizarre fusion of touching, tasting, and smelling, our experiences would be extremely limited: the experience of space-time would be significantly reduced, impoverished down to memory and a highly precarious immediacy, an environment with skinny future possibilities, a milieu with no (or little) advanced warning.

Touch, taste, and smell are sometimes called "proximal" senses, whereas sight and hearing are "distal" senses, with vision being the most "representational" of the senses. Further delineating the senses, touch is most clearly aligned with actuality and presence, taste and smell are mainly domains of presence but marked by limited modes of absence, whereas both hearing and vision generate fields populated with possible objects of attention, realms of space-time that allow for kinds of possible follow-up by the body and its other senses. Smell and taste admittedly open to the "now gone." For example, we can retain the taste of something recently eaten.[25] Smells, too, often linger after the source of the smell is removed. This partly explains the deep connection between smell and memory. Smell attunes to something there to be smelled, and what is to be smelled is often only a sign of something that is near, or is at a distance, or is now absent, but, at any rate, definitely was there. Smell, then, admittedly, opens to certain kinds of distances and liberates possible pasts.

For humans, though, the main perceptual sources of distant possibilities come through hearing (the prey sense) and vision (the predator sense).[26] The close connection between vision and predator on the one hand, and hearing and prey on the other hand, underscores their primal origins. But this should not leave the impression that the terminus of worldly commerce always culminates in touching, smelling, and tasting. In fact, the most intimate sense, that of tasting, is also the most exclusive; we taste very little of the whole of experience. Rainbows, sunsets, stars, paintings, musical compositions, fairy tales, and epic dramas are not for tasting. Although infancy blends touching and tasting, the child soon enough learns that much of the world will not be tasted nor smelled. Indeed, of all that "there is" in the world, comparatively little can be touched and held, smelled or tasted. Thus the world we experience gains much of its depth and dynamic intensity by hearing and vision, both of which provide the bulk of the content for episodic memory and consciously controlled imagination. Vision and hearing, as two distal senses are also, not surprisingly, the two that have been most successfully subject to digitizing and turned into media content (e.g., books, radio, TV, music, movies, etc.).

Whereas vision tends to objectify life's eventfulness into a steady visual field and offers a silent horizon of possible future movements, hearing registers only the dynamic activity or action around us; it is able to capture what is inherently evanescent.[27] Erwin Straus nicely expresses this fact as "to hear is to already have heard."[28] Hearing tightly attunes to the process-nature of reality and conveys the eventfulness of existence. Walter J. Ong thus suggests that you can see a dead elephant, touch a dead elephant, and even smell a dead elephant, but if you hear an elephant, you'd better look out![29]

Vision, like the other senses, spatializes space in its own unique way. Vision conveys the sense of permanence, a sense of the unchanging, as no other sense can. We can move an object from one location to another, rotate it, and, despite such changes, the object shows itself as unchanged throughout the movements. The eye opens us to the static, the inert, and the lifeless. It discerns colors that adhere to three-dimensional objects, and so, surfaced objects compete with each other for occupancy of particular spaces.[30] Objects stand next to one another, simultaneously juxtaposed, and some objects can block other objects from view depending upon one's vantage point. Note, too, that vision exclusively deals with surfaces.

Hearing, in contrast to vision, opens us to interiorities: we can knock on an object and hear whether it is relatively hollow or solid. Sounds also go through walls in ways that light cannot, and sounds always seem to infiltrate us and surround us. We find ourselves resonating with sound, penetrated by it, engulfed on all sides by it. People, too, can make their interiors, their inner depths, their distant pasts, their hidden fears and private aspirations, known to each other (and even known to themselves) as the human voice allows for the presencing of such unseen depths.[31] Sound makes manifest that part of the individual that is *not* a surface. Furthermore, sounds separate from their sources, making the source or origin of a particular sound sometimes difficult to locate, and, more importantly, sounds—without visible surfaces and inherently evanescent—easily overlay the visual field without crowding out what is seen. Whereas vision shows surfaces in the distance, sound adds unseen depths and dimensions to the visual field. In the overall field made possible by hearing, sounds present themselves as part of a vast interiority and an all-inclusive realm of process and action. Thunderclaps, dogs barking, babies crying, leaves rustling, and rivers flowing in the distance, we vibrate to such sounds and dwell in the animated connections they provide. And one of the most striking features of sounds is that one can always add more sound. Sounds admittedly can drown or cancel each other out, but sounds have no extension other than through time.

Sound is the ideal medium for articulate thought and symbolic activity because it is unseen and is not extended, as are colored three-dimensional objects. Internally produced speech-sounds generate the mysterious sense of thought's omnipresence. Susanne K. Langer well captures how verbal symbols naturally hide themselves:

> Peaches are too good to act as words; we are too much interested in peaches themselves. But little noises are the ideal conveyers of concepts, for they give us nothing but their meaning. . . . Vocables in themselves are so worthless that we can cease to be aware of their physical presence at all, and become conscious only of their connotations, denotations, or other meanings. Our conceptual activity seems to flow *through* them, rather than merely accompany them, as it accompanies other experiences that we endow with significance.[32]

Because words can be said silently, internally to oneself, they easily elude our attention and we simply experience the "content" of thought. More will be said about the self-effacing nature of language and symbols in chapter 3, but, for now, suffice it to say that people commonly talk to themselves without recognizing that fact. It is as if our inward discourse routinely goes into dreamlike autopilot, where fantasy, phrases and expressions, song-lyrics and other flotsam and jetsam of consciousness, stream along without us having too much concern over their consistency, coherence, or intelligibility to others.

Compared to the gut-wrenching depths of despair and the heart-filled glow of hope that humans can experience, other animals have very meager future possibilities. They do not live in anguish. They do not agonize over having to make something of themselves. They mostly open to a "not yet" that is positioned within space, even if a very distant space. The animal body—without the resources of language, symbols, and communication technologies—seems naturally inclined to use vision as a metaphor for time. Even in human vision, time seems to be a kind of spatial container. The long expanse of the visual field opens "the now" by carrying some of the past and future along. The visual field, with its open expanses and receding horizon lines, serves as a primordial grounding—more than metaphorical—for experiencing the continuity and elongation of time, the experience of possible spatial distances. We can walk through an open field and see objects in the distance grow nearer and nearer at each step. The steady permanence offered by objects in the visual field coupled with our ability to move through space enables us to experience time as elongated and thick, as an extended domain between past and future with receding horizons in opposite directions.

But what is in the future is not merely spatially remote. Not all possibilities exist in space; not all distances, actual or possible, are spatial. As just suggested, there are many possibilities, largely those opened through language and discourse, that are not reducible to spatial possibilities at all. They are possibilities *in* time, possibilities *of* time. Georg Simmel, in his essay "The Transcendent Character of Life," well captures the odd nature of temporal distances as he reviews the tight-minded logical empiricism that subtly falls prey to a species of the A-Naturalist Fallacy. He writes,

> The present, in the strict logical sense of the term, does not encompass more than the absolute "unextendedness" of a moment. It is as little time as the point is space. It denotes merely the collision of past and future, which two alone make up time of any magnitude, that is, real time. But since the one is no longer, and the other is not yet, reality adheres to the present alone. This means that reality is not at all something temporal. The concept of time can be applied to the contents of reality only if the atemporality, which they possess as present, has become a "no more" or a "not yet," at any rate a nothing.[33]

To suggest that reality is always, only, and exclusively "the now," is to commit to an overly circumscribed sense of time and reality. The now, as William James would agree, is saddle-bagged by protentions and retentions, meaning that human perception unfolds as an articulate gathering along.

The "no longer" and the "not yet" must somehow be part of "the now." We might accordingly ask: how big can "the now" be? Spoken language, as one commonplace illustration, depends upon the integration of past-present-future; it is a leaping ahead that retainingly awaits its own completion. It unfolds through time in just such a way that the prior becomes intelligible only through the later. The lived-body—especially in its resources for thought—manages both actualities and possibilities by integrating different horizons of spatial and temporal distances.

When athletes kick a ball toward a goal, throw a dart at a dartboard, or hit a golf ball toward a hole, they use their powers of touch to guide a projectile to a particular spot within a visual field. They intend to delimit and actualize a "shot" from the many possibilities imagined. Whereas the visual field presents imagination with a wide expanse of possibilities, touch attempts to target one and to bring the possibility into an actuality. In these ways, similar to the hunting of predators and the fleeing of prey, possibilities appear to be spatial; vision provides an expanse of possible directions for movement, of which touch will actualize only a fraction. But notice how different this is from someone asking us for information about our childhood. We bear the possibility of telling the truth (as best we remember) just as we have the possibility of telling lies. Here we find realms of possibility not reducible to space. Likewise, the possibility for someone to fall in love or to fall out of love, to give up on their religious beliefs, to come to new modes of self-understanding and new levels of spiritual potency, these are grossly mischaracterized if reduced to possibilities simply "in" space.

To exist is to be that time that is made for possibilities. And possibilities are not merely hidden actualities in space; not all possibilities are "somewhere not here." Time is not space, and time is not something located "within" space. But time is real and it offers its own modes of distances. Humans, as language-using animals, dwell in temporal possibilities, live out their days by attending to temporal distances. In fact, some distances are made of nothing but time. Lived-though temporality—existence—is basically a species of negativity, one of non-being or negation. To exist is to entertain what was and will be; it is to transcend the "here and now" of the senses; it is to articulately open within a denial of what is merely the "here and now" of immediate contact. Obviously, not all possibilities are eventually actualized; some remain forever out of reach. Perhaps they were failed attempts or goals slowly abandoned or possibilities simply overlooked and neglected. At any rate, humans can live in the anguish of the missed opportunity and the failed attempt. And even the past as past is only a possibility, for "where and when" is that distant past which no one can remember?

Each person is a place and moment of all that ever has existed and all that ever will exist. We, each of us, did not come *into* the world but rather we have come *out* of it. People are something the Earth is doing. Alan Watts captures this well where he suggests, "Just as a tree flowers, so the earth peoples," to which we should immediately add the addendum, "*and people world.*" Again: the earth peoples and people world. What does this mean? It means that the world worlds itself through bodies that transcend themselves; flesh and sensory organs self-efface for the sake of a manifold of different relations and connections: physical, sensory, retentional, emotional, representational, imaginative, and so on. Human bodies are Earth's way of folding back upon itself in different ways and at different levels of interaction. As Margulis and Sagan put it, "Self-transcending life never obliterates its past: humans are animals are microbes are chemicals."[34]

VISION AND WAYS OF NOT-SEEING

To look is to disclose what's there in its much-at-onceness. It is to see multiple items, colors, distances all arranged and organized according to one's line of sight. Vision conveys the experience of the simultaneity of different objects as well as their permanence in ways unrivaled by the other senses.[35] Sight, as far back as Plato, has been hailed as "noble" and the "king" of the senses, meaning that it hierarchically dominates the perceptual field as the governing discloser of reality but nevertheless remains highly dependent upon the lowly functions of movement, hearing, touch, taste, and olfaction.

When we wish to compliment people, deeming them particularly sagacious and perceptive, we use terms such as "visionary" or "seer." But, make no mistake, to look at the world includes at least three ways of *not* seeing.

First, we have eyelids. This means that visible aspects of the world disappear when we close our eyes. Although the world in total does not go away, eyelids successfully hide what we wish not to see. So long as what we wish not to see is only something seen—an image—eyelids effectively eliminate such items from experience. Infants are quick to learn that they can banish some things out of existence by simply closing their eyes and keeping them shut. The opening and closing of eyes is perhaps the earliest recognition of being and non-being; it serves as a basic bodily metaphor, a micro-archetype, for them. With the ability to open and close our eyes at will, we can make the visual world appear and disappear at the blink of an eye.

Second, eyes see whatever is visible, but unless there is something wrong with them, they do not see themselves. This is partly what Drew Leder refers to when he writes about *The Absent Body*. All of the body's senses, not just sight, exhibit a "focal disappearance" such that routine operations render any particular sense absent while it makes present what it is not. Eyes are openings, holes that light pours through, and they function by making themselves disappear for the sake of what they are not. Eyes hide themselves in making present the visible world. We need a mirror or reflective surface to see our own eyes, and, even when we can see our eyes in a mirror, a gulf remains between our eyes as objects and our acts of seeing. When we look and try to see our own seeing, the seeing is whole and undivided but the seen eyes can be focused on only one eye at a time.

Third, to look is to selectively look in a direction. Here, then, nestled together are two more modes of negation: a negation within negation. To look is to look "here" rather than "there"; it is to focus upon one item rather than another; it is to select out a particular object from the visual field. But the total visual field itself is already engulfed by fuzzy edges of nothingness on all sides: top, bottom, left, and right. This means that to look is to have taken some kind of stand or position in the world; it is to have brought about an entire arrangement of the body, one that includes facing a direction, and furthermore, one that can change along with a turning of the feet or a turn of the head. Vistas and aspects otherwise unnoticed come into view. Upon further consideration, then, this fact of selective perception according to the position of the body proves to be even more haunted by absences than it first appeared. David Abram well identifies several modes of absence that show themselves within the parameters of the visual field where he writes,

> We are hunting for modes of absence which, by their very way of being absent, make themselves felt within the sensuous presence of the open landscape. . . . The *beyond-the-horizon* is just such an absent or unseen realm. . . . Is there *another* unseen aspect, another absent region whose very concealment is somehow necessary to the open presence of the landscape? . . . The back of my body is inaccessible to my vision and yet I know that it exists. . . . Yet while pondering the unseen aspects of my body, I soon notice another unseen region: that of the whole *inside* of my body. The inside of my body is not, of course, entirely absent but it is hidden from visibility in a manner very different from the concealment of my back, or of that which lies beyond the horizon. It is an instance, I suddenly realize, of a vast mode of absence or invisibility entirely proper to the present landscape—an absence I had almost entirely forgotten. It is the absence of what is *under the ground*.[36]

One's body, the clearing that makes room for the world, is caught by absences on all fronts: the horizon line of vision recedes off into something one cannot fully see and the limits of one's hearing make it so that some things are too far away or too quiet for one to register. We have a backside that we cannot see, and we also cannot see our insides (and all of their odd operations) without it costing us our life. The very ground under our feet, in all of its mysterious depth, hides itself and is absent from conscious awareness.

When we look at anything at all, we inherently bear a perspective; we see how things appear from that distance and point of view.[37] Unfortunately for common sense, all of the above is routinely used as evidence for the conclusion that perspective is an obstacle to truth, something that keeps truth, or at least an objective view of the world, always out of reach. Granted that the word *objective* can be quite problematic, perspective is not necessarily a limitation to truth and objectivity. In many ways, visual perspective makes experience (as well as certain kinds of perceptual truth) both actual and possible.

The A-Naturalist Fallacy Reconsidered

We need to carefully reconsider the A-Naturalist Fallacy, which most broadly refers to various imagined separations between humanity and nature, where we comprehend less than the whole of nature by taking humanity to be other than natural. The A-Naturalist Fallacy appears in many places and in different guises. One avenue into reconsidering it—and trying to guard against it as we proceed—will be to suggest that two different issues need to be reviewed, assessed, and strategically integrated.

First, conceptual ambiguities lurk within the notion of "representation," mainly because the human body is a complex multisensory network capable of strangely looping back upon itself and its relationship with the larger environment in different ways.[38] This is also partly an issue because the body, never merely an object within space, has come "into" the world by literally growing "out of" another person, and, in doing so, is *of* space, is thick with it, in just such a way that the world has already made room for it.[39] Bodies are *of* space, never merely *in* it. And, to be, at all, is to be suspended and bound within countless constellations of various relations, only some of which are representational. Second and closely related to the first issue, relations between things are not things and yet they are as real as things.[40] It is by addressing these two different issues, tying them together as it were, that we can best proceed.[41]

For a brief preliminary example, we might compare how sunlight tans our skin with how sunlight affords acts of looking: if we walk out into the sunlight and close our eyes, we can feel the warmth of the sun on our skin. The light rays have overcome great distances, and, as they make their contact, they register their actuality—whether we are attending to it or not—such that we could receive a burn if we stay in the sun too long. Now compare such actuality to the kinds of possibilities afforded through vision. Even though both processes amount to the body's interaction with light waves, suntans are evidence of the sun overcoming distance, making actual contact, and leaving its mark upon the skin. No matter how "actual" the presence of the visual field, it presents itself as a horizon of possibilities for future action in the distance. Indeed, without the sense of sight, we would be at a loss to quickly locate shade, and, in contrast, more than any other sense, sight discloses where, if at all, shade can be found.

We should note, too, that when we look to objects in the distance, one object resists our gaze so powerfully that it can annihilate our vision permanently. In fact, staring directly at the sun has blinded more than a few people in the ancient world. Is there not something quite interesting in the fact that we cannot stare at that which made our vision possible?

THREE EXEMPLARS

The body's positionality, directionality, and visual perspective make certain kinds of distance and perceptual truth both actual and possible, and yet embodied perspective amounts to nothing substantial, nothing added to matter. It is the world of relations delimited and configured according to one's body, but it is not itself a thing. It does not have a measurable extension in space. Perspective is the gravitational center that detotalizes the whole visual field into a particular constellation of delimited relations based on a particular vantage point. From there, different distances and elements are organized and cast as different parts of the whole.

The Rainbow-Observer Phenomenon

Let's examine the classic case of a rainbow.[42] Recall the question, if a tree falls in a forest and no one is there to hear it does it make a sound? We can also ask, are any rainbows "in 'the' sky" if no observers "are there" to see them?

A version of the A-Naturalist Fallacy shows itself here. In general, for a rainbow to appear in the sky, several elements must all be present and in the right arrangement. There must be sunlight, moisture in the air, and an observer must be at a fortuitous angle and at the right distance. When all of those elements are present in the right arrangement, we see a rainbow and can say, "There is a rainbow in the sky."

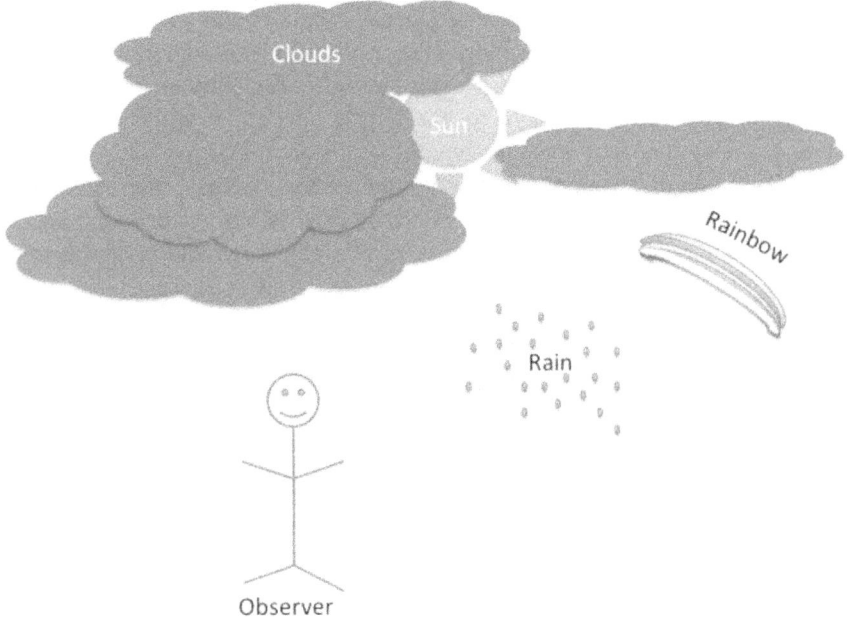

Figure 2.1. The Rainbow-Observer Phenomenon

Now, if one were to ask, "Would the rainbow 'be there' without any sunlight, if, say, the sun were completely covered by thick clouds?" people routinely respond, "No, you need sunlight for a rainbow to occur." Similarly, if we were to ask, "Would the rainbow 'be there' if the sky had no moisture in the air?" once again, people are pretty quick to say that moisture is one of the components necessary for a rainbow. But if we move to the observer, and ask, "Without an observer at a particular angle for viewing, is the rainbow 'there' in the sky?" many people become committed to a naïve belief that the rainbow is "there" with or without observers. They would be wrong. The point here—a little bit more sophisticated than the proverbial "tree falling in the forest with no one there to hear it" question—is not simply that the different light waves are "there" and that observers are needed to perceive those as colors, to "turn them into" colors. No, the much more important conceptual point is that without observers, there is "no 'there' there." This is why, when different people see the "same rainbow," there are in fact as many rainbows as there are observers. Each person sees a slightly different rainbow, and rainbows move relative to particular observers. This also explains the joke about those who would seek a pot of gold at the end of the rainbow. Admittedly, there are still sun and clouds and moisture, doing what they do, but without some observer located somewhere, there are no rainbows. Does this mean that rainbows, then, don't *really* occur in nature? Are they simply a subjective, psychological projection? No, not at all! That would be the A-Naturalist Fallacy rearing its head again. The more general and important point is that we are part of the way that nature reflects back upon itself to make such distant phenomena possible and actual.

Observer-Dependent Relations

Consider a second example, one where two people face each other over a table that has six objects upon it. Once again, I am attempting to show how observers partly make the scene, that relations are as real as things, and that in some basic sense, perspective—rather than an obstacle to truth—is what makes some kinds of perceptual truth possible and actual.

Figure 2.2. Observer-Dependent Relations

In this case, we can describe how things appear for Observer A and for Observer B. Moreover, we can assume a fair measure of intersubjective agreement in their assessment of how things look from the perspective of the other person.

For Observer A, the triangles stand "in front of" the ovals and squares (the ovals and squares stand "behind" the triangles). For Observer B, the squares are "in front of" the ovals and the triangles; the ovals and triangles stand "behind" the squares. For Observer A, the white objects are on the "right-hand side" of the table, whereas for Observer B, the white objects are on the "left-hand side" of the table. Note that although both observers see the objects from their own perspective, they have a sense of how those objects appear to the other person; each person's perspective includes a metaperspective regarding how things appear from the other person's perspective. That is, these are real relations on the table and they are subject to intersubjective agreement; persons are not locked within a solipsistic view of things.

But now ask, *independent of any and all observers, how are those items related to one another*? Again, try to imagine that there are no observers at all. At one extreme, we perhaps could say that, bereft of all observers, there is no way to delimit and coherently address what "is there." Even in our imagination, while considering them as possibilities, in trying to entertain what the table looks like without observers, we seem to occupy a certain vantage and maintain an angle of imaginative approach. Obviously, items on the table do not pop in and out of reality depending upon whether people are present or not. We might suggest that the items on the table have inherent properties and something like objective similarities between them in terms of shapes, sizes, and maybe even colors (i.e., measurable light waves). But it makes no sense to speak of any object being "in front of" the others or "behind" the others or "to the left or to the right" of the others without an observer. These are not merely represented relations, as if they, the relations, were independent of us and merely discovered by us. Granted that our eyes may be representing these objects in the visual field—as possibilities for future touch or interaction—but, hopefully obviously at this point, the sheer position of one's body is not representing those relations. It is how they come to *be* at all. One's body, its forward directionality and positionality, performs the work to cause them to come into existence, even if vision and the intellect can then surreptitiously treat all our relations as merely something represented. These relations (e.g., "behind," "in front of," etc.) are real relations in the world, not simply "subjective" interpretations. This is evident enough in the fact that each observer can recognize how the objects appear to the other observer. With all of that, such relations are nevertheless not "there" independent of observers. We need to make room for these kinds of phenomena or we slip into the A-Naturalist Fallacy. We fall prey to imagining that all relations must be present independent of people or they are merely subjective.

The Unlooked-At Mirror

For a final illustration, imagine an art exhibit where two chairs and two paintings are strategically placed at different angles before a mirror so that whoever sits in either chair has one of the paintings perfectly fit and framed within the surface of the mirror. The mirror is so clear and clean that if a person focuses for just a little bit, it seems as if the painting is there before them and that they are looking directly at it, rather than just looking at the mirror. The highly polished mirror seems to disappear completely for the sake of the painting. Here, two different people look at the exact same object, the mirror, and yet each person sees a different painting, and they also do not see what the other sees.

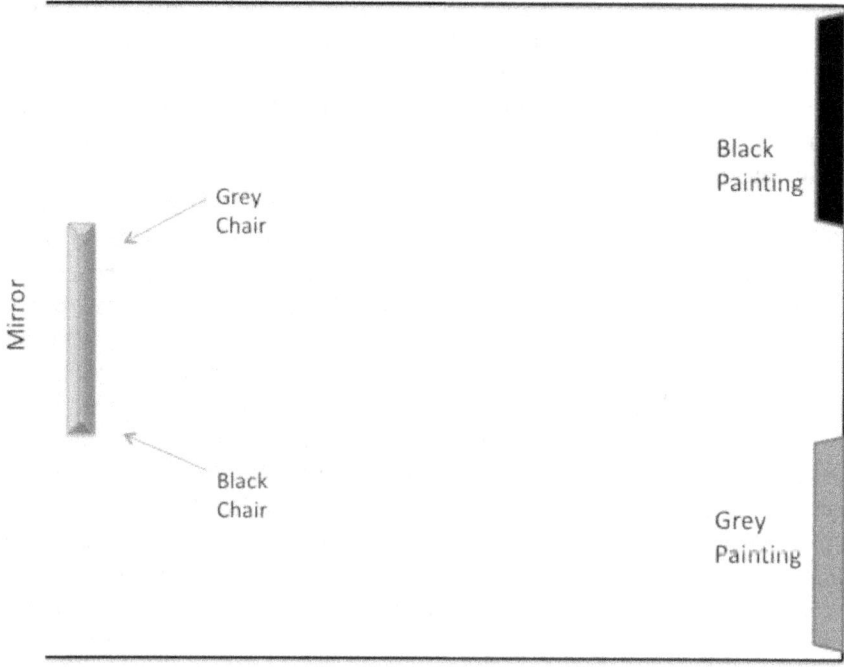

Figure 2.3. The Unlooked-At Mirror

The person sitting on the grey chair sees the grey painting while the person sitting on the black chair sees the black painting. To suggest that either person is only representing the image confuses things on many levels, though it is mainly because a very interesting variant of the A-Naturalist Fallacy is smuggled in as we attempt to talk about the world independent of observers.

Let's start with a couple of questions. Is each person simply representing a painting? How can the reflection be a mere representation? The word *representation* makes it seem as if the image of the painting is already "there" to be re-presented, and yet the image of the painting does not even show itself until (and unless) a person is sitting in one of the chairs. When someone sits in a chair, that person's body performs a kind of work and thereby constitutes relations as much as represents them.

Try it this way: without anyone in the room, absolute observerlessness, what, exactly, is showing in the mirror? How could that possibly be represented, given that one needs to be at some angle of incidence to perceive any object in the mirror at all? Obviously, I am not advocating for a kind of subjectivism, as if reality is made up by people. On the contrary, the point is simply that relations are as real as things, and some of those relations come from sheer distance, physical location, positionality, and bodily direction. It obviously makes sense to talk about the chairs being in the room without any observers, and it makes sense to say that there is a mirror there, and that there are paintings in the room, too. One might even be willing to haggle about the inherent properties of the chairs or of the paintings, showing relations that seem to be discovered by people and that continue independent of (and after) observation. In this case, it does make sense to speak of representing the chair, or talk about representing the paintings, or even the mirror and its particular properties (although it is hard to look upon a mirror without immediately perceiving whatever is disclosed upon its surface according to angle of incidence). Anyone could walk around the chairs, take them in from many different distances, angles, and perspectives. Note too that the actual paintings have depth and substance and allow for multiple vantages and angles of viewing (and can be touched, smelled, or even tasted), whereas either painting that can be made to appear as an image fully in the mirror is in fact a particular vantage upon, and distance from, the mirror.[43] Those are fair enough, but it stretches what we meant by "representation" in the previous case to then also suggest that we, in sitting in one of the chairs, simply "represent" either the chair or the image in the mirror. The image in the mirror isn't anything but light; it is already a kind of representation, but our actual bodily presence, its directionality and delimited field of vision, strategically positions us, does the work, and *causes* the image to happen in—to "be there" in—the mirror. An observer might furthermore represent that image in many ways—in memory, imagination, speech, and drawing—but it is fundamentally something constituted and only secondarily represented; it is not something wholly and merely "represented" by the observer. Hans Jonas writes,

> One might point to the built-in spatial orientation which the physical directions of the body provide with the organic sense of right and left, front and back, up and down—a sense always actualized by some rudiment of motion. . . . We may therefore say that the possession of a body in space, itself part of the space apprehended, and that body capable of self-motion in counterplay with other bodies, is the precondition for a vision of the world.[44]

I have gone into these three exemplar cases to illustrate some pervasive ways that we underestimate how our sheer bodily presence and sensory-motor capacities make certain kinds of relations both actual and possible.

We do not merely nor exclusively represent items from our environment; our bodily presence causes certain kinds of relations to come into being—various possible distances in space and time—but, admittedly, we also can then discover and represent those by other sensory means. Hence, Deacon stresses,

> Work is a more complex concept than mere cause, because it is a function of relational features. And relations, both actual and potential, are precisely where the action is. . . . A constraint is not an intrinsic property but a relational property, even if just in relation to what is possible.[45]

We can thus appropriate his insight for the present purposes to show that constraints, ones that naturally perpetuate themselves, give focused direction to causality and enable bodily work to be done: the body's positionality and forward orientation builds in constraints that enable a certain kind of perceptual work to occur. Hence, my eyes represent what appears in the visual field, but that actual delimitation of a particular visual field is always already constrained by the fact that my eyes are on the front of my head and I must face what I wish to see. Optimal looking always implies an optimal distance from that which I wish to see, and I cannot see what is behind me without turning my head. These are not simply "limitations" of the body, but rather they are part of the inbuilt constraints through which the body gets its work done.

Also, it needs to be underscored before moving on that in all three of these cases, in order to differentiate between "caused relations" and "represented relations," we are forced to imagine what is not the case, and in principle cannot be the case: *observerless visual fields*. It is only by being able to imagine what is not the case, what by definition must not be the case, that such truths can be disclosed. I explore this more in chapter 3, but for present purposes I simply stress that our experience of the passage of time is similar to all three of these cases. Past and present and future are real and they are part of the world, but they are not "there" independent of observers.

What could be more beautiful than a good sunset? When is the last time you took a moment to enjoy one? Like rainbows, sunsets are "there" in the horizon only with the assistance of observers: the earth is rotating, moving through space, and it is because we occupy a certain position that the sun seems to "set" over the horizon. Were there no people (or other organisms) here to see them, they would not exist. The sun is both rising somewhere and setting somewhere and both of these are always happening simultaneously. Fortunately for us, this is not what we directly experience. Our highly limited vantage, and our ability to turn and face West, provides the ground for such treasures to become available. *Each of us is the setting of the sun.* This means that some of our greatest assets come not from what we personally can possess but from the way the earth possesses us, from how the earth makes purchases upon itself though the fillable vacancy that is the body. The sunset is among our greatest riches despite evading all private ownership. As the mystic Douglas E. Harding rightly observes, "[T]his kind of ownership is the only real kind."[46]

The "addition" that bodies with sensory capacities add to the world cannot be measured by any study of the total spatial volume a body occupies, as if the addition is merely increased extension. And bodies do much more than represent relations. The body, as it is lived—not the body as a measurable object—is a flight beyond its fleshy boundaries. It is the way the world opens to itself; it includes perspectives and it delimits those relations that constitute the situations in which we find ourselves.

THE HEADLESS WAY AND THE WORLDING OF THE WORLD

One of the most playful yet elusive accounts of absence and nothingness can be found in Douglas E. Harding's classic text *On Having No Head*. Harding recalls the single greatest day of his life as when, while walking in the Himalayas, he suddenly realized that he didn't have a head. This was no ordinary absence. It was a room-making nothingness that made room for everything, a vacancy eminently filled. As Harding states, "I had lost a head and gained a world."[47]

Have you ever noticed that you don't have a head? Seriously, look for yourself. What do you see? Don't think about it. Don't rely on what others have told you. Just look. One's face is the emptiness through which the world pours in; headless bodies are the way the world worlds. This, it must be stressed, is not properly speaking a "belief" about something; it is a direct experience.

Harding suggests a simple exercise may help you see your headlessness. Begin by placing one of your hands out in front of you, pointing your index finger to where you think your face should be, and then, try to see, *to carefully look at*, the place to which the finger is pointing. When you look to where your finger is pointing, what, exactly, do you see? Try it now. When I do the exercise, I see nothing, pure emptiness!

Now, undoubtedly, we can see the head that sits atop another's shoulders. Everyone else has a head, but, each of us, *for ourselves*, is fundamentally without one. This also means that we, as Harding would say, are never actually "Face-to-Face" with one another in our interactions. Rather, we are "Face-to-No-Face," as we can see someone else's face but only because of the room-making absence of our own. Thus, when we look at others, they seem to be whole objects extended within space, figures against a ground. We see them from head to toe, if only from a given perspective and at a certain distance. It is quite natural, then, to infer analogically that we are just like everyone else. We think to ourselves: "I am simply a thing in the world, just as others appear to me." Hence, when we look to another person, see a face, and say to ourselves, "I guess that is how I am as well," we overlook and undersee the most obvious fact of all. The question is not, "Am 'I' an object like everyone else?" but also and more fundamentally, "Is everyone else a subject (i.e., an absence) like 'I' am?" Accordingly, we would be much better served if, when we look to others, we were to say to them, "Pardon me, but I recently realized that I don't have a head, and I was just wondering if you have discovered that you are headless as well?" This can be the beginning of a fine conversation.

Headless interlocuters have the basis for genuine community, one found not through age, race, sex, nationality, culture, or even belief. Regarding all other possible similarities and differences, people can disagree or simply not be sure if their experiences are identical: your "blue" may be slightly different than my "blue." An action that seems "reserved" to you might seem "uptight" to me. We might be the same age and yet my sense of "old" might be different than yours. And so on. In contrast to these, we find in headlessness an equally available experience of the expansive nothing that we all are. This is partly why Harding stresses that headlessness is the most universally communicable experience "since there's nothing in it to differ about, nothing to go wrong, nothing idiosyncratic or merely personal and private. In headlessness we find common Ground at last."[48]

Before advancing any further, a few caveats should be made regarding the dominance of visual metaphors and the apparent over-reliance upon the sense of sight in "the headlessness way." First, we already spent considerable time identifying sight's unique status as a human sensory capacity. Of all the body's senses, vision generates a field that is the most expansive and far-reaching, one most open to a multiplicity of items simultaneously juxtaposed and hence experienced as standing possibilities. Second, with our eyes closed, we nevertheless can attend to the absolute stillness, the silent, stationary, and abiding emptiness that makes room for the articulate thoughts, spontaneous words, and inner images that fade in and out of conscious awareness. Third, "headlessness" is obviously and admittedly a metaphor for the self-effacing nature of the lived-body: it fundamentally refers back to the primordial emptiness that awareness *is*, and it also obliquely refers to all of the processes in the body that function despite the fact of us being completely ignorant, *utterly unknowing*, of how they actually work (e.g., we mysteriously grow hair, digest food, heal wounds, recover from illnesses, etc.).[49] Finally, Harding offers useful preemptive advice regarding possible critics where he writes that "the very suggestion of headlessness is for many people profoundly offensive, and there's no end to the objections they will raise. Never mind: headlessness is for living always, for sharing occasionally, for arguing about never."[50]

Infants soak up the world around them, "taking it all in" as it were. Beginning with no awareness of themselves as objects in others' visual fields, they naturally experience their headlessness. Then, throughout childhood, each of us learned to trade the worlding of the world that we are for a socially agreed-upon view. We became objects within the world of other objects. This is what some psychologists call "confiscation"—a profound alienation and estrangement from direct, primary experience. We slowly learned to overlook our true being (i.e., headless capacity for world) and instead focused upon the "individual," the bounded thing, the sack of skin that others (or mirrors) can locate within space.

Hence, the "headed grown-up" comes to pass. Growing up basically entails learning to overlook the most obvious feature of experience. As Harding suggests, "[O]ur learned view of ourselves from outside begins to overshadow, to superimpose itself upon, and eventually to blot out, our original view of ourselves from inside. . . . Instead of containing our world, it now contains us—what's left of us."[51] The whole of our being gets more and more shrunk down: we go from being the entire scene to a tiny part within it, some kind of thing amidst other things. By the time we are adults, we take the self that is seeable in the mirror to be the "real" us.

Now, for contrast and a reminder, stand in front of a mirror and carefully look at the difference for yourself. The image of you that can be seen in the mirror, that strange object amidst other things in the world, seems so tiny and self-contained compared with the vast clearing that you are in your headlessness. Your headlessness, in fact, makes room for much more than the image that can be seen in the mirror. It discloses the whole mirror, the wall the mirror is attached to, the entire visual field, and so on. Nevertheless, many people buy the social narrative and come to see themselves in terms of their social identities, their names, their egos, how they appear on the surface—things that are incidental and comparatively inconsequential. As Harding suggests about many people in their development from infant to adult, "instead of getting through to the central Absence-of-anybody they got stuck in the peripheral presence of a very human somebody."[52]

This also means that, as Harding suggests, "While I appear to others over there (viewing me from a distance) to be a mobile and limited human thing, I am really here (viewing myself from no distance) this immobile and unlimited and non-human No-thing."[53] The meaning of the gulf between "there" and "here" is basically that we are both one and many; in one sense, we are, as nothing, all the same as each other, but in another sense, we are different than each other, each person completely unique in a unique body with a unique temperament and with a unique life-history and unique set of practical competencies. The view "looking out" is one of difference, unique to me, my circumstances, particular vantages and perspectives, while the view "looking in" reveals a universally shared emptiness—the Nothing that each of us fundamentally is. Harding puts it simply: *"As something I am merely that thing, as no-thing I am all things."*[54] Part of the task, then, is to become "adept at two-way looking—at once looking in at No-thing and out at everything."[55] These two different views need ongoing synthesis: the outward view of things to be seen and the inward looking to the nothing that one is, and this "two-way looking" needs to be engaged simultaneously.

Such "two-way looking" is a practical form of daily mediation that helps dissolve the subject-object divide. It is one of the exercises that can help the "headed grown-up" become a "headless seer." One of the clearest ways to illustrate the Still Emptiness, the Nothingness of one's being, is to practice two-way looking while closely attending to what actually shows itself as one moves through space—not what one imagines happens but what actually makes its appearance if one takes the time to look. Upon close inspection, one's headlessness remains absolutely stationary no matter how one moves about. Look for yourself. The scenery and landscape move while the clearing that is no-head remains utterly motionless. Harding writes, "Walking across the room, I look *down*, and my head (no-head) is the infinite and empty Stillness in which those arms and legs are flailing."[56] This stillness and emptiness that shows itself as we move through space (e.g., in a car or on train) furthermore reveals that, at that level of analysis, everyone shares equally in non-being. Each person is a place and moment of the Holy THAT of which there is no whicher, the primal mystery of being itself.

> This very spot, this observation-post of mine, this particular "hole where a head should have been"—this is the Ground and Receptacle of all existence, the one Source of all that appears (when projected "over there") as the physical and phenomenal world, the one infinitely fertile Womb from which all creatures are born and into which they all return. It is absolutely nothing, yet all things; the only Reality, yet an absence.[57]

Harding further suggests, "Intrinsically, we all are one and the same, and there are no others,"[58] or stated otherwise, "the headless one remains the Only One, and sees itself as the Alone, and faces its Solitariness. At this level there are no others."[59] The key part of the phrase is, "At this level."

To clarify these claims, we can tease out at least three layers of selves: two that show up from the "view out" and one that appears only through the "view in." First, there is the embodied individual (with a particular age, race, sex, culture, etc.) who looks out at things in the world. Second, there is the particular self (with an age, race, sex, culture, etc.) who is seen as an object in the world, someone who is "there" for others to see (the body I imagine others see, the body that I can see in a mirror). Finally, there is True Self, sheer capacity for world, *Awareness Itself*, that which makes room for all by hiding itself and which can be seen only by the "view in." Harding disambiguates some of this where he writes, "The timeless and absolute consciousness which you are (for which some reserve the term Awareness) must not be confused with its temporal and relative aspect, as it takes on and discards endless functions, forms, and realizations."[60]

Consider a case for illustration purposes. A bride and groom, both slightly past their teenage years, walk down the aisle during a wedding ceremony. As they proceed, many people look upon them. The flower girl and ring boy, ages five and six, look at the couple and see "old" people. Simultaneously, the grandparents see the couple as too young to be getting married. The couple thus appears "old" or "young" depending upon who is looking. It cannot be overstated that this is more than a difference of "interpretation," and it is, strictly speaking, also more than different "representations" of the couple. There is a fact of age; people are a certain age in addition to any representations of those ages; they are at temporal distances from one another. A body is subject to sociohistorical formation and influences, and it has an age and a relative perspective on items in the world, but awareness per se does not. It is as old as life itself. The invariant Nothingness that allows for all perceptions to be made room for, inner or outer, is a perennial resource shared by all individuals, if only they take the time to look at the elusively obvious.

BEING-FOR-OTHERS AND EXISTENTIAL INCOMPLETENESS

Had the universe come into existence such that it was experienced by a single, solitary consciousness, then it would have successfully made itself and created the conditions for reflection back upon itself. It would have served as the foundation for itself and successfully removed contingency from its being. But such is not the case.

The previous account of headlessness admittedly slightly underplays the existence of others and seems to slide into an idealist position. By Sartre's terminology, Harding's thinking somewhat tends toward what he would call "sadistic bad faith," one attentive mostly to the "unseen seer" (the "unlooked-at looker").[61] This contrasts with "masochistic bad faith," which focuses upon an "unseeing seen" (the "non-looking looked-at"). By Sartre's lights, although we are headless for ourselves (i.e., *being for-itself*), we should not deny or underestimate the fact of otherness haunting our being: we are partly *being-for-others*. In fact, our being is ineradicably "being-for-itself" as well as "being-for-others," and Harding's practical technique of "two-way looking" acknowledges as much.

Stressing that consciousness cannot be a solitary relation of negation, Sartre writes, "The scattering of being-in-itself of a shattered totality, always everywhere, always at a distance, never in itself, but always maintained in being by the perpetual explosion of this totality—such would be the being of others and of myself as other."[62] In one sense, then, consciousness is one and the world is many, but, in another sense, the world is one and there are many pockets of emptiness (i.e., consciousnesses). Being-for-itself, as suggested in chapter 1, is parasitic upon being-in-itself. This means consciousness is not the source of what is; being-for-itself is the source of the "being there" of what is; being-for-itself is the source of all figure–ground differentiations, possible distances, and contextual configurations, but it is *not* the source of being-in-itself.

We are not independently ourselves, not in full possession of our identities, and nothing separates us from others. A fully self-contained person or a single solitary consciousness is, both in principle and in fact, an impossibility. To imagine ourselves as wholly alone is to try to make us the foundation of ourselves, to be the ground of ourselves, to cover over history and our convoluted and mysterious ancestry, to forget that we did not make up the language that we speak or invent the artifacts that enable us to do what we do. It is to pretend that we do not have a navel; it is to nullify the latent possibilites suggested by our teeth, our tongue, our sex organs, and so on.

We do not have full control over how others apprehend us, but, nonetheless, what others see of us is us even though it eludes our awareness. For example, others can know of us prior to our birth via ultrasound and can recall facts about us from infancy even though we don't remember any of it. They can see facial expressions that we failed to hide. We can have kale stuck in our teeth, or we can mispronounce or misidentify a word without knowing it. We can have a stain on the back of our pants. We can walk through a busy parking lot and not be sure who, exactly, is seeing us. We can believe that we are successfully hiding ourselves, but, all the while, through comportment and demeanor, reveal ourselves as nervous or tired or perhaps intoxicated. We are not as hidden from others as we commonly believe: social politeness and etiquette encourage us to downplay our tactical advantage over others. We, all of us, are object-things in the world, entities that others can approach, handle, and manipulate, and whose fragility others can exploit. This means that any division between self and others is more problematic than it first seems: part of our being, our *being-for-others*, comes into the world only through others.

Well beyond seeing more of us than we see, others can realize aspects of us that are not part of our direct experience. For example, we never know if we have a beautiful or ugly face, never know exactly how young or fat we look, because these partly depend upon who looks at us.[63] And if one's face is seen to be "ugly" or "beautiful," this is a fact *for-others*, not a fact directly for oneself. It is a rather horrifying thought that we do not fully possess ourselves (not even our faces!). What could be more dreadful than the fact that others take an equal share in what we often presume to be our most private possession. But wishing it away does not change the situation.

The presence of the other is thus the possible negation of *our* world as *ours*, and the possible negation of our subjectivity, of us as transcendence, of us as headless. Others turn our world into *a* world, one of many different possible configurations of space-time, including countless ones where we are not at the center. This is partly why Sartre suggests that "Hell is other people." Others are never merely items within experience, reducible to objects before us, for others can, at any moment, look back upon us, steal our world away from us, render us into a thing among other things.

Conflict is always possible, even if it is only the nonverbal tussle between "looker" and "looked-at," that pedestrian struggle where those who ogle at others can be looked back upon, turned by the Other into the "looked-at."[64] When I look at others, especially when I stare at them, they can see my seeing, see where I'm looking, and can judge any judgment I may offer. The other *as other* is the subjectivity who can contest my look or reappropriate my gaze. Hence, despite the fact that I only can see the other's physical form, any act of recognizing the other *as an Other*—and not a mere surface-bound object—is a grasp of them as capacity for world, as a freedom, a site of transcendence. They, too, are headless (i.e., being-for-itself). This is plainly evident in the case of love because "the lover does not desire to possess the beloved as one possesses a thing; he demands a special kind of appropriation. He wants to possess a freedom as freedom."[65] It is only by recognizing the other's no-face, their headlessness, their being for-themselves, that we can appreciate both who the other is as transcendence and how we can be revealed as thingly presences. It is only because we can be seen by others that shame, guilt, and embarrassment are possible.

Not surprisingly, many people try to hide from their being-for-others; they try to maintain a self-assured stance that thoroughly undermines the other's look, perhaps wishing to imply that any and all others are purely objects or have no real claim upon them. But alas, others cut our world down to size, render us a satellite caught in their gravitational orbit, and this happens at multiple levels, not merely through their looking at us. For example, we walk through the park and notice another person there. Each of us is a particular clearing of space-time from a particular vantage, and, accordingly, distances unfold differently for each of us. Each spatializes the scene such that relations of distance roll out from each person's headlessness, making each self the gravitational, perceptual center from which things are arranged and actions coordinated. For me, the other initially seems contained within my field of vision, subject to the arrangement of space and distances set according to my body. But for the other, the reverse is true. I appear as an object within the other's visual field—something that the other places within the environment. The other person arranges the space around me and decenters me. In fact, there might even be a third party, another other, who sees both of us but whom neither of us see. Such an other can sneak up on either of us and surprise one or both of us. This example illustrates that others disclose us factually and help us learn a profound truth about ourselves: in addition to being the nothing, the emptiness, which makes distances and figures-against-grounds possible, we are also thingly, at least in our being-for-others. We are objects in the world, subject to others' looks, subject to being placed in the world that others make possible, and, ultimately, subject to the modes of self-relation made possible by the human body's multisensory capacities.

Whereas some people adopt a life strategy that sadistically writes off how others perceive them, many people become masochistic to themselves. They become overly concerned with how others see them. They try to get a hold of what others see, even though degrees of noncoincidence remain between how others see them, how they see themselves, and how they think others see them. Note the range of what is at stake here by attending to the difference between, on the one hand, people in their late teens—aspiring "celebrities"— who elect to have plastic surgery because they think it will help them in their careers and, on the other hand, children born with facial disfigurements who themselves first suspect something is wrong because people routinely greet them with grimaces, winces, and pained looks. In the latter case, it would seem inadequate to simply tell children with disfigurements that their true riches are in their headlessness, even if this is a profound truth at some level. No, the fleshy face that is absent for oneself but which others possess is very real. Nothing separates one from others, and so it makes sense that the child, parents, and society at large would, if they could, surgically correct facial malformations. In contrast, elective cosmetic plastic surgery is a sign of confiscation. It is very likely a symptom of people who have not appreciated their headlessness and who do not know who they really are. Admittedly, whole cultures can engage in elective plastic surgery and, as we are thingly in some real ways, no one is immune to its temptation.

Note, in this context, some of the dynamics that enter *between* self and others, as we admittedly are not others, though in some ways we cannot even be ourselves without others. There never has been a self without others already present. Others are a mutual condition of sociohistorical existence, not simply items within an individual's perceptual experience. Others so thoroughly infiltrate the inner recesses of identity and self-understanding that one's very sense of subjectivity comes to be intersubjectively constituted—a kind of latent byproduct of ongoing social interactions. Therefore, although the ancient stoics have lent much wisdom in suggesting that one should be indifferent to anything outside of one's control, things are not so clear regarding what others directly say to us about us, as this is beyond our control but not something to which we can remain impervious. It poses significant challenges for the stoic position: for better or worse we developmentally become ourselves in the presence of others, and they are a shaping factor in how we grow to understand and experience ourselves. Laing, Philipson, and Lee have made this point painfully clear:

> Self-identity is a synthesis of my looking at me with my view of others' view of me. These views by others need not be passively accepted, but they cannot be ignored in my development of a sense of who I am. For even if a view by another of me is rejected it still becomes incorporated in its rejected form as part of my self-identity. My self-identity becomes my view of me which I recognize as the negation of the other person's view of me.[66]

For example, someone might think that I'm selfish, and I might think that I'm not. They might say to me, "You are selfish," to which I am free to respond with "No, I am not." I do not necessarily need to accept their definition of me, but the view that has been negated becomes part of my identity if only in its disavowed state: I am stuck with a sense of being someone who is misunderstood, someone who others mistakenly think of as selfish.

In rendering us and completing the image of us that is not for us, others are capable of much more than alienating us and estranging us from our full and rightful possession of the world. They can also *complete* us, in quite beneficial ways, though these also flee from us. If heaven metaphorically refers to a kind of sovereign subjectivity (and the Garden of Eden is here and now for the headless seer), then, in contrast, hell metaphorically refers to the fact of others, the degree to which our being-for-itself is denied. Hell is when we are left with a shrimpy being, one dwarfed down to a skin sack within an objective world populated by others who lay genuine claims upon our being. But when these two are combined—somewhat similar to how we try to appropriate the love of the beloved, possessing a freedom as freedom—others can look upon us and see not mere things, but human beings in striving, beings who remain caught in the ongoing project of having to be their possibilities and whose endeavors unfold within expanding contexts of meaning. Here, then, we find new dimensions of aesthetic enjoyments, new dynamics of artistic existence.

The very otherness of others, that they are positioned outside our experience, gives them what Mikhail Bakhtin calls a "surplus of seeing," a "transgredience" that enables them to contextualize our strivings and projects into an artistic whole, one that escapes our direct experience. Others are able to consummate us in our ethical strivings in ways that we, as always at a temporal distance from the selves we are still becoming, cannot complete ourselves. Bakhtin eloquently identifies some key differences between how we experience ourselves and how that experience is transformed when wrapped up by the look of others. In the main, we live our own lives with a sense of temporal and spatial incompleteness, with projects that are still outstanding at various distances, and hence, we relate to the impending "not yet" with ethical intensity; we, for ourselves, are ethically concerned over having to be our possibilities. Others, by their outsideness, cloak our strivings, unify them aesthetically, and turn them into artistic wholes. I quote Bakhtin at length:

> What constitutes that organizing principle of my life from within myself (in my relationship to myself) is solely my consciousness of the fact that in respect to all that is most essential I do not exist yet. The form of my life-from-within is conditioned by my rightful folly or insanity of *not coinciding*—of not coinciding *in principle*—with me myself as given. I do not accept my factually given being; I believe insanely and inexpressly in my own noncoincidence with this inner givenness of myself. I cannot count and add up all of myself, saying: this is *all* of me—there is *nothing more* anywhere else or in anything else; I already exist *in full.* . . . I know that in the other as well there is the same insanity of not coinciding (in principle) with himself, the same unconsummatedness of life. . . . This position of outsideness makes possible (not only physically, but also morally) what is impossible for me in myself, namely: the axiological affirmation and acceptance of the whole present-on-hand givenness of another's interior being. . . . In this outside position, *I* and the *other* find ourselves in a relationship of absolute mutual contradiction that has the character of an event: at the point where the other, from within himself negates himself, negates his own being-as-a-given, at that point I, from my own unique place in the event of being, affirm and validate axiologically the givenness of his being that he himself negates, and his very act of negation is, for me, no more than a moment in that givenness of his being. What the other rightfully negates in himself, I rightfully affirm and preserve in him, and, in so doing, I give birth to his soul on a new axiological plane of being. . . . For me, the other coincides with himself, and, through this integrating coincidence that consummates him positively, I enrich the other from the outside, and he becomes aesthetically significant—becomes a hero.[67]

Because we, for-ourselves, are incomplete beings, all of our strivings are experienced as forms of ethical action, something yet-to-be-completed, and, yet, the outsideness of others enables them to consummate us and our projects into a totality that thereby includes aesthetic dimensions and turns our ethical strivings into artistic accomplishments. This is no doubt partly why top-notch athletic competitions overflow with aesthetic dimensions that pass underappreciated by the active participants themselves. A player rushing for a ball or trying for the perfect shot lives in the incompleteness of the still-unfolding action, ethically, whereas we, the spectators, view it aesthetically because we wrap it up as a whole. We can look at a child striving to piece together a puzzle. While children are enraptured in the project, transcending themselves into the spatial-temporal possibility of a completed puzzle, we, onlookers, cloak their ethical striving and experience it as a beautiful moment.

We, as social beings, cannot be our entire selves without others. The whole picture of ourselves can be completed only with their help, and, even here, the whole evades us, eludes any individual's direct experience. We are not others and they are not us, and yet, none of us could be ourselves without the otherness that others provide.

DREAMLESS SLEEP AS THE NON-BEING OF CONSCIOUSNESS

One of the most pervasive but subterranean modes of non-being stitched into human life is the veiling of the entire world during dreamless sleep.[68] It entails a radical and all-encompassing giving up on all cares, all projects, and all engagements. Everything else is momentarily put on hold. During dreamless sleep "there are" no distances, no objects, no differences, no similarities, no relations, no nonrelations, no religions, no politics, no you nor me, not even the passage of time. In fact, if one were never to wake up, one would never know exactly how much time had elapsed. Dreamless sleep is arguably one of the most thorough, inclusive, and undeniable modes of non-being within conscious life. What could be a clearer indication of the nothingness within life than that nightly erasure of consciousness during dreamless sleep?

One's own dreamless sleep is that odd nowhere when "I," as conscious subject, do not exist for myself, and, to say as much is to agree with Bergson that one never directly experiences oneself in a spell of deep sleep. It is not a conscious experience per se. Fair enough, but we all know of that hidden nothingness we seek after a hard day's work. In this regard, it simply doesn't matter that dreamless sleep is never directly experienced by anyone: it enters conscious experience in a roundabout way, from the back door as it were. In waking up from a deep sleep, we compare how sapped and drained we felt earlier, before we went to sleep, to the refreshed and rejuvenated state we now feel. Moreover, although we do not directly experience the gap that is dreamless sleep, we, upon waking, vaguely experience having been dreamlessly asleep.

Moving from one day to the next, we undergo dreamless sleep even if that fact can be repressed, conveniently papered over, strategically downplayed, or just ignored. But, if we're going to be candid and honest about it, consciousness, in its basic functioning and operations, owes much to its own diurnal self-erasure; as obvious as it is paradoxical, consciousness is greatly indebted to—and relies upon—recurrent events that amount to the non-being of consciousness. Douglas E. Harding identifies the paradoxical ways that non-being is etched into human life where he writes,

> Indeed it is as if the gods invented sleep . . . expressly to make final nonsense of my claim to self-continuity, decreeing that to stay conscious I must periodically fall into a deep trance, that to keep my wits I must nightly lose them . . .[69]

Hence, even the most vigilant people, the most committed and dedicated, eventually need to get some sleep at some point. They must rest if they are to continue on in their projects, and this is another way of saying that chronic insomnia is an exhausting and debilitating disorder. Not surprisingly, sleep deprivation has been used throughout history as a reliable, cheap, and easy means of torture. Sleeplessness is draining, and, if persistent and unrelenting, can lead to both physical ailments and mental health problems. Consciousness gains its energy, vivacity, creativity, resilience, and resourcefulness by the body being well rested. Correlatively, without any need for conscious intervention or meddling, the body somehow "knows" how to heal itself while we sleep. Admittedly, sleep provides no guarantee to health, potency, or creativity, but, on the other hand, we can find ourselves unable to feel creative or be resourceful when suffering from deep-down body fatigue. It is hard to deny that a good night's sleep cleans the slate and prepares consciousness for agile movement.

Day after day the sun goes down and darkness sets in all around. When the lights are dimmed and we cannot see the distances separating things from each other or the distances that separate things from us, a sense of the void becomes palpable. While lying in bed late at night and unable to sleep, our thoughts themselves become, as William Gass writes, "beacons that one burns against the darkness."[70] The archetypal battle between being and non-being is registered by consciousness, if only subliminally, as the unending war between the light of day and the dark of night. Children, we can recall, are routinely afraid of the dark, partly because they cannot see what might suddenly appear. Elias Canetti's masterpiece *Crowds and Power* begins with the following lines:

> There is nothing that man fears more than the touch of the unknown. He wants to *see* what is reaching toward him, and to be able to recognize it or at least classify it. Man always tends to avoid physical contact with anything strange. In the dark, the fear of an unexpected touch can mount to panic.[71]

Darkness, where the "too-sudden" often equates to the "too-late," is its own mode of non-being. This also suggests that we could not be any more vulnerable than when we sleep. Accordingly, in order to feel comfortable enough to get any sleep, we select hidden sleeping places, lock our doors, set up guards, and so on.

Common sense has long noted an apparent parallel structure between life at the micro scale and life at the macro scale: a single day from sunrise to sunset is similar to an entire lifetime from birth to death; the daily venture from morning to evening somehow parallels the journey that goes from cradle to grave. Using this perceived parallel in their reasoning, people throughout the ages have considered death itself to be a special kind of deep sleep from which people eventually reawaken. The temptation to believe in life after death comes largely from the fact that we daily go to sleep, give up on all concerns, and yet wake up the next day. The fact of waking up—of making it through the night—lends intelligibility to belief in an afterlife. (Also, undoubtedly, the cycle of the seasons, the fact that spring returns after the dormancy of winter, is another metaphorical source of the sense that life lives on after death. Were humans to hibernate through the winter, one might suspect even deeper convictions regarding the possibility of life after death.) However, although sleep and death seem analogous, each a metaphor for the other, there is also a sense in which significant differences between these two are overlooked.

With death, the cycle goes birth-life-death, from nonexistence to existence to—presumably—nonexistence again. This means that at one point you were not, now here you are, and soon enough you won't be any more except as persisting for others in their existences. With sleep we can account for the experience in two different ways: we can say that we go from awake to asleep to awake again, or, just as equally, we could say that we go from asleep to awake to asleep again. As we are routinely awake longer than we are asleep, we might be tempted to start the cycle with awakeness. But the cycle also could be started with sleep, especially when we take into consideration the amount of sleeping we do during infancy or when we are sick. For beings such as ourselves, "being awake" (i.e., conscious waking life) seems to occur atop and depend upon the nutritive ground of dreamless sleep, not the reverse.

We are not simply awake beings who occasionally need to get some sleep, but rather we are just as equally dreamless sleepers for whom being awake is a periodic and limited achievement. People, though, seem stubbornly unwilling to recognize the obvious for what it is. They seem to believe, and proudly so, only in that self who can be seen within the world of awake consciousness.

At the least, we are *both* awake beings and dreamless sleepers. We are partly vegetative, an earthly ground, and sleep is the proof and daily reminder. At some levels of consideration, we are thoroughly vegetative—*and constantly so*—and dreamless sleep serves as the prompt to keep us from forgetting this fact. We grow tired, need to give up on the existential project of delimited and possible relations, and we recess into the *undifferentiated*.[72]

We all have seen someone asleep who then woke up, but what we do not see, except in horror movies or fantasy films or dreams, are the dead coming back to life. Someone who was presumably dead but who now is alive is someone who was prematurely declared dead. The death of one's body is the permanent loss of all of those unique relations of distance and possibilities that were one's own; what was uniquely one's own is now gone. But dreamless sleep is significantly different. We can wake up and incorporate the lapses into our self-understanding. We can know the obvious though elusive truth regarding ourselves. We are, each and every one of us, partly nothing through and through.

Our awake lives tell only part of the story of who we are, and dreamless sleep gives testimony to the fact that we are not in full possession of ourselves. It clearly discloses how we are also a recessive ground of being, partly the undifferentiated. This is, to a certain extent, Drew Leder's point when he writes, "In deep sleep, we discover . . . radical anonymity."[73] Meditating upon our own dreamless sleep, then, reveals a useful companion to the "two-way looking" exercise within the headless way: as attending to the absolute stillness and emptiness that is one's headlessness frees up means for creativity and handling life's challenges, so, too, does acknowledging one's fundamental need for sleep: the daily dissolve of conscious awareness helps us grasp an even deeper mode of non-being etched into existence. It liberates resources for self-understanding, for grasping who one really is.

We can wake up and remember—if only as a rejuvenating lack—the non-being of consciousness that we had been and that we partly are. It is a universally shared nonexperience. Our awake lives are double-posed with absence: we can both recall as well as anticipate the non-being of consciousness that laminates our everyday existence.

BODILY ABSENCES, INCOMPLETENESS, AND MODES OF BODILY NON-BEING

How amazing to be born into a body with billions of years of developments, adaptations, modifications, and survival value already built into it. The human body is a supreme exemplar of the self-negating cosmos.

We are incomplete beings, both in space and time, and we bring that incompleteness with us wherever we go. We are a bacteriological zoo, a colony of microbes, a digestive tract on legs, a visual expanse by which possibilities for action are clearly displayed.

Of space and not merely *in* it, *of* time and not merely *in* it, the lived body is the source of all delimited and possible distances, of those relations—spatial and temporal—that give birth to otherwise unrealized possibilities and to new dimensions of experience. We, for ourselves, are never just figures against a background. Rather, we are the precondition for any figure against any ground whatsoever.

We are headless capacities for world, the room-making nothingness that makes room for everything. But we are also "thingly" before others, entities whose completeness, for good or ill, depends upon their participation.

We are places and moments that can meaningfully differentiate ourselves from the Earth for only limited times and only in partial, restricted ways. We are dreamless sleepers, beings who do not merely need sleep to restore our health, but beings whose complete and utter undifferentiation in dreamless sleep can be brought into awake consciousness as a reminder of who we really are: incomplete beings, dependent and non-self-sufficing beings, beings wholly on loan to ourselves, living out our days in borrowed space and on borrowed time.

NOTES

1. Ronald David Laing and David Graham Cooper, *Reason and Violence: A Decade of Sartre's Philosophy, 1950–1960*. (New York, NY: Pantheon Books, 1971), 107–108.
2. See Jean-Paul Sartre, *Being and Nothingness*, trans. Hazel Barnes (New Jersey: Gramercy, 1956).
3. The practice of circumcision represents a kind of negativity whereby the body is "corrected" by removing the foreskin. Once a religious tradition, it is for many parents today a matter of "hygiene." We can note here an interesting linguistic inversion: "circumcised" is the unmarked term, whereas "*un*circumcised" in the marked one.
4. Ronald David Laing, *The Voice of Experience* (New York: Pantheon, 1982), 135.
5. Arthur Koestler, *The Ghost in the Machine* (London: Pan, 1967), 87.
6. Terrence Deacon, *Incomplete Nature: How Mind Emerged from Matter* (New York: W. W. Norton and Co., 2012), 416.
7. Lynn Margulis and Dorion Sagan, *What Is Life?* (Berkeley: University of California Press, 2000), 97.
8. The environment for early life remains murky, under water that is. Philip Ball writes, "And we tend to forget, landlubbers that we are, that until comparatively recently, an aquatic environment was the sole milieu for life on Earth. The planet has apparently hosted living organisms for an astonishing 3.8 billion years of its 4.6-billion-year history, and yet the colonization of the land began only around 450 million years ago," in *Life's Matrix: A Biography of Water* (Berkeley: University of California Press, 2001), 222–23.
9. Lynn Margulis and Dorion Sagan, *Acquiring Genomes: A Theory of the Origins of Species* (New York: Basic, 2002), 150.
10. Lynn Margulis, *Symbiotic Planet: A New Look at Evolution* (New York: Basic, 1998), 34.
11. Margulis writes, "Abortive cannibalism in single-celled protoctists resulted in a truce called sex," in *Symbiotic Planet*, 100.
12. "All organisms large enough for us to see are composed of once-independent microbes, teamed up to become larger wholes. As they merged, many lost what we in retrospect recognize as their former individuality," in Margulis, *Symbiotic Planet*, 33.
13. Margulis and Sagan, *What Is Life?* 97, 114, 140, 137.
14. Margulis, *Symbiotic Planet*, 90–91.
15. Even if technology enabled people to postpone death indefinitely, humans can't all live indefinitely without either ending procreation or finding other means of reducing the population.
16. Margulis and Sagan, *What Is Life?* 153–54.
17. Margulis and Sagan, *What Is Life?* 156.
18. Bacteria are so varied and strange, so resilient and omnipresent, that Francis Crick, one of the co-discoverers of the helical structure of DNA, actually suggested that they were perhaps kinds of seeds sown from extraterrestrials. See Margulis, *Symbiotic Planet*.
19. Margulis and Sagan, *What Is Life?* 19.
20. Margulis and Sagan, *What Is Life?* 166. For more on the evolution of the eye through symbiosis see Margulis and Sagan, *What Is Life?* 203–204. We can note here that mammalian eyes are located in skulls and that the bacterial ancestors to eyes produce calcium as their waste byproduct.

21. Margulis and Sagan, *What Is Life?* 49. They furthermore suggest, "Life is matter gone wild, capable of choosing its own direction in order to forestall indefinitely the inevitable moment of thermodynamic equilibrium—death. Life is also a question the universe poses to itself in the form of a human being," in *What Is Life?* 214.

22. For those disconcerted by the idea that humans evolved from colonies of bacteria, there may be some comfort in learning that, using the "clade system" for categorization of species, humans are also fish. See the MinuteEarth YouTube video titled, "You Are a Fish," https://www.youtube.com/watch?v=yyeDgBm1Du8.

23. See Corey Anton, *Selfhood and Authenticity* (Albany: State University of New York Press, 2001).

24. What separates us from the air or from the ground? Nothing!

25. I recently went to the store and saw some "Sweet Potato, Potato Chips." I thought, "Well, I have never had those before; let's give them a try." Later that evening, I opened the bag and put a chip into my mouth. My immediate response was a tacit recognition that the chip did not have salt on it. Now, I don't know why I thought it would have salt on it, perhaps because potato chips are usually salted. But this one did not have any salt and I seemed to taste the lack of salt; it literally tasted like an *unsalted* chip. Seriously, there is no such thing as an "unsalted" chip, and yet I experienced one for myself. "Unsalted" is not a property of a chip. There isn't anything that a scientist could disclose about a chip "in itself" which could reveal the "not being salted." If there is, then there are also many other characteristics not had: it is "unbleached," "not sugar-coated," and so on.

26. See Diane Ackerman, *A Natural History of the Senses* (New York: Random House, 1990).

27. See Walter J. Ong, *The Presence of the Word: Some Prolegomena for Cultural and Religious History* (Binghamton, NY: Global, 1967); Walter J. Ong, *Orality and Literacy: The Technologizing of the Word* (London: Methuen, 1982).

28. See Erwin Straus, *The Primary World of Senses* (New York: Free Press of Glencoe, 1963).

29. See Ong, *The Presence of the Word*.

30. Black and white are, properly speaking, not colors on the spectrum of visible light, but rather, they are registered from complete absence of stimulation on the retina and complete stimulation of the retina, respectively.

31. See Ong, *The Presence of the Word* and *Orality and Literacy*. See also Corey Anton, "Presence and Interiority: Walter Ong's Contributions to a Diachronic Phenomenology of Voice," in *Of Ong and Media Ecology: Essays in Communication, Composition, and Literary Studies*, eds. Thomas J. Farrell and Paul Soukup (Cresskill, NJ: Hampton, 2012).

32. Susanne K. Langer, *Philosophy in a New Key: A Study in the Symbolism of Reason, Rite and Art* (New York: Mentor Books, 1942), 61–62.

33. Georg Simmel, *On Individuality and Social Forms: Selected Writings*, ed. Donald N. Levine (Chicago: The University of Chicago Press, 1971), 359.

34. Margulis and Sagan, *What Is Life?* 217.

35. Much work here is drawn from Hans Jonas, *The Phenomenon of Life: Toward a Philosophical Biology* (Chicago: The University of Chicago Press, 1966); Erwin Straus, *The Primary World of Senses*; Erwin Straus, *Phenomenological Psychology* (New York: Basic Books, 1966); Diane Ackerman, *A Natural History of the Senses*. See also my own earlier works: Corey Anton "Beyond the Constitutive/Representational Dichotomy: The Phenomenological Notion of Intentionality," *Communication Theory* 9, no. 1, (1999): 26–57; Corey Anton, "Discourse as Care: A Phenomenological Consideration of Spatiality and Temporality," *Human Studies: A Journal for Philosophy and the Social Sciences* 25, no. 2, (2002): 185–205; Corey Anton, "Futuralness as Freedom: Moving toward the Past That Will-Have-Been," in *Media and the Apocalypse*, eds. Kylo-Patrick R. Hart and Annette M. Holba (New York: Peter Lang, 2009), 189–202; and Corey Anton, "Presence and Interiority."

36. David Abram, *The Spell of the Sensuous: Perception and Language in a More-Than-Human World* (New York: Vintage, 1996), 212–13.

37. All of this, of course, has its counterpart within language. Burke nicely captures this where he writes, "Even if any given terminology is a *reflection* of reality, by its very nature as a

terminology it must be a *selection* of reality; and to this extent it must function as a *deflection* of reality." See Kenneth Burke, *Language as Symbolic Action: Essays on Life, Literature and Method* (Berkeley: University of California Press, 1966).

38. See Douglas R. Hofstadter, *I Am a Strange Loop* (New York: Basic, 2008).

39. See Maurice Merleau-Ponty, *Phenomenology of Perception*, trans. Colin Smith (New Jersey: The Humanities Press, 1962); Maurice Merleau-Ponty, *The Visible and the Invisible*, trans. Alphonso Lingis (Evanston, IL: Northwestern University Press, 1968).

40. This is partly what William James meant by "radical empiricism."

41. What does it mean to say that relations are as real as things? This can be tricky: there are many different kinds of relations both inorganic and organic, and some relations can be made evident only by comparisons across different levels of analysis. Consider the case of water. In his interesting book *Life's Matrix: A Biography of Water*, Philip Ball notes that life on this planet became sustainable largely because of the quite anomalous properties of water. One of water's oddest qualities is that it is one of the very few fluids to expand when it transitions to a solid. H_2O molecules, when they are in a liquid state, loosely bond and then break apart only to quickly reattach to neighboring molecules. When water temperature falls below thirty-two degrees Fahrenheit, the molecules change their position slightly with regard to each other; they take on a stable hydrogen bond with neighbors. As this occurs, the micro-distance between the molecules slightly increases and expands. This not only changes the specific heat and provides for increased insulation, but, on the level of everyday perceived experience, we find the "hardness" of ice compared to the "wetness" of water. Those phenomena, as such, do not occur at the level of the molecular bonding per se. But, unless one wishes to commit the A-Naturalist Fallacy, that does not mean they are not real, nor that the experience is somehow illusory. We must change levels of analysis to compare what at one level could be described as little other than a slight change in the angle and stability of connection, with what at another level could be experienced as the "wetness" of water and "hardness" of ice. Hence, water seems like one thing and ice seems like another thing, but hardness and wetness are not different substances. To us, they are different things, having different properties. But relations, not things per se, make such phenomena possible. We should note as well that water is a molecular compound: hydrogen, a colorless, odorless, tasteless, highly combustible gas, and oxygen, a highly reactive nonmetal, are able to join together such that something new is added to existence despite the fact that no new matter has been added to the universe. The relation between these two basic elements is not a thing, and yet something very real comes out of it. One of the interesting examples that Deacon mentions is the combination of the elements sodium and chloride, both of which are highly reactive metals (e.g., sodium bursts into flames if it comes into contact with water), and yet when sodium and chloride combine, they form common table salt. Two different elements, each of which is unstable and toxic to human beings on its own, become highly stable when combined and play a crucial role in maintaining human health. Both water and salt are extant parts of the world, vital components of life as we know it, and both illustrate how relations are as real as things.

42. See two different cases of the rainbow: one in David Bohm's book *On Dialogue* (New York: Routledge, 2004) and one in Alan Watts's chapter, "The World Is Your Body," from his book, *The Book: On the Taboo against Knowing Who You Are* (New York: Vintage, 1966).

43. Antoine de Saint-Exupéry writes, "For a mirror, too, holds nothing, and the forms that fill it have neither weight nor stay," in *The Wisdom of the Sands*, trans. Stuart Gilbert (New York: Harcourt, Brace and Company, 1950), 6.

44. Jonas, *The Phenomenon of Life*, 154–156.

45. Deacon, *Incomplete Nature*, 141, 388.

46. Douglas E. Harding, *On Having No Head: Zen and the Rediscovery of the Obvious* (Carlsbad, CA: InnerDirections, 2002), 97.

47. Harding, *On Having No Head*, 24.

48. Harding, *On Having No Head*, 78.

49. Harding in fact stresses that his friends who are without sight have confirmed to him their direct experience of headlessness.

50. Harding, *On Having No Head*, 94.

51. Harding, *On Having No Head*, 70.

52. Harding, *On Having No Head*, 87. Morris Berman, in his illuminating chapter, "The Basic Fault," well captures this elusive transition from the "headless infant" to the headed grown-up, and he notes how it runs concurrent with, and seems to be a function of, two different cultural practices: on the one hand, the amount of physical touch people experience from infancy, and, on the other hand, the availability and use of mirrors. The point here is that some cultures seem better able to help their members deal with this transition from the kinesthetic or somatic self (e.g., who I am as capacity for world) to the abstract imagined self (e.g., what shows up when I think about others seeing me). Some people (and whole cultures too), those who receive abundant touch in particular, are more somatically grounded, more "located" within their absent bodies and their capacities for world, whereas others, those who receive little caring touch, are more concerned with how others see them, how they think they are seen by others. Whereas the former can be quite comfortable in situations with prolonged moments of silence, the latter can find silence a terrifying existential threat. Something similar happens, Berman points out, in response to the use of mirrors, as mirrors easily fool us into thinking of ourselves as complete and fully present objects in space, and they also amplify the sense of separation between people and within people. Depths of self-consciousness run parallel with awareness of self as distinct from others. With mirrors, photographs, and, now, visual recoding devices, we see our bodies as if they were no more than surfaces, unmarked by absence. But no matter how much we try to make ourselves objects for ourselves, we remain mysteriously at a distance from ourselves, somehow strangers to ourselves. *Coming to Our Senses: Body and Spirit in the Hidden History of the West* (New York: Bantam, 1989).

53. Harding, *On Having No Head*, 96–97.
54. Harding, *On Having No Head*, 97.
55. Harding, *On Having No Head*, 87–88.
56. Harding, *On Having No Head*, 96.
57. Harding, *On Having No Head*, 45.
58. Harding, *On Having No Head*, 100.
59. Harding, *On Having No Head*, 121. The key phrase here is, "*At this level.*" As a side note, I once asked Richard Lang, one of Harding's well-known students, the following question: If you and I stand next to each other before a mirror and we look at the two images we see in the mirror, how many No-Faces are there? He immediately said, "One," and I replied, "Really, not two?" He maintained, "There is only one No-Face." No-face is nothing and so there cannot be boundaries between consciousnesses at this level. Differences, distances and separate objects can be located only as we "look out," never as we "look in." For more on the finer relationships between Sartre, Harding, and dreamless sleep, see "Dialogue with Richard Lang (Who Are We?)" https://www.youtube.com/watch?v=hDfd5tZvpIw.
60. Harding, *On Having No Head*, 86.
61. Admittedly, some of this is oversimplified: Harding stresses the practice of "two-way looking" which offers a nice parallel to Sartre's notion of "good faith." Moreover, one might well argue that Harding's position provides an attempt at "angelic good faith" rather than a move toward sadistic bad faith. For clearest evidence of Harding's "good faith," see the "The Distant View—Humanity," in Douglas E. Harding, *The Hierarchy of Heaven and Earth*, (London: Shollond Trust, 2011), 75–82.
62. Sartre, *Being and Nothingness*, 300.
63. As Morris Berman notes, "To the end of our days we continue to check ourselves out in front of the mirror or search ourselves out in a group photograph, to 'see what we look like,'" in *Coming to Our Senses*, 40. Hence, we never really know what others see when they look at us.
64. It should be noted that "gaze laws" in some southern states granted the government the prerogative to arrest African American males for simply looking at white females. For more on the ways that bad faith plays out in race relations see Lewis Gordon, *Bad Faith and Anti-Black Racism* (New York: Prometheus, 1999).
65. Sartre, *Being and Nothingness*, 367.
66. Laing, Phillipson, and Lee, *Interpersonal Perception*, 5–6.
67. Bakhtin, *Art and Answerability*, 127–129.

68. See Anton, *Selfhood and Authenticity*; Corey Anton "Dreamless Sleep and the Whole of Human Life: An ontological exposition," *Human Studies: A Journal for Philosophy and the Social Sciences*, 29, No. 2, (2006): 181–202.
69. Harding, *The Hierarchy of Heaven and Earth*, 186.
70. See Gass, *Habitations of the Word*.
71. Canetti, *Crowds and Power*, 15.
72. Sartre writes, "Whatever may be the original undifferentiation of being, non-being is that same undifferentiation *denied*," in *Being and Nothingness*, 14.
73. Drew Leder, *The Absent Body* (Chicago: The University of Chicago Press, 1990), 59.

Chapter Three

Language, Absence, Negation, and Context

SYMBOLS, THE BODY, AND INTERNAL NEGATION

"Nothing," the word in English, bears meaning even though it does not have a tangible referent. Indeed, there can be no material referent for "nothing" and that is precisely the point! With this word at hand, we can refer to what is not the case or point out a relevant absence or indicate that other elements have been omitted or even speak about what can never be the case. Also, because words are linguistic distinctions, they, in addition to any ostensive definition they might have, are partly defined by semantic relations of similarity, opposition, or contrast to other linguistic distinctions. Accordingly, "nothing" includes a wide range of meanings such as "an inconsequential occurrence" or "totally empty" or "no *particular* something" or "what people were wearing at the nude beach" or "what we have planned for the upcoming holiday weekend" or "what we regrettably ate for breakfast today" or "what is left in the bag after all of the chips have been eaten" and so on. But symbols—and language and communication in particular—contain many layers and levels of non-being, many forms of constraint that introduce functional absence, and, hence, the nothing at stake throughout this study, as has been shown already in chapters 1 and 2, is obviously much more than the various meanings of a single word.

Jean-Paul Sartre sets the context for further interrogation where he writes, "The problem of language is exactly parallel to the problem of bodies, and the description which is valid in one case is valid in the other."[1] Just as the lived-body is an absent body, a self-effacing body, so too, the language that we speak is, for us, a flight beyond itself—an absence that makes room for more than itself. And, just like the body, it is a flight easily truncated by others, as our words can appear quite thingly to the foreign other who can reveal us as chattering animals. Others who do not dwell in the expansive space and time that language makes possible for its speakers—those who don't know the language—stand on the "outside" of it, as it were, witnessing the emoting and gesticulating person. The ancient Greeks used the term *barbarian* to describe those who did not speak Greek partly because they heard foreign speech as unintelligible soundings of "bar-bar-bar." Admittedly, we do not hear the "noisiness" of our native tongue as we hear it in foreign tongues. If we travel to a country where we do not know the language (or tune into a media station where people are speaking an unknown tongue), we cannot identify the beginning or ending of particular words; we are not dwelling in their meaning horizons. Moreover, the heard sounds vanish as quickly as they appear. Words of unknown languages seem to be little other than evanescent noises that are occurring within the space–time of auditory fields.

For native speakers of a language, in contrast, their words are much more than—much other than—evanescent noises; they constitute an articulate gathering, a leaping ahead that retainingly awaits its own completion. A mother tongue is the primary vehicle for transcending the immediate here and now; language enables items of care, often distant in space and time, to be freed up and made available for articulate consideration. With language we rove over all things, taking hold of and considering what remains too distant for even the most long-sighted vision. It is humanity's primary means for reaching beyond the present moment. People can talk about what happened earlier in the day or what they are going to do over the weekend, or, more importantly, they can consider what they are going to do with their lives, how they plan to live out their days, what they hope to achieve in this world. Hence, the sounds of our mother tongue spontaneously disappear from awareness for the sake of an attention to the meanings that they make possible—with their intelligible space and time horizons. Only others help us discover the strangely physical nature of our words. If people were wholly unexposed to any foreign languages, they might never realize that they speak "a" language, for they would appear to themselves (and to other native speakers) to speak thought itself. For native speakers of any language, the meaning and the sounds so fuse together that the sounds are simply experienced as an emotional-volitional articulation of the meaning. Interestingly, if people do not speak a language but are fairly familiar with it, they can find it easy to make stereotyped speech sounds of that language. They also can mimic the regional dialects of their own mother tongue, where one's own native tongue sounds somewhat different in rate, prosody, expressiveness, and assonance. And yet when asked to make stereotyped sounds of their dialect in their own mother tongue, people are at a loss. Despite hearing it all the time, in fact incessantly, people simply do not know what their language sounds like to those who don't speak it.

Language is linguistic legerdemain; it enables people to pull both hats and rabbits out of thin air or out of squiggles on paper. It, like consciousness itself, is not what it is and is what it is not. Exemplifying what Sartre means by "internal negation," spoken words effectively convey their message when vocalizations are negated as sounds and become meaning itself. Maurice Merleau-Ponty writes,

> In a sense the thought of the negative provides us with what we were searching for, terminates our research, brings philosophy to a standstill. We said that philosophy needs a contact with being prior to reflection, a contact which makes reflection possible. The "negintuition" of nothingness *is* the philosophical attitude that puts reflection and spontaneity in a sort of equivalence.[2]

To dwell in the meaning of words is, basically, fundamentally, to spontaneously entertain something absent through something present. Meanings are eidetic, not empirically available. Although they seem "on" the words or "in" the words, this is true only for those who already know enough of the language to perceive the sounds as the words they are.

Consider the writing inscribed across the entrance gates of Plato's Academy: "ΑΓΕΩΜΕΤΡΗΤΟΣ ΜΗΔΕΙΣ ΕΙΣΙΤΩ," translated as "Let no one ignorant of geometry enter here," also translated as "Let none but geometers here." To be a student in Plato's academy, one needed to be familiar with essences, universals, types, and other entities whose nature remains always beyond the confines of the empirical world. To understand geometry one needs to grasp more than what the senses can perceive directly. The formal relations that make up the essential characteristics of triangles pertain to *all* triangles, meaning that they cannot be exhausted by any particular, actually extant, triangle. Each and every right triangle that one can draw represents a universal, essential right triangle. When a teacher draws a triangle on the board, we must pay no attention to the color of the chalk and must disregard any differences of thickness in the line. We also need to overlook any observable nonproportionality and attend only to the ideal triangle, the triangle that this empirical item on the board enables us to contemplate. It is because essences reside on the backside of things, casting the light by which the things of the senses become intelligible, that people need to study geometry. We can do geometry only by dealing with particulars as universals, eidetically constraining what is empirically present as if it were *not* exclusively what it is, as if it is something other than itself. The same can be said of ideas such as "the beautiful," where we are not interested in this particular beautiful sculpture or in this particular beautiful face or in this particular beautiful painting, but rather we are interested in grasping the beautiful *per se*, the essence arrested out from all empirical particulars. But we need not follow Plato down the path toward Eternal Forms causing the particular things as imperfect replicas. We can settle for less by identifying essences in two different ways: first, general types of things can occur by having shared properties but they also can occur by having shared absences (e.g., being unsalted). Second, they can be abstracted out from particulars by operations of eidetic negation. As we overlook the density and depth of empirical particulars and attend to imagined forms of invariance, we grasp essentials. Much needs to be *ignored*, *overlooked*, and *neglected* (i.e., *constrained out*) to effectively engage such lofty considerations.

But this dynamic pertains to more than geometry and abstract ideas such as beauty, for, as you read the words you currently are reading, you must negate their sheer physical presence, or, as Alphonso Lingis would say, "vaporize the substrate."[3] Transcending the physical marks on the page to recognize their meaning amounts to negating them as they are: silent printed letters. Every word that we find intelligible must hide part of its materiality if the invariance, its essential meaning, is to show itself. That is partly why the printed word in a uniform font is far more easily transcended and seems far less "thingly," than a sloppily handwritten letter or a printed statement with several of the words in different fonts and accents.

For even further illustration, imagine that you hear a dozen people, one after the other, say aloud the expression, "good guacamole requires ripe avocados." Here, although each speaker has a slightly different volume, a different rate of speaking, a particular style of pronunciation, a unique set of vocal qualities, and so on, across all these differences we can hear the "same words." We experience invariance across the variation. The dozen different speech acts occurred at twelve different times, in a particular order, with variety throughout. And yet the same words can be heard because we can internally negate the nonpatterned elements of the sounds, discounting all irrelevant differences.[4] We constrain attention to listen for sameness across differences. This admittedly can be more challenging when listening to non-native speakers. In these situations, we might struggle to disambiguate the invariant words behind the wider latitude of pronunciations, intonations, rhythms, and cadences. (Note that invariance recognition occurs at additional levels, for people can discern avocados from other fruits in the grocery store, and they can examine the range of colors and degree of firmness for particular avocados; they can discriminate between those that are overripe, ripe, not-yet ripe.) Invariance recognition thus occurs on multiple levels, and, as all of it trades on non-being, it amounts to constrained absence.

Words, therefore, can become vehicles for meaning only insofar as thought accomplishes itself though forms of internal negation, and internal negation is not an explicit or overt act of outright denial or opposition. Internal negation refers to the structure of consciousness and language, their spontaneous and prereflective character, and how materiality relates to experience. Just as my body, through its senses, opens to distances beyond itself and makes room for both actual and possible situations, so too are speech and language, as extensions of the body, part of our means for transcendence. Consciousness, always embodied within various forms, transcends its materiality by internally negating it. One therefore need not seek some kind of "transcendent" realm for ideas, for we can acknowledge them as always on the horizon of the material world while somehow on the backside of it, beyond it in principle.[5]

People can and often do, prereflectively and in "thoughtlessness," spontaneously blurt something out and successfully achieve a thought or meaning without realizing the particular words they employed in that achievement. In the spontaneity of interaction, spoken expressions easily hide themselves from awareness as speakers attend to what the words are about; the meaning-horizon makes its showing at the expense of attention to the wording per se, at least initially for the speaker. No doubt hurt feelings within interactions can occur as people reregister what they just said, often having it pointed out and perhaps slowly repeated back to them by someone else. This also means that words *for-ourselves* have a different being than they do *for-others*, and that is partly why we're never exactly sure what others take from what we say. Words are not private property. Just as aspects of our bodies are us but can flee from us, so likewise, we can mean more or less than what we think we do, depending upon who is listening to us.

As is the case with the body, our very sense of subjectivity comes to pass only through an intersubjectivity; the otherness that language provides helps us to become ourselves, and we can only learn the language from someone who likewise learned it from someone else; we came to ourselves, became self-conscious, only after having been dependent upon an other who had already been otherized by an other, and so on. Language is therefore the Ancient Other, the Primal Ancestor, who imparts similarity while also making each of us an other for others and for ourselves.[6] We, those speakers of a particular language, are the same in that we now are interchangeable with each other, at least regarding "the language" we both speak: either of us can say what we both can understand. Through language we can co-ponder aspects of the world, and, with analytic precision, we can disentangle our subjective and relative perceptual and sensory perspectives and be aware of others' views as "similar to" but "different than" our own. Language gives us the distance to come back to ourselves as if we were an other.

Sight may give the most expansive perceptual domain for the direct experience of possibilities, but spoken language radically opens to even further possibilities. Compared to sign-systems of other organisms, language is a *difference in kind*, not simply a *difference of degree*. Humans do not merely inhabit an environment nor are they primarily installed in their immediate surrounds. They *exist* in a *world* opened through languages, symbols, and communication technologies. People dwell in the immense expanse of whatever can be expressed about what was, what is, and what will be. They also open to those strange domains of non-being: what was not, what is not, what could have been, what should have been, what cannot be, what is unknowable, what should be, what ought to be but is impossible, what remains only a fiction, and so on.

This study began with questions regarding nothing and non-being. We found that the least controversial claims regarding nothing were those that suggested that language, at the very least, includes expressions for "nothing," and that we cannot without self-refutation deny that people verbally negate by saying "is not," "no," and "don't." Kenneth Burke suggested that "the negative" is a marvel of language and that we need to study how the command "Don't!" developmentally precedes and grows into the "Is Not." He also explained how persons as self-conscious agents with a sense of conscience are birthed through a drenching in the "thou-shalt-nots" of their culture.

Ahead, we explore some of the sociohistorical developments of negativity that have been propagated, distributed, and normalized. These are mainly constraints built into language habits that, by way of strategic neglect or omission from awareness, enable certain kinds of cognitive work. Before going on to explore many different ways that absence, incompleteness, negation, and non-being pervade language and symbol use, we need to review two relevant and related evolutionary precursors: dreams and mammalian play.

DREAMS AND MAMMALIAN PLAY AS EVOLUTIONARY PRECURSORS TO LANGUAGE

As a spontaneous, undirected, and unconscious flow of symbols, dreams are a mode of psychic communication that evolutionarily predates the emergence of language use. Welling from the depths of the collective unconscious and also from the root cellar of an individual's unconscious, dreams are a form of anonymous and private communication, one shrouded in mystery, obscurity, and possibility. Across the great diversity of life, it remains uncertain exactly which organisms dream, but mammals, as organisms with highly complex nervous systems and sophisticated internal representational capacities, show clear evidence of dreams (REM sleep). Dreams are a symbolic language that all mammals unconsciously speak, but, as far as we know, only humans talk about dreams—their dreams, the dreams of others, and even the dreams of other organisms. Dreams are bits and pieces of conscious life recycled, played with, and imaginatively drawn upon by the unconscious in its effort to make sense of experience. Dreams are possibilities actualized, cryptic symbolic representations that are experienced as "reality" while we sleep. In its unconscious attempt to make sense of waking life, mulling over possibilities as it were, the dreaming body produces what the dreamer experiences as "reality" and what the contemporary awake adult knows as "a dream." The unconscious body thus employs unwilled and subterranean symbolism in its spontaneous attempt to digest earlier experiences or prepare for upcoming events and engagements. For these reasons, dreams are soaked in non-being.

There are, additionally, two obvious ways that non-being characterizes dreams. First, what is occurring in a dream is not occurring outside it. Second, dreams are a mode of symbolism that lacks analytic and self-reflexive resources. This means that we cannot methodically reflect upon the fact that we are dreaming while we dream. Night by night we entertain a world that is not real, a world that is not what it appears to be. Admittedly, in a different sense, dreams are very real in their own right, part of nature itself. How else would one explain the fact that people can wake up in a panic from a nightmare or that sleeping bodies can be so taken in by dreams that they can achieve orgasm. Nevertheless, no matter how real dreams seem while we are dreaming, awakeness reveals them to be other than what they had appeared to be. The reality of the dream for the dreamer is very different than the reality of that same dream when the person wakes up and realizes the dream was "just a dream."

Sigmund Freud long ago pointed out the operations of "displacement" and "condensation" in dreams. Burke, following out these lines, suggests that the dreamer is so lazy and charitable that the loosest, lamest, and roughest approximation, the vaguest image, can well serve the purposes of symbolic substitution during a dream. Also, as Gregory Bateson points out, while we dream we cannot employ strict logical or mathematical rules for categorizing reality. The dreamer cannot, for example, rigorously and consistently differentiate between, on the one hand, "'all' and 'some,'" nor, on the other hand, between "'not-all' and 'none.'"[7] These different observations summatively point to experiences dreamers know all too well: during a dream, one can walk into a dwelling that does not look anything like one's house, and yet, one still has the distinct sense that it is one's house. From within a dream, someone can talk with us, and, even though we do not recognize this person by face or voice, we somehow know who it is. We can be sitting on a rollercoaster next to a co-worker and then abruptly be in a car talking with a neighbor, and the sudden transition from one scene to the next is not the least bit disconcerting. In the dream, the dreamer just rolls along with whatever presents itself moment by moment.

Dreams present an engaging but ultimately illusory sense of how things stand between our environment and ourselves: they present an "I" or "me" as simply *in* the dream, a figure serving as the organizing principle, the gravitational center, for the parade of imagery and flow of interaction. The other people who appear in our dreams can approach us and say things that surprise us, even though, all said, our slumbering consciousnesses produce not just "the me" that appears inside the dream, but the other people, the objects and artifacts, the scenery, the entire dream itself! None of us is simply the self who appears within a dream; each of us creates the whole dream even though we experience ourselves as only one element within it.

To name a dream as "nothing but a dream"—to know that what we just experienced was fortunately or unfortunately *only* a dream—is to come to terms with the non-being of dreams. It is also to recognize an event that beckons reflection and further interpretation. Dreams partly exemplify evolutionary precursors to language because, like statements within language, the symbols within our dreams already are interpretations and yet call for further interpretations. Emil M. Cioran identifies some of the implications here where he writes, "Only the madman enjoys the privilege of passing smoothly from a nocturnal to a daylight existence: no distinction between his dreams and his waking. He has renounced our reason."[8] Moreover, what are we to make of the fact that ghosts and spirits, throughout the ancient and medieval world, routinely made their appearance in dreams? Were people really contacted by spirits or angels? Were they simply fooled or had they renounced "reason"? Maybe they thought others would be gullible or at least unable to disprove such visitations. A significant shift in self-understanding occurred when dreams, in the wake of Freud, became something "psychological" rather than "otherworldly." Ambrose Bierce, in talking about apparitions within dreams, provocatively observes, "There is one insuperable obstacle to belief in ghosts. A ghost never comes naked. . . . To believe in him, then, is to believe that not only have the dead the power to make themselves visible . . . but that same power inheres in textile fabrics."[9] But perhaps the connection between clothing and belief in ghosts is deeper than it would first appear. I return to this issue later in chapter 4.

Synthesizing resources from memory and imagination, dreams are fantasy and projection; they are speculation and unconscious considerations of possibilities. In fact, no matter how "true" any of our dreams turn out to be in some sense, they are nonetheless abstractions, and they themselves are *not* what they are about. Some of the impulse to language and to truth, the drive to overcome self-deception and to get clear on what, exactly, is going on, is precipitated when we wake up from a dream. Dreams are the daily prompt to the fact that things may not be as they seem, the eye-opening reminder of how thoroughly, even if only momentarily, we can be both self-deceiving and wholly deceived.[10]

Another important evolutionary precursor to human language is mammalian play.[11] In his essay "A Theory of Play and Fantasy," Gregory Bateson suggests that we can best understand how spoken language evolved the capacity to make denotative propositions by first grasping how mammalian play contains the rudiments of abstraction and metacommunicative framing. The phenomenon of play thus provides important clues to understanding how the possibilities of denotative language evolved out of (and still ride atop) mammalian sign-systems.

To appreciate how play paves the way for one of the distinguishing characteristics of human language (i.e., denotation), we must first underscore how complex and varied are the sign-systems and modes of communication of other animals. Animals communicate in various ways: though chemicals, odors, sounds, physical markings, contact, and the like. They give mating calls, warning cries, engage in territoriality displays, and maintain complex social relationships, but, given all of that, they do not make denotative propositions about features of the world. Their communication manages actual relation-states in local contexts of engagements, but it does not abstractly contemplate possible truths about aspects of the world. Hence, one of the ways that human language significantly differs from other animal sign-systems is in its capacity for making denotative statements.

More than expressing emotion, claiming territory, showing good will, threatening force, displaying intention or hiding intention, language holds the perennial possibility of making propositions about aspects of the world, including statements about things not present or even statements about what was not said. Clearly, human communication is not reducible to making denotative statements, for we too are animals who, whether we intend to or not, give off emotive signs and various forms of intention displays, even as we speak denotatively. Moreover, compared with many other speech genres that we employ throughout the day—such as making requests, issuing commands, declining invitations, raising questions, delivering jokes, imitating others, praising or blaming, and so on—denotative utterances occupy a relatively small portion of our language practices. Nevertheless, the possibility of denotative statements is always imminent. We can, at a moment's notice, generate denotative statements about anything that calls for such attention, whether it is some item in the present situation, something from the past or future, something that someone said earlier in a different context, or something that didn't happen but should have.

Denotative language, as categorical and dealing with abstract types, bears propositional content. As such, regarding any denotative statement, we can ask: Is the proposition true or false? For example, someone can say, "The cat is on the mat" or "My car is in the garage." In such cases, there is a fact of the matter and others can make a judgment regarding the veracity of the statement. How are denotative utterances possible? Well, they require, at the least: (1) *denotative language* (i.e., words with a semantic or categorical meaning that enable reference outside of language), (2) *meta-linguistic references* (i.e., words for talking about language and aspects of verbal communication itself such as "truth," "statement," and "say," etc.), and (3) *metacommunicative framing* (i.e., nonverbal cues, tones of voice, postures, distances that help listeners determine whether something was said in earnest or in jest or ironically or as a question, etc.). Depending upon the context of the statement, we may have all that we need to judge whether a statement is true or false. For example, if someone says, "The cat is on the mat," we may or may not be able to examine the extra-verbal situation to see if the cat is, in fact, on the mat. But if the person says, "'The cat is on the mat' is an expression in English that rhymes," those who speak the language well enough to understand the statement already have all the facts needed to make a judgment regarding the truth-value of the proposition.

Some nonhuman animals, mammals in particular, have metacommunicative framing capacities. This means that even though they are incapable of advancing denotative utterances, they can communicate about their communication with multileveled messages. During moments of play, as Bateson suggests, mammals convey messages that also include metacommunicative cues for interpreting those messages. By framing their behavior and interaction through metacommunicative cues, mammals are able to signal that they are playing rather than fighting. While "playfully" nipping at each other, they are able to differentiate between a nip and a bite such that the nip "means" a bite but it does not mean what a bite would mean. Bateson describes the situation as follows: "[T]he nip denotes the bite but does not denote what would be denoted by the bite."[12] The nip is similar to the bite, but it is occurring at a different level of abstraction; it represents the early possibility of consciously playing with signs themselves. As Bateson states, "Not only do the playing animals not quite mean what they are saying but, also, they are usually communicating about something which does not exist."[13] More than action or reaction, the phenomenon of play gives evidence of mammals responding to each other's codified, multileveled messages. Said otherwise, the nip, an iconic sign, represents the bite, makes an allusion to its possibility or perhaps to an absent bite, whereas an actual bite is a concrete moment within interaction. The bite establishes a relationship, whereas the nip is a metonymic sign, a behavioral synecdoche. The beginning of a sequence, evolutionarily speaking, comes to abstractly represent the whole sequence. Anthony Wilden well captures this evolutionary transition:

> The nip represents the presence and the absence of the bite. . . . The world of the communication of the bite is full of real differences; with the nip, gaps begin to appear, something akin to the zero-phoneme, or to the space between one and two. And whatever else the nip may be, it is NO-THING. The nip begins as a real metonymy (a part for the whole, related by contiguity) and becomes a symbolic metaphor (something standing for something else, related by similarity).[14]

Play therefore reveals the initial stages of multileveled codification through shared abstractions, which also means the beginnings of the possibilities of deceit, threat, histrionics, and tactical manipulation. It marks a significant step toward denotative utterance if only because play requires recognition of different kinds of signs and also demands awareness of different levels of abstraction and interaction.

The signs deployed during play move beyond involuntary and symptomatic display and give clear evidence of conscious control and strategic design, if only to limited degrees. The evolutionary leap between Bateson's two meanings of the word "denote," even though both still refer to nonverbal signs prior to the emergence of language, represents a gap between two different logical types of interaction, or, more precisely stated, it signifies the evolutionary emergence of logical typing per se.

Human life overflows with phenomena similar to mammalian play: theatrical performances, enacted stories, fictions, fantasies, television programs, cinema, and so on. When we sit in a theatre and view a theatrical production or film, something occurs on stage or on screen, a something that we say is "not real." The characters, including their stage names, occupations, and social statuses, are all just pretend—a dramatic illusion that the actors and actresses perform. When two thespians kiss, the staged kiss means "a kiss" but it does not mean what a kiss would mean. The two people are engaging in behavior that is not what it appears to be; it needs adequate communicative reframing to be correctly understood, and, depending upon the play or film, it may demand multiple viewings and layers of interpretation.[15] Nevertheless, the obvious should not be overlooked: almost all the fighting, conflict, and violence watched in popular films and television is fake. The images, sounds, and enactments *mean* fighting, *mean* conflict, and *mean* violence but do not mean what actual fighting, conflict, and violence would mean. This further implies, as Bateson suggests, "We face then two peculiarities of play: (a) that the messages or signals exchanged in play are in a certain sense untrue or not meant; and (b) that that which is denoted by these signals is nonexistent."[16] Admittedly, there is still something occurring: people are sitting in a theatre and there is something playing on the stage or screen. But the event witnessed is a *story*, a playful rendering of what remains somehow absent. In performing their characters, the actors and actresses become vehicles for what they are not. Actions are not simply what they appear to be; they have become metaphors and symbols that stand for something else. Not only do audience members spontaneously laugh and cry to such scripted scenes, but also they respond to the characters in the stories. Some adults send personal, heartfelt letters to television characters rather than to the actors or actresses who portray those characters. These facts well illustrate how caught up in fantasy people can become; they take performed characters to be what they are not.

George Carlin, with great comedic flair, pointed out that newspapers can print an obscene word if they strategically pretend to avoid using the "real" word. They simply print the questionable material with one of the word's letters as an asterisk (e.g., "sh*t" or "f*ck"). Here, a kind of nonword invokes another word, refers to it, but does not mean what the invoked word would mean. This is somewhat similar to adults resorting to partial spelling of unseemly words or using acronyms when discussing difficult topics in front of young children. In all these cases, people manage to express something to others and come to shared understandings by a roundabout indexing of what is *not* being expressed. To express what we want to say without having to say it, we employ veiled codes, drop subtle hints, and use other forms of innuendo.

In examining human communication we find many different layers of abstraction.[17] Hollywood, for example, goes to extraordinary measures in efforts to increase the realism of shadows cast from cartoon figures. Think of how much money is spent annually telling stories about what is not the case and what will never be the case. As Marshall McLuhan wrote about the early days of film, "The world eagerly lined up to buy canned dreams."[18] That is precisely what movies are. Never before have dreams been able to be "put in a can" and collectively enjoyed. Admittedly, biographies and documentaries can be quite fascinating, and, although these are products of our ability to tell it like it *was*, people generally spend much more time dwelling in what is *not* the case, and what will *never* be the case. Popular films from *Avatar* and *Avengers* to *Star Wars* and *Zootopia* go far beyond realism. They are evidence that people love fantasylands and collectively dwell in their imaginations.

Undoubtedly, people are capable of making denotative propositions, but the stubborn fact remains that very little of communication is just that. All day long, not just to themselves but also to others, people bullshit their way through the day.[19] They opine and preach, speculate and wonder, daydream and fantasize, contemplate and conjecture, joke and tease, push phony narratives, indulge in wishful thinking, watch epic dramas on stage and in film, zombie out to old TV shows, and binge Netflix. Along the way, they hop around according to ideologies that have come to inhabit their bodies.[20] In his efforts to help people become more critical of their ideologies and more aware of the humble organismal roots of language and communication, Ernest Becker writes, "Communication is largely self-deception, a disguise of power-rooting. . . . . [P]eople get together not by communicating with one another but by sharing appetites and power-allegiances."[21] The words, claims, and beliefs that people think on a day-to-day, hour-by-hour basis are, in actual content, much more make-believe and play—more "hot air"—than many people seem to realize.

Language is a playful intersubjective dream, a collective hallucination where whole cultures and subcultures "make it up as they go along," cobbling together viewpoints that mainly serve the interests of who they believe they are. To speak another's language is to gain partial entrance into the waking dream that is their life. We of course have the capacity to wake up, contemplate the truth, speak the truth, and hold others and ourselves accountable to it; but we are more primarily self-deceiving dreamers who are playing around. Most of the time we are not dispassionate, clear-headed truth-tellers. We seem to love a good story more than we love the truth, especially if the truth is difficult while the story brings comfort and provides a warm sense of security.

Courageous willingness to accept that humans have the capacity for wholesale deception and self-deception is a necessary precondition for honesty and veracity in public affairs and in self-relation. A most uplifting, humbling, and beautiful kind of pain, easily the most forgivable of all inflictions, comes from exposure to the truth. The pain of truth is a healing wound, for without truth there cannot be acceptance or wisdom. But it remains uncertain just how possible it would be for all (or most) of us to look beyond the veil of our own socioeconomic and cultural identities, beyond all our political allegiances and religious affiliations. We would need robust and viable alternatives, self-understandings and cultural practices that can be both honest and frank but also moving and enriching. Perhaps it is partly about telling a more inclusive story about humanity and life, one whose truth is obvious and which makes no appeal to any dogma whatsoever. What would that look like? I return to this issue in chapter 4.

NON-BEING IN LANGUAGE STRUCTURE AND CONTENT

Elmar Holenstein's book titled *Roman Jakobson's Approach to Language* stands as one of the most impressive works on language and communication theory, especially the chapter titled "Perspectives of a Comprehensive Theory of Language."[22] Holenstein provides a wide-ranging framework for analytically grasping what goes on as we speak with one another. At a minimum, spoken language is a multilevel, multimodal, and highly complex phenomenon. It includes different kinds of dynamics: facial expressions that accompany whatever is said (e.g., "smiles," "frowns," "grimaces," "blank stares"), speech sounds symptomatic of the speaker's emotional state (e.g., "excited," "bored," "tired," "worried"), sounds that register sentiment regarding the interlocutor (e.g., "friendly," "indifferent," "condescending," "ingratiating"), intended meanings clarified by sonorous contours (e.g., "jests," "asserts," "commands," "inquires"), object language that occurs across a variety of levels of abstraction (e.g., "horse," "mammal," "animal," "organism"), words for different levels of language itself and genres of utterance (e.g., "word," "statement," "discussion," "argument"),[23] words for semantic values (e.g., "pet," "food," "lover," "friend"), words for prepositional relations (e.g., "over," "under," "next to," "on"), indexical shifters (e.g., "here," "there," "this," "now"), and, of course, the most odd of all linguistic signifiers, the syntactical "not."

With these dynamics in mind, we can begin by noting that all the words within our utterances have two kinds of linguistic bonds. Specifically, words are connected to other words by two different kinds of relations: *paradigmatic similarities* and *syntagmatic combinations*. Along the paradigmatic axis (also called the *vertical axis*) we select units from a stock of similar units, whereas along the syntagmatic axis (also called the *horizontal axis*) we combine units contiguously with other units, each creating a context for others.[24] To put it simply, we draw upon semantic elements and syntactically combine them, and each word "gains" its meaning both paradigmatically and syntagmatically. A simple illustration is the statement, "The man walks down the street."[25] The combination of these words into a whole unit achieves an utterance meaning, but that meaning can be paraphrased by paradigmatic substitutions, which implies that words always have other words that are similar in meaning or sound structure that could be employed. Rephrasing the statement, someone might say, "The person walks down the street" or "The person hustles down 43rd street." As a motivated rhyme, we might follow up with: "He got right up and on the beat." The paradigmatic axis thus represents the vertical depth of the code as well as language's static nature.

For a second example, compare the statements "I see your point" and "I see the point of a spear." The word "see" means different things in each statement. In the first statement, it could be replaced by the word "comprehend" or "grasp" or "understand," whereas in the second statement it could be replaced with "am looking at." The word "point" also bears a different meaning in each statement: in the first we could substitute the word "argument" or "position" or "claim," whereas in the second statement the word "point" could be replaced by the word "tip." This example illustrates how semantic meaning depends upon both an absent bank of *possible* substitutions and a word's placement within the syntagmatic axis. It also illustrates that we, as listeners and readers, do not delimit and specify a word's meaning without first identifying the context in which it occurs. Such syntagmatic synergy gives great flexibility to language. This can be seen where people employ nouns as verbs: they thereby can speak of "wet leaves papering a street" or tell of "how the habit of anger raisins the heart."[26]

A fact that cannot be overstressed in this context is that the paradigmatic axis is *in absentia* whereas the syntagmatic axis is *in presentia*. This means, basically, "The combined units are actually present in a sequence. The paradigmatic groupings exist potentially in the memory of the speakers."[27]

Hence, what makes a given expression intelligible is a massive and largely absent code and the absent transformational rules for combination, both of which play pivotal roles in the acts of interpretation, rephrasing, translation, and so on.[28] Regarding the example, "I see your point," the whole statement might be rephrased or restated as "I understand what you are saying" or "you have made your idea clear to me." In a practical sense, this means that if we are talking with people and want to know that they understand what we are saying, we sometimes need to hear them say back to us what we said to them but using different words; otherwise we can't be sure if they understand. They could simply be parroting back what we said. But if they can change the words and we can recognize the absent invariance across the different expressions, then we feel understood and feel as if they understand.[29] The need for this back-and-forth shows that there is no way to reduce linguistic meaning to what is wholly present within a given statement. The meaning of our statements is both *present* in the syntagmatically combined words and also *absent* as possible similar substitutions. Without substitution and rules for combination, all language translation would be impossible.

Any word within a sentence can be replaced by a similar word and this shows how expressed utterances are tips atop a massive and invisible berg of potential: all the words in absentia. Along these lines, Igor E. Klyukanov points out the key role that nothing plays in communication were he writes:

> The quintessential element of the overall communication universe, then, is nothing but nothing, which, as the most potent source of meaning, gives rise to everything. . . . It is not easy yet essential to accept the fact . . . that the nature of communication continuously comes into being from nothing.[30]

The nothing at stake in discourse occurs in different guises and at different levels, and it functions in part because relations are not things but are real nonetheless. Relations are essentially no-thing, nothing but arrangement and organization. This is most evident if we make changes along the syntagmatic axis while making no new paradigmatic substitutions. For example, we can rearrange words in a sentence, not add or subtract any word, and yet completely change the meaning of the sentence. A simple example is "The dog tried to eat the man" and "The man tried to eat the dog." Here we find quite other than a simple reversal of transitive relations: in the former case, the dog is attacking, attempting to devour the man, whereas in the latter case we find something akin to a moral repugnance or gustatory revulsion to the act of eating dog. We might even think the latter perhaps meant an aborted attempt at eating an unsavory hotdog. For one more example, consider the difference between the statements "The defense shredded the evidence" and "The evidence shredded the defense." In the former statement, the word "shredded" refers to a criminal tampering with material relevant to a legal case whereas, in the latter statement, the word "shredded" basically means "defeated completely." The important theoretical point, in both examples, is that no new words are added, but as their arrangement changes so too does the *entire* meaning of the statement. Hence, there are several senses in which negativity in the form of difference and distinction pervades linguistic structure.

At this juncture, as a way of easing the advance into additional forms of non-being in language and communication, we perhaps should step back, slow down, and examine the underlying elements of spoken language: phonemes. One can see them either as abstractions generated out of the science of linguistics or as the most concrete and basic building blocks within language. In either case, they are no-thing at all. In fact, as Holenstein points out, "In identifying a phoneme, we are guided not by a sensory quality, but by an oppositional relation between sensory qualities. We ask, 'Did you say *ma* or *pa*?'"[31] Phonemes are not things and they have no self-standing, independent meaningful identity. Hence, Holenstein writes that phonemes, like the "letters" of the genetic code of chromosomes, "have no positive, constant, and general meaning,"[32] and Jakobson observes, "All phonemes designate nothing but mere OTHERNESS. . . . The phoneme is not identical to the sound, nor it is external to the sounds . . . it is *the invariant in the variations*."[33] This also means that, "phonology aims not at positive, absolutely defined qualities, nor at just any differences between qualities, but alone at those differences that distinguish one meaning-differentiating element from another."[34] Maurice Merleau-Ponty nicely reinforces this idea where he writes, "[P]honemes, too, which are the real foundations of speech, since they are reached through the analysis of spoken language and have no official existence in grammar and dictionaries, by themselves *mean nothing* one can specify."[35]

Language, obviously then, is not simply the stock of already known words (i.e., lexical entries found in the dictionary). Such a narrow orientation to language is acceptable for some purposes, maybe for the taskmaster grammarian in grade school, but language, as an open system, remains subject to novel expressions, slang, and the coining of new terms. These are partly what make language so handy, dynamic, and subject to sociohistorical change. With suffixes (bound morphemes) such as *ish*, we can turn a noun into an adjective. Biting a slice of pizza, we can say it has a "lasagnaish" taste or we can say that a soup is pretty "soggy dogish." Because much of the language we experience has been handed down to us from others, and often in printed text, we easily forget that all languages have a history. What we receive as traditions and institutions were originally neologisms springing forth from novel situations.

A little after the rise of the vanishing point in Renaissance paintings and after the invention of Guttenberg's movable-type printing press, both with their implied notions of infinity,[36] William Shakespeare, perhaps not surprisingly, radically deepened the language, fortifying and thickening its paradigmatic axis. He did so by his use of the prefix "un" and the suffix "less" With these, he coined in print many words whose meaning derived from grabbing already-existing words and making them into new and negative words. With the prefix *un*, Shakespeare brought some three hundred new words to English, including *unreal, unaware, untrained, unlettered, uneducated, unpublished, unhelpful, uncomfortable, undress, unsolicited, unwilling, unlock,* and *untie*.[37] Tagging the suffix *less* onto the tails of words, he coined in print the terms *dauntless, viewless, noiseless, remorseless,* and *worthless*.[38]

Additional examples of negative morphemes added to words that therein deepened the paradigmatic axis include *anonymous, disgruntled, illicit,* and *discombobulated*. Marks of absence so thoroughly cover over their earlier roots and counterparts that they leave them unknown or in desuetude. Indeed, who today uses the words *onymous, gruntled, licit,* or *combobulated*? Along parallel lines, Daniel Boorstin writes of how far such micro-negativity has advanced into modern culture, leading to overall reorientations:

> This is the age of contrivance. The artificial has become so commonplace that the natural begins to seem contrived. The natural is the "un-" and the "non-". It is the age of the "*un*filtered" cigarette (the filter comes to seem more natural than the tobacco), of the "*un*abridged" novel (abridgement is the norm), of the "*un*cut" versions of a movie. We begin to look on wood as a "*non*-synthetic" cellulose. All nature then is the world of the "*non*-artificial." Fact itself has become "*non*fiction."[39]

With little more than phonemes and morphemes, people infect everyday sensory experience with non-being, and, in time, people's sensibilities regarding what appears as natural comes to change and evolve. Moreover, the more important theoretical point is that difference and apposition limns the semantic load of each and every word.

Because language makes room for newly minted words, and because words occur at multiple levels of abstraction, when we use a word categorically, placing a particular item within a class, we need to make clear what is inside and what is outside the class. This also means, as Bateson suggests,

> Within a culture, we have a consensus about what sort of things that are going to be the "not" objects of the subject that we are talking about. . . . [P]lay is one of the ways in which we learn what the "not" objects are and what the system of stratification of the "not" object is.[40]

His point is that in creating a category or genre—by saying what something "is"—we need to show what the category excludes, meaning that we need to say what is *not* included within the category. Moreover, the phenomenon of play helps organisms learn to differentiate between "what is" and "what is not" to be included. Here Bateson uses the word *not* at two different levels of abstraction (two different logical-types) and stresses the importance of discriminating between those. If only for psychological reasons, we need a "double-frame" for distinguishing what is *not* to be taken as items within a class. This is why Wilden claims,

> Boundaries are the condition of distinguishing the "elements" of a continuum from the continuum itself. "Not" is such a boundary. . . . The metalinguistic function of "not" is in fact what generates the higher order paradox, for "not" is the boundary of an empty set, which like "the class of classes not members of themselves" is both a member of itself and not a member of itself.[41]

Animals, in their varied forms of communication, can engage in kinds of refusal or withdrawal, but they are not making classes within hierarchical scaffoldings of abstractions, nor are they employing categories that include different logical types. Language, within its syntactical "not," does precisely that. "'Not' . . . is a metaword, a rule about words, a word with the symbolic function of changing the meaning of all the other words associated with it."[42] The syntactical "not" is essential for denotation but is nevertheless a main source of paradox within language.

At points in his writing, Bateson suggests that his ambiguous use of the word "denote" precipitated paradoxes: when he writes that "the nip denotes the bite but does not denote what would be denoted by the bite," he claims that he is violating the theory of logical types because he is employing the word "denote" in very different senses but treating them indiscriminately: the bite does not "denote" per se and the nip does not either, but the nip stands as an evolutionary precursor to logical-typing differences within mammalian codifications.[43] More than a symptomatic sign, the nip marks the early evolutionary beginnings of abstract meaning. At other points, though, Bateson recognizes the problem to be more categorical, more inherent in the multileveled meaning of the syntactical *not*. Bateson powerfully illustrated this later claim at the 1956 Macy conference, where he gave a lecture titled "The Message: 'This Is Play.'" He began his talk by going to the chalkboard, writing "class of chairs" on it, drawing a circle around that and then saying, "We live in a universe of nameables. Within that universe we make classes. Let me here make the class of chairs." He then said to the audience, "I now want you quickly, without thinking too much about it, to name for me some of the '*not* chairs.'" Audience members started yelling out examples of what are not chairs, and Bateson went back to the chalkboard and wrote out some of their examples. Then he drew a larger circle around everything on the board so far. Following up on this animated interaction, he stated, "You have suggested 'tables,' 'dogs,' 'people,' 'autos.' Let me suggest one now: 'tomorrow.' Does it make you a little uncomfortable when I say 'tomorrow' is not a chair?"[44]

Bateson's example nicely clarifies how kinds of logical-typing violations occur—and how paradoxes emerge—once evolution makes way for sign-systems as complex and multileveled as language. Said simply, when we specify the class of "chairs," we also need to identify those items that are "*not* chairs," but these range from those things that "properly speaking" are "not chairs" (i.e., are of the same logical type or level of abstraction, e.g., tables, lamps, automobiles, etc.) to those things that are "improperly" not chairs (i.e., are of the different logical type or of a different level of abstraction, such as "tomorrow," "love," the word *chair* itself).

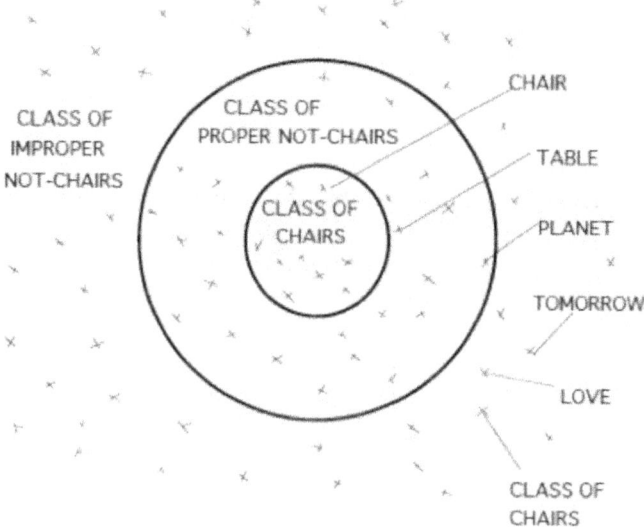

Figure 3.1. Diagram for discussion purposes referred to as *onionskin*. Josiah Macy Jr. Foundation. From Bateson's 1955 lecture/group discussion, published in 1956.

Whereas the logician and mathematician demand that we do not draw this outer line, as it would precipitate paradox, Bateson's point is that matters within evolutionary biology are not so straightforward. Language is inherently paradoxical because people necessarily draw that line; this metalevel distinction is part of the process by which, as Bateson suggests, people "pull themselves up by their own bootstraps."

We define words not only by inclusion but also by *exclusion*, and the latter occurs on more than one level of abstraction. There is a cognitive "double-framing," a two-tiered bracketing, that allows for intelligible management of "what is" and "what is not" the case. Bateson called this diagram the "onionskin" and used it to describe "the paradoxes of abstraction." The inner line is "legitimate" as it separates items that are of the same logical type, whereas the outer line is, logically speaking, "illegitimate." One cannot draw the outer line without precipitating paradox, but that is precisely the line that has to be drawn for psychological reasons. As Bateson writes,

> When a logical class or set of items is defined—for example, the class of matchboxes—it is necessary to delimit the set of items which are to be excluded, in this case all of those things which are not matchboxes. But the items to be included in the background set must be of the same degree of abstraction, i.e. of the same "logical type" as those items within the set itself. Specifically, if paradox is to be avoided the "class of matchboxes" and the "class of nonmatchboxes" (even though both these items are clearly not matchboxes) must not be regarded as members of the class of nonmatchboxes.[45]

Perhaps obviously, the "double-framing" of negation around any defined items means that the "not" haunts whatever "is." Not only do items take on a conceptual coherence according to proper definition and exclusion, but also, exclusion operates on multiple levels, sometimes within the meaning of a single word.

We can recall from chapter 1 that Bergson makes a useful distinction between affirmative propositions and negative propositions, suggesting that the former is largely psychological and epistemological, whereas the latter includes social, rhetorical, or admonitory dimensions. Bergson writes,

> Thus, whenever I add a "not" to an affirmation, whenever I deny, I perform two very definite acts: (1) I interest myself in what one of my fellow-men affirms, or in what he was going to say, or in what might have been said by another *Me*, whom I anticipate; (2) I announce that some other affirmation, whose content I do not specify, will have to be substituted for the one I find before me.[46]

He offers the following example: "The ground is not damp." Here the speaker preempts someone who might be wrongly thinking that the ground is damp, and the speaker also makes no affirmative statement regarding present conditions. His point is clear enough and insightful, but, as I suggested in chapter 1, things are a bit more complicated than the example suggests. Bergson makes it seem as if an act of denying requires the use of the syntactical "not," as if countless words do not already carry denial or negation within their meaning. In contrast, I have taken pains to show that negativity is more deeply entrenched in the semantic horizons of words because the underlying semantic structure of language is oppositional.

One of the founders of modern linguistics, Ferdinand de Saussure, well captures the purely relational character of the most basic elements of spoken language: "Concepts . . . are purely differential. They are not defined positively by their content, but negatively by their relationships with the other terms in the system. Their most exact characterization is to be what the others are not."⁴⁷ Consider, for the purposes of illustration, the contrasting conceptual pair "expensive" and "cheap." Each word already bears negativity in it. Each is an evaluative term and potentially advocates a kind of negative response, a possible turning away or withdrawal, as in, "I don't want it because it is cheap" or "I don't want it because it is expensive." This does not deny that, depending upon the context of the utterance, each word could be used for advocacy. One could say, "Wow, impressive, that ring looks very expensive" or "I needed to buy it because it was on sale and was so cheap." At the very least, each term is defined by not being its opposite. Words are not labels slapped upon some thing or state of affairs. Rather, they are elements within a system haunted by semantic opposition—including possible negative admonishments buried in the paradigmatic axis. Nestled within the meaning horizon of countless words lies a sense purchased by negation. As Burke points out, "A great many terms like *opposition, antithesis, alternation, contrast, contradiction, reciprocation, balance,* and even *succession,* can be summed up as pairs of elements or processes that 'negate' each other."⁴⁸

We can see, then, how both consciousness and language, as always haunted by non-being, are anathemas to materialist reductionism. Walter Kauffman writes,

> There are no opposites in nature. What would be the opposite of this rose or that Austrian pine? Or the sun, or of this human being? Only human thought introduces opposites. Neither individual beings nor classes of such beings—such as roses, pines, or human beings—have opposites; nor do colors, sounds, textures, feelings.
>
> But are not hard and soft opposites? As abstract concepts they are; but the feel of a rock and the feel of moss are not. It is only by disregarding most of the qualities of both experiences and classifying one as hard and the other as soft that people *think* of them as opposites. . . . No specific degree of heat or coldness has any opposite, only concepts do.⁴⁹

We can accept his point by simply underscoring that we, as humans, are precisely that part of nature through whom thought and conceptual opposites come to be. Otherwise, we once again succumb to the A-Naturalist Fallacy.

How about the old question, "Is the glass 'half-full' or is it 'half-empty'"? This seems at first appearance to offer two options, one that focuses upon what "is there" and one that focuses upon what "is not there." What gets obfuscated is how non-being haunts even the half-full glass, hence the word "half" in each expression. Also, either way of looking, as a selection from possibilities, is already infected with the negation of the other possibility.

Incorporating the negativity nestled within the semantic space of individual words (e.g., *undressed* or *dead*) and enriching the negativity found within propositions (e.g., "It is not raining today, hasn't rained for a week now, and might not rain tomorrow nor the next day"), we find additional modes of negation pervading the clauses and phrases that employ verbs to specify and handle "grammatical mood." Grammatical mood, commonly conveyed through syntax and verb agreement, designates and specifies forms of absence and non-being; it expressly makes room for consideration of possibilities. For example, the conditional mood, the subjunctive mood, and the interrogative mood are ways of registering what could be done or should be done *if* "X" is the case, what we hypothesize or what we wish to be the case, and what we seek to question and interrogate, respectively. Grammatical mood thus allows speakers to consider hypothetical cases and to speculate without strict adherence to actual facts of the matter. It enables people to reflect on counterfactual conditionals. In this way, non-being hides on the "inside" and "backside" of verbal expressions such that only speakers of the language could entertain such empirically absent dimensions. As a simple illustration of non-being haunting being throughout grammatical moods, consider a few sentences: Julius Caesar, one of most influential rulers in the Western world, "is dead" and "has been" for a long time, meaning that he once "was alive" but he "no longer is." Now, for those of us who "exist today," his "being" is reduced to his "having been," meaning he is physically absent yet remains part of the world's historical unfolding. If he somehow "were alive" today, knowing how he "has been treated" historically and "if he were offered" a chance to go back and change some of his actions, "might he do otherwise than he did" at first opportunity?

Non-being is the lifeblood and source of vitality within grammatical moods, and different grammatical moods are aptly suited for handling possible relation-states, for dealing with suggested actions based upon conditional or eventual relation-states, and also for asking questions about doubtful, probable, or potential relations (i.e., not currently actual ones). Moreover, even the indicative mood, in addressing or inquiring regarding what is actual, remains haunted by non-being: as we indicate, we specify, restrict, demarcate, and delimit.

If two items are similar, we can indicate their similarities by spelling out common properties. But any *differences* between two items, as Bateson has pointed out, cannot be located in either item:

> Difference, being of the nature of relationship, is not located in time or in space. We say that the white spot is "there," "in the middle of the blackboard," but the difference between the spot and the blackboard is not "there." It is not in the spot, it is not in the blackboard, it is not in the space between the board and the chalk.[50]

He adds,

> When I wipe the blackboard, where does the difference go? In one sense, the difference is randomized and irreversibly gone, as "I" shall be gone when I die. In another sense, the difference will endure as an idea . . . as long as this book is read. . . . But this enduring karmic information will be information about an imaginary spot on an imaginary blackboard.[51]

There are, then, many different kinds of difference, both real and imagined, both actual and possible.

Within the scientific method broadly construed, "the null hypothesis" proposes that there are no statistically significant differences between two or more specified populations or measured variables. If we use the expression "there is *no* statistical difference between X and Y," at least two layers of negativity already show themselves, as any concept of "difference" is already haunted by negation. It should also be of interest that scholars rely upon the word "variable." Variable, as a term and concept, is primarily grounded in negativity. A variable *as variable* is not itself; it means an empty marker to be filled in by something else. It is a functional absence, a placeholder. "X correlates with Y" illustrates how metalinguistic resources, especially those grown out of alphabetic literacy, are designed to handle abstract possibilities pure and simple.[52]

Non-being, by way of functional absence, also operates at the level of whole arguments. One of the most powerful rhetorical tropes is known as the *enthymeme*. It basically refers to a kind of syllogistic reasoning where one of the premises is missing. Aristotle thought enthymemes were among the most powerful rhetorical tropes, partly because people persuade themselves in being able to follow along, filling in the missing pieces. For example, a full syllogism is, "All men are mortal. Socrates is a man, and, therefore, Socrates is mortal." An enthymeme, in contrast, is: "Socrates is mortal because he is a man." If you were able to follow that enthymeme, you did so by filling in the missing premise, "all men are mortal." Most advertising relies upon enthymemes, where strategic omissions enable listeners and readers to participate in the ad's persuasive appeal.[53]

Finally, we can round out this examination of the non-being within linguistic structure and content by observing that we cannot talk about the "supernatural" or even the "natural" on "their" own terms. Perhaps obviously, all talk about the "supernatural" is, by default, partly an analogical borrowing from other realms with identifiable forms of reference—what Burke calls: natural order, verbal order, and sociopolitical order.[54] Burke clarifies how any discussion of the supernatural draws upon these other three orders:

> No matter how firm may be one's convictions that his terminology for the supernatural refers somehow to a real order of existence, there is the obvious fact that he necessarily borrows his terms from the prevailing three worldly orders. At the very start, therefore, he must concede (and if he is thoroughgo-

ing, he willingly does concede): His statements are but metaphorical, analogical, mere makeshifts for talking figuratively about a supposed superhuman realm that, no matter how real it may be, cannot be adequately discussed in human terms.[55]

One can talk about the supernatural only in terms of what it is not. All talk about God or the Divine, to the extent that it does not limit itself to negative theology, discusses God in terms that trade upon notions of the natural world (e.g., God is a being, sits on throne, has a sex, etc.), terms that stem from the verbal realm (e.g., God as the Word, God speaking to people, making covenants), or terms that stem from the sociopolitical realm (e.g., God as Lord, King, someone who "rules" over people).

Scientific or naturalist orientations do not escape a somewhat similar fate; they, too, talk about things in terms of what those things are not. That is, we commonly think of words as signs for things, but the situation is dialectical and reversible, meaning that things can be the signs of words. In fact, we sometimes need to ask ourselves, as Burke asks, "What Are the Signs of What?"[56] Whether talking about "selfish genes" or describing the "active role" of sperm in fertilizing the "'passive' egg" or speaking of lions as "kings" of the jungle or talking about the "machinery" of mental processes or discussing the "language" of insects, anthropocentricism abounds as things of the world are metaphorically infused with the compass of language and culture.[57] We talk about nature using countless words whose meanings are analogically borrowed from the human realm. As Burke writes:

> Whereas the supernaturalist has had to recognize explicitly that his words about the supernatural are but analogical, figurative, metaphorical, the naturalist would persuade us that his nonverbal realm is available to us in its immediate sensory aspects, completely free of verbal and sociopolitical elements. But if the things of nature are, for man, the visible signs of their verbal entitlements, then nature gleams secretly with a most fantastic shimmer of words and social relationships.[58]

Items of nature, parts of the so-called nonverbal realm, cannot be talked about on their own terms, for they have no terms other than the ones we give them. "The orderliness of 'nature,'" talked about and delimited as such, is already other than "itself"; it has been otherized in and through its entanglements with the sociopolitical order and the verbal one.[59]

CONTEXTS WHERE NOTHING HAPPENS

Humans live in the world of achievable relations, in the contexts created out of the semantic and syntactical spaces that language makes possible. For example, the words you are reading right now are in English, on the page or screen, part of this book, in some particular space, after the big bang but before the big crunch. Obviously, other relations could have been mentioned but were not, yet those that were mentioned have become possibilities actualized and delimited. Language thereby creates and laminates the contexts in which "what is not the case" can show its falseness and "what is not there" can reveal its absence. Without language to frame and contextualize situations, without language to delimit a particular horizon of possibilities, what is "not" cannot be revealed in particular. As Sartre suggests, "The world does not disclose its non-beings to one who has not first posited them as possibilities."[60] For example, if we say "this room does not have any elephants in it," people can look around to verify that fact for themselves. Now, if we say, "there are no zebras in the room," people might take a peek and then agree with that fact as well. But the trouble begins if people forget the context that the words created, and, basing their judgment solely on sensory perception, they conclude that these assertions refer to the same fact of non-being; they get seduced into thinking that the "not-being there of any tigers" has precisely the same content as the "not-being there of any zebras."[61] Hence, they might argue that these statements refer to the same fact—to the fact that "there are no African animals in the room." That would be yet a third claim, slightly different than the other two, and we'd have to check.

"Context" remains one of the most inadequately theorized aspects of human communication. Richard L. Lanigan has provided some of the most important correctives to popular oversimplifications.[62] At a minimum he suggests that we differentiate between the phenomenon of "information," which operates through various "contexts of choice" (e.g., contexts of selection and combination), and the phenomenon of "communication," which incorporates information yet surpasses it by including a "choice of context." Without choice of context, we do not have the requisite conditions for communication; we have only possibilities of information.

With nebulous boundaries, context sometimes remains intangible and loosely situated in both space and time. It also is subject to re-contextualization to differing degrees at any moment, and that means that it cannot be analyzed as if it were a material thing. Two people can be sitting together and having dinner, which could also be described as a man and a woman on a date, or also described as a married couple out celebrating an anniversary meal. What is all too evident in the visual field can remain subject to different interpretations depending upon how the occasion is framed and contextualized. The word "date" itself is just one example. Young people today feel too much pressure if a mealtime encounter with a possible romantic partner is labeled "a date." Instead, they will frame such interaction as "talking" but not as going on a "date." This example also shows that contexts do not always remain vague and undefined.

Certainly, recurrent kinds of situations and patterns of interaction occur. We have words to designate them: a "date," a "job interview," a "birthday party," a "work outing," a "funeral," and so on. This also means that once we have established a sense of context and have codified occasions for coordinated actions with others, we have set the conditions for absence and non-occurrences to become meaningful events in their own right. If I call someone every day at 8:00 a.m. and one day I do not call, the absence means *something*, at least to the person who normally receives the call. This also means, as Bateson argues,

> The letter you do not write, the apology you do not offer, the food that you do not put out for the cat—all of these can be sufficient and effective messages because zero, *in context*, can be meaningful; and it is the recipient of the message who creates the context. . . . [T]he income tax people will become alerted by the declarations which you did not send.[63]

Holenstein conveys similar insights where he brings Jakobson's work on linguistics to nonverbal communication and social interaction. He writes, "In clothing there is also a parallel to the linguistic 'zero sign,' which can be most conspicuous, for example, when someone turns up at a particular occasion without a head covering or a tie."[64] Here attendees may experience a noticeable absence, and the person inadequately attired may feel embarrassed for the transgression. But the fact remains that the transgression itself cannot be grasped by looking exclusively to the person who is *not* wearing the head covering or tie. Where, if not within the context itself, including in the minds of attendees, is the transgression located?

Consider, too, how a wedding band commemorates vows and a ceremony now unseen. To place a wedding ring upon one's finger in certain cultures is to make known that, even if one is currently unaccompanied, one is "not single." Moreover, at a certain age the absence of a wedding ring, a sheer nothing at all, can be a meaningful sign to others. Again, because of sociohistorical context, a hand without any jewelry, a hand simply as it is, with nothing else, can be enough to announce that one is "not married." Some people even "advertise" their status as single by wearing a ring on a neighboring finger, as if to intimate a message that equates to: "I am not against wearing rings, and my 'ring finger' is available."

In their classic book *Pragmatics of Human Communication*, Watzlawick, Beavin, and Jackson suggest, "One cannot not communicate."[65] Their point is that within interaction and communicative contexts, there is no equivalent to non-behavior and that, given that all behavior has some possible communicative value, communication occurs well below the level of spoken messages and intentional exchanges.[66] Sometimes the communicative exchange amounts to subtle attitudinal postures—practices of deference and demeanor—which convey the following three meta-messages: "This is how I see myself. This is how I see you. This is how I see you seeing me."[67] Without necessarily intending to or without self-conscious recognition, people exude behavioral signs that embody those three meta-messages. Nevertheless, some strategists realize this and try to get their expressions under conscious control, performing gestures and facial expressions that seem spontaneous but in fact are calculated. People can pretend to like each other, try to hide their attraction to one another, act as if they respect another's view, pretend to be interested when they are not, etc. Such nonverbal situations remain ambiguous: are others being genuine? Or are they intending to subtly convey certain messages? Are they perhaps trying to deceive? Are we simply projecting and perceiving what is not really there? Interaction becomes more like a game or a kind of play than anything else. Such dimensions of interpersonal relations illustrate interesting layers and modes of non-being lurking behind and within human communication: *affectation, contrivance, exaggeration, hint, posing, posturing, pretense,* and, of course, *plausible deniability.*

Knowing that people cannot not communicate, knowing that their sheer presence or spoken language also gives off sign-material that can be taken as information about their mental state, intentions, previously stated claims, and identity more generally, individuals strategically *avoid* certain places or particular others or topics of conversation. Erving Goffman nicely captures this spirit where he writes, "Social life is an uncluttered, orderly thing because the person stays away from the places and topics and times where he is not wanted and where he might be disparaged from going."[68] The world thus maintains its orderliness and appears to be a tidy affair partly because people have learned to avoid going where they know they don't fit in, where they cannot compete, and where they know they are not welcome, and so on. People know what *not* to do and what *not* to say. There is, as Goffman suggests, "much to be gained from venturing nothing."[69]

Imagine that you are at work. You learn though the grapevine that a co-worker is hosting a party and apparently many people received an invitation but you did not. Was a "message" conveyed? How about those who come home later than expected, and, when asked where they have been, make a slight hesitation in their response? Sometimes such "deception cues," although nothing in themselves, serve as a gap that gives up the game. Or, at the least, the inquirer can be confident that there is some kind of relevant absence present. According to the television detective Columbo, there are three things to look for at any crime scene: what's there now that wasn't there before, what was there before that isn't there now, and what has been moved.

Silence, the unheard context of all contexts, is nothing in particular but it rides along on the backside of whatever is heard. It serves as the ground upon which one sound disappears to make room for the next. Miles Davis is known for having said, "The most important notes are the ones you don't play," and, in *The Community of Those Who Have Nothing in Common*, Lingis writes, "Since communication is, for the receiver, actively separating a figure from the background, then in the absence of the background there can be no figure either.... John Cage once emerged from a soundproof room to declare that there was no such state as silence."[70] Cage in fact took this insight to the extreme when he composed and performed "Silence," a "piece of music" that lasted four minutes, thirty-three seconds, and it was just that, silence. But perhaps obviously, the piece is, as a performance of non-being, much more than what is not heard. In trying to comprehend the nature of context, we, like Cage, are, as R. D. Laing writes, "at the outer reaches of what language can state, but we can indicate by language why language cannot state what it cannot state. I cannot say what cannot be said, but sounds can make us listen to the silence." To which he adds, "This zone, the zone of no-thing, of the silence of silences, is the source. We forget that we are still there all the time."[71]

THE "DON'T" AND THE SECRET SACRED SIGN OF NEGATIVITY

Human beings, as living organisms, gain their initial sense of negativity in their exercise of responding to preferences in their immediate environment. As beings capable of moving away from what is regarded as undesirable or moving toward objects of desire, humans—in their sheer animality—already have some basic sense of managing possibilities and thereby experience the rudiments of moral decision-making. But individuals grow into their sense of self-conscious agency (and conscience) only after a thorough steeping in their culture's "thou-shalt-nots." As social order requires cultural members to avoid places where they are unwelcome and to refrain from actions that the culture deems unacceptable, persons are subjected to a flurry of negativity. They are shaped by self-perpetuating constraints: they inwardly sustain the social negativity, carrying it over in how they think, and, in this manner, conscience plays a pivotal role in informing people's decisions and in guiding their actions.[72] Said from the inverse angle: a person who never has heard (or not sufficiently internalized) "No!" "Stop!" and "Don't!" does not grow into a self-aware cultural agent, does not develop a conscience, but instead becomes something akin to a "sociopath" or "psychopath." Not surprisingly, then, parents raise their children by telling them not to touch, not to stare, not to play in the street, and not to wiggle around so much. Children are commanded to stop horsing around, to stop talking so much, to not be a nuisance, to keep off the grass, to not trespass, and to not forget to flush the toilet. They are told to clean up after themselves, to not leave their toys lying around, to quit playing with their food, to stop picking their nose, to not stay up late, to avoid certain foods, and to keep away from certain kids at school. They are advised to knock on a closed door before entering a room, told that one does not go into a neighbor's house or pool without invitation, and further told not to invite themselves over. They are admonished to not waste their time and to not be foolish with their money. This litany of examples of cultural "Don'ts" could be extended at length, but the important point for the present discussion is that somewhere along the way, children are usually subjected to two very concrete, meta-level experiences of negativity: first, they must *share*, meaning that they are pressed to "*not* hoard goods," and, second, they are required to *take turns*, meaning they are demanded to "*not* monopolize access to possessions." Both of these yearnings for justice are a kind of negation atop negation. This partly means that youths already have, however rudimentary, a budding notion of *mine* and they are routinely blocked from that orientation with two practical reorientations of "not-exclusively-mine." To be fit for society and social interaction, individuals must overcome, at least to some extent, their egocentric impulse to dominate space and time.

But adolescents soon enough learn about possession, ownership, wealth, inheritance, and private property generally construed, and they learn to take such things very seriously.[73] Preoccupation with socioeconomic status comes to the forefront of thought and decision-making in young adulthood, and moral views regarding why people end up either rich or poor inform cultural members' practices and self-understanding (e.g., the "fate" of birth, industriousness, laziness, luck, competence, happenstance, charity, exploitation of others, etc.).[74] These become the fabric of everyday life and of conscience too, with a set of social structures and underlying personal beliefs to keep the whole system working. Things of the world become other than merely what the eyes can see; they are now things *possessed*. People accordingly learn to go about *their* daily business, to not take what is not *theirs*, and to not worry about what is not *their* problem. By the time adolescents reach adulthood they have come to see the entire world enshrouded within the invisible dimension of negativity.[75]

There is, unquestionably, a tight but deeply repressed connection between the "don't," private property, money, and conscience. Rather than having to continuously say "don't" to others, one's possessions and properties constantly yet silently announce "mine," "hands off." Few relations in the social world, perhaps with the exception of sexual relations, are as complex and nebulous, somehow all pervasive and yet cloaked in mystery.[76]

Money, an element within a system of substitution, is an item of instrumental value, not an object inherently valuable. If one were completely alone on a deserted island, having no food or fresh water but only a stockpile of money, the non-being of money would be more than evident. It is not valuable as an end per se; its only real value is in its exchange for something other than itself. This also means, as unfortunate as it is ironic, that someone, as Burke points out, "can even starve to death hoarding the symbols that would buy him more than he could eat in many lifetimes. And men will kill themselves trying to amass more and more of the monetary symbols that represent good living."[77] Burke suggests that money, like language, becomes a material embodiment of transcendence, the closest humans come to moving beyond their animality: it makes possible modes of noninvolved action at a distance, "as with the coin tossed to a leper,"[78] and it makes the word *everything* more than a vague abstraction, for people can want everything and express that desire by loving what seems to give them everything: money. Georg Simmel hits upon the negative character of money and how its modes of absence bear functional value where he writes, "We know more about money than about any other object because . . . it is a thing absolutely lacking in qualities and therefore cannot, as can even the most pitiful object, conceal within itself any surprises or disappointments."[79] We want money because it is a universal wishing well: we want *other* things, and those others who take our money for the things they provide to us also want the money for other things. For all of these reasons, and because money always obliquely refers to all those others who are willing to exchange something for it, money is others at-hand. And, lots of money is a crowd, a powerful one unleashed at will.

Why do some people make so much money while others make so little—often with no unambiguous rationale for pay differences? Why do some people possess more than they possibly could use while others don't have the basics for survival? Burke offers much insight where he claims that social inequality partly sustains itself without continued effort because people do not know what others do to earn their money; it remains a secret. For example, what does a hedge-fund manager do all day? How about a contractor, dentist, farmer, lawyer, lobbyist, politician, or street sweeper? What time did they get up and how many hours will they work? Who sets their calendar, and what, exactly, does their average workday and workweek look like? We simply don't know, and such all-encompassing mystery, its own mode of non-being, helps keep social inequality from being thrust into people's faces. Moreover, people have been taught to refrain from asking others about their salary or how much they saved or inherited. Not knowing these specifics enables people on both upper and lower ends of the economic ladder to keep dissonance and guilt at bay. In gated communities, working in offices with private keys to the executive toilet, people simply don't talk about the mystery of salary and possession, and accordingly, social inequality and the opaque structures and varied beliefs that serve it routinely evade scrutiny.

But why, exactly, would private property and social inequality generate senses of guilt or dissonance? Well, at a minimum, we are animals whose very bodies are on cosmic loan to us, and it seems presumptuous to speak of ownership, especially beyond one's own lifetime. Inheritances, landed properties, or owned properties that one has never visited stand out as clearly odd or strange. We cannot find such practices or institutions anywhere else in nature. Someone might object, and, taking a naturalist slant, suggest some animals do have private property, just to a limited degree. Even if we grant the obvious appeal of such an argument—as some animals do have dens, caves, or dwellings and many also have territories—the differences between animal occupancy and human possession are just too significant: other animals need to occupy their dwellings, mark them, and "police" them themselves. In contrast, once people own a piece of property it is theirs—because they paid for it or it was given to them—which also implies that unknown others (e.g., security guards or law enforcement officers) will be paid to defend it for them, even in their absence. The difference here seems to be *in kind* rather than merely one *of degree*. Denying the radical difference here amounts to a denial of culture itself.

Intergenerational private property does not spontaneously happen on its own; it demands many forms of constraint and labor for its continuance. This implies, then, that people want much more than merely power. They know that sheer capacity to exercise power at a distance is not what matters most in the human realm. No, what people seek is *authority*; they want a legitimate exercise of power, because, once deemed legitimate, power can then perpetuate itself or at least not bog down in internal friction nor consume itself in the heat of resistance and contention. Not surprisingly, religious texts, governmental bodies, "natural law," and the state apparatus all routinely serve the primary function of authorizing and sanctioning property rights for both individuals and society.

In his *The Rhetoric of Religion*, Burke spells out how Christian notions of redemption, via Christ on the cross, connect back to money, property rights and the sense of conscience, all of which grow out of the "thou shalt nots":

> [T]he principle of negativity will enable men to build up vast empires, all based on this distinction, which says in effect: "Thou shalt not take these things of mine, nor I of thine." Myriads of myriads of laws, deeds, contracts, precepts, prison sentences, educational policies, businesses, revolutions, religions, etc., etc., will be erected atop these simple beginnings: things . . . in themselves are positive, but . . . in becoming labeled "mine" and "thine," take on the secret sacred sign of negativity. . . . The negative, as so ingrained through the subtleties of "conscience," will build up a sense of guilt equally as vast and complicated as this bundle of negatively protected properties. And from this sense of guilt there will arise the yearning for a new and all-inclusive positive, the demand for a supernal sacrifice literally existing and somehow serving by his suffering both to cancel off this guilt and to sanction the perpetuating of the conditions out of which the guilt arises.[80]

With its notion of Christ dying for people's sins, Christianity has a multifaceted and hazy connection to money and private property. Although it is relevant to trace Christ's sacrifice to the Garden of Eden story from the Old Testament and to the notion of "original sin," the appeal of Christian redemption and salvation comes, at least in part, from the experience of negatively sanctioned property rights and the logic of substitution that money helps to facilitate.

Money, like language, is a system of substitution, and, as such, it operates through functional absence. It not only precipitates a sense that everything has its price, but it also leads, in a roundabout way, to the notion that someone's actions can serve as a "payment" for another's wrongdoing. Burke writes, "For money introduces the principle of *redemption*. That is, money will give them [people] the idea of redemption by payment.... [I]t implies that one person can suffer for another, as 'payment' for the other's guilt."[81] Hence, once people have built their lives around private property, often at others' expense, and once they have coupled that with the wish to be forgiven for such practices while also wishing to continue on with business as usual, they now need some kind of redemption, some kind of amends for what they know, at least on some level, is morally questionable.[82] At this point in history, many people seem to believe, or want to believe, or perhaps want others to believe, that the redemption already happened (or is happening or will happen), and, therefore, everything is fine if only people accept Jesus and the message of Christianity. It is worth recalling that by the time of the rise of the Roman Empire (one of the first world powers to not cancel private debts older than six years old and to institute forms of debt bondage), social inequality was so extreme that many people opted for Christianity, with its impending promise of the end of the world. Here we are today, over two thousand years later, still waiting, and the situation does not seem to be getting any better.

What will it take for people to accept that there has not been, and never will be, such a sacrifice on their behalf? Can they wise up and acknowledge that any possible justice and fairness will be accomplished in this world or it will not be achieved at all?[83] If people come to believe that their only hope is for God to save people from themselves, they have covered over some of the most robust moral possibilities in existence. They are missing something very important regarding who they are: the meaning of life itself, and also, their connections to others and to the earth.

At some level of awareness, people who are "well off" know, or at least suspect, that some of the social inequality in their culture is partly their responsibility but they may not know the most viable solution. Also, they don't want to give up what they have. They have grown complicit and comfortable within a system that they know is morally questionable, but to call it into question seems to cut against what they have come to understand as their "self-interest." Imagine people with a serious substance abuse problem who are hurting others, hurting themselves, and who know that they are unable to stop in their unhealthy, destructive lifestyle. This is what money has become for some people. Greed has literally taken over their lives, reducing people, places, and things to price tags. It is sometimes said that "love of money is the root of all evil." This is probably not the case, but we should not deny how much anxiety, defensiveness, guilt, and rationalization appears when thinking about the topic or discussing it publicly. And the problems of social inequality seem even more pressing today, partly because we can witness a rise in the billionaire class, and people, generally speaking, are not well suited to comprehend the scale differences in numbers that large. For example, how long is one million seconds? It is a little over eleven days. How long is one billion seconds? It is about thirty-two years. If someone makes $100,000 a year and is allowed to keep every cent of the money with no taxes, how long would it take the person to accumulate $1 million? Ten years. But now, if someone makes $100,000 dollars a year and is allowed to keep every cent of the money with no taxes, how long would it take the person to accumulate $1 billion? Ten thousand years. Who cannot see the moral ramifications at stake here? When some people have billions of dollars while others are destitute and starving, this is more than extreme economic inequality; it is, just as equally, a moral crisis.

These are contentious waters and it is worth moving cautiously. Much ink has been spilled over the past few centuries regarding wealth and class, and people get heated—their sense of conscience gets riled—just thinking about property rights, money, and social inequality. Almost everyone seems to agree that social inequality is a problem, but they disagree on its source and solution. We might lessen some tension by openly asserting that we would be in error to argue that private property is "not natural." To think so simply succumbs to one more version of the A-Naturalist Fallacy discussed earlier. I have tried to safeguard against oversimplifications of nature by introducing the A-Naturalist Fallacy, suggesting that all that happens, by the very fact of it happening, falls within the domain of the natural. Nature, as a whole that includes humans and their dealings, is varied, multileveled, and has many forms and modes of being and non-being that do not appear elsewhere in nature (e.g., art, math, monetary systems, science, religion). But we need to be careful not to fall into an a-historicist fallacy that thereby takes a particular practice or institution as a given, covers over the contingencies of its historical development, and treats it as inevitable or the only possible way for a given society to continue or survive.

Overpopulation is already a major problem in many of the world's cities, and, as climate change makes fewer and fewer places habitable, there will be even more struggle over land ownership and immigration. This is not, however, to argue against private property or to suggest that it is inherently wrong or immoral. It is simply to state that people, in gaining a self-awareness as they were also gaining a conscience, have learned how to reason about moral possibilities and how to question their assumptions, just as they learned that sharing and taking turns are part of what it means to be a good member of society. Moreover, some of people's earliest memories can testify to how willing they were to share with others before they discovered themselves as merely "things in the world." Many of the problems of greed and massive social inequality can only be dealt with through political change, tax laws, and legislation, but some of that can be facilitated through a significant revision of how we understand ourselves and our place in the cosmos. Buckminster Fuller orients us in the right direction where he writes, "There are no passengers on Spaceship Earth. We are all crew."

NOTHING IN THOUGHT AND LANGUAGE

Kenneth Burke suggests that one cannot truly be at home in one's language until one has become comfortable with irony. It is not until people can say, "Oh, I've had just a fine day," while meaning the opposite, that they enjoy the full sense of language. Not only is it the case that, as George Steiner suggests, "Language is not a description of reality but an evasion from it and an answer to it," but our symbolic abstractions allow endless applicability partly because no word or sentence is attached to a once-and-once-only state of affairs.

Countless expressions, thoughts verbalized, enable speakers to talk about something by talking about something else. In a particular context having no ties to farms or farming, one can say, "Don't count your chickens before they've hatched." Or someone might summarize the details of a business meeting with the line, "Well, it's evident that 'the squeaky wheel gets the grease,'" and this can be said despite the fact that at no point during the meeting did anyone mention wheels or items needing lubricants.

In the world of discourse and language, there is neither a first word nor a last word, just an ever-incomplete dialogue indefinitely under way. And, as Ralph Waldo Emerson reminds us, people are only half themselves; the other half is their expression. Moreover, Marshall McLuhan and Quentin Fiore invoke the thinking of Meister Eckhart to point out, "Only the hand that erases can write the true thing."[84]

It is easy to overlook or underappreciate that we are animals making sounds; we often take those sounds too seriously, too literally. We are symbol-using animals, and symbols are *not* what they represent. Count Alfred Korzybski rather famously observed, "Whatever one might *say* something '*is*,' it is not."[85] He furthermore suggested that "the word is not the thing" and "the map is not the territory." Alan Watts pointed out that you cannot eat a menu. In even more practical terms, grades are abstract letters, and a degree is nothing but a piece of paper. Any good teacher reminds students that the grades and degrees are not the skills and competencies that those grades and degrees are supposed to represent.

All signs are characterized by some absence, and some signs are drenched with negativity on multiple levels. Symbols more generally considered enable an articulate management of what is remote in time or space, and, as such, they can handle what is possible only because they themselves are abstract. Thought, too, is abstract: it selects and delimits, decontextualizes; it deals mostly in *possible* relations.

Words are inherently selective abstractions, real in their own regard but *not* the things to which they refer. Thought, no matter how true, cannot be other than a representation, a kind of actualized possibility, and this is why, as Burke would say, we need to watch our thought and language as we would eye a mean dog. *Neti, neti.*

NOTES

1. Jean-Paul Sartre, *Being and Nothingness*, trans. Hazel Barnes (NJ: Gramercy Books, 1956), 374.

2. Maurice Merleau-Ponty, *The Visible and the Invisible*, trans. Alphonso Lingis (Evanston, IL: Northwestern University Press, 1968), 64–65.

3. Alphonso Lingis, *The Community of Those Who Have Nothing in Common* (Bloomington: Indiana University Press, 1994).

4. Also, in a similar way but at a different level of abstraction, when we use a general word such as *person*, we are talking about something essential, or as Burke would say, an abstract title, something that cannot be restricted to any *particular* existing individual. Any actual existing particular human person would have to be tall or short, would have to be of this age or that age, would have to have lots of hair on the head or little or perhaps none at all. Finally, and perhaps obviously, *categories* is a word, but this does not suggest that the world independent of humans is bereft of naturally recurring types, even types partly operating through modes of functional absence. See Terrence W. Deacon, *Incomplete Nature: How Mind Emerged from Matter* (New York: W. W. Norton and Co., 2012); also see Corey Anton, "Lanigan's 'Encyclopedic Dictionary': Key Concepts, Insights, and Advances," in *Communicology for the Human Sciences: Lanigan and the Philosophy of Communication*, eds. Andrew R. Smith, Isaac E. Catt, and Igor Klyukanov (Pittsburg: Duquesne University Press, 2017), 49–70; Corey Anton, "Syntagmatic and Paradigmatic Synergism: Notes on Lanigan's 'Encyclopedic Dictionary,'" *The Atlantic Journal of Communication* 25, no. 1 (2017): 48–63.

5. Burke writes, "Indeed, since Hegel equates Thinking with Being and since Hegel reminds us that 'pure' Being is indistinguishable from Nothing, and since thought according to Hegel is essentially dialectical, we here have the means for spinning Thought, Being, and Dialectic from the principle of negation," in Kenneth Burke, *Language as Symbolic Action: Essays on Life, Literature and Method* (Berkeley: University of California Press, 1966), 437.

6. See Corey Anton, "Technology, Hypocrisy, and Morality: Where, Oh Where, Has All the Hypocrisy Gone?" *Explorations in Media Ecology: The Journal of the Media Ecology Association* 17, no. 2 (2018): 119–35.

7. See Gregory Bateson, *Steps to an Ecology of Mind* (New York: Ballantine, 1972).

8. Emil M. Cioran, *The Temptation to Exist*, trans. Richard Howard (New York: Arcade, 2012), 40.

9. Ambrose Bierce, *The Devil's Dictionary* (Mineola, NY: Dover, 1993), 42.

10. Just as waking up after dreamless sleep serves as a metaphor for the idea of life after death, so too—because awakeness affords the ability to differentiate dream from reality—we find an analogical comparison wherein life might be a dream of sorts and death an awakening from the dream. More than one religious tradition has believed that life is a kind of dream in the mind of a sleeping god. Sympathies for an afterlife partly come from the repression of one of the conscious mind's most profound and traumatic discoveries: a coherent sense of the difference between dreamland and the awake world.

11. The same could be said of "threat" and "histrionics." See Bateson, *Steps to an Ecology of Mind*.

12. See Gregory Bateson, "A Theory of Play and Fantasy: A Report on the Theoretical Aspects of the Project for Study of the Role of Paradoxes of Abstraction in Communication." *Approaches to the Study of Human Personality*. *Psychiatric Research Reports* no. 2 (1955).

13. Bateson, *Steps to an Ecology of Mind*, 135.

14. Anthony Wilden, *System and Structure: Essays in Communication and Exchange* (London: Tavistock, 1972), 251.

15. Do they practice the scene, practice it often, and try to get it just right? As "nothing" separates a staged kiss from a real kiss, who finds it surprising that those who perform in romantic roles sometimes inadvertently fall in love? The meta-communicative frame of "pretend" or "play," as basically nothing, can break down. In this regard, more interesting than the frame, "this is play," is the frame, "Is this play?" See Bateson, *Steps to an Ecology of Mind*.

16. Bateson, *Steps to an Ecology of Mind*, 135.

17. See Linda Elson, *Paradox Lost: A Cross-Contextual Definition of Levels of Abstraction* (Cresskill, NJ: Hampton, 2010); Corey Anton, "A Levels Orientation to Abstraction, Logical Typing, and Language More Generally," in Linda Elson's *Paradox Lost: A Cross-Contextual Definition of Levels of Abstraction* (Cresskill, NJ: Hampton, 2010), 183–201.

18. Marshall McLuhan, *Understanding Media: Extensions of Man* (Corte Madera, CA: Gingko, 2003), 391.

19. See Harry Frankfurt, *On Bullshit* (Princeton, NJ: Princeton University Press, 2005).

20. See Burke, *Language as Symbolic Action*.

21. Ernest Becker, "The Spectrum of Loneliness," in *The Ernest Becker Reader*, ed. Daniel Liechty (Seattle: University of Washington Press, 2005), 124. Also see Lee Thayer, "Saying So: The Lie of the Mind," in *Pieces: Toward a Revisioning of Communication/Life* (Norwood, NJ: Ablex, 1997).

22. See Elmar Holenstein, *Roman Jakobson's Approach to Language: Phenomenological Structuralism*, trans. Catherine Schelbert and Tarcisius Schelbert (Bloomington: Indiana University Press, 1976); also see Richard Lanigan, *The Human Science of Communicology: A Phenomenology of Discourse in Foucault and Merleau-Ponty* (Pittsburgh: Duquesne University Press, 1992); Anton, "Syntagmatic and Paradigmatic Synergism."

23. It should be noted that meta-linguistic words are routinely employed as "empty intentions." This means someone can "say" that someone had "said" something without "saying" exactly what was "said." We thus make reference while leaving unspecified the particular content. See Corey Anton, "About Talk: The Category of Talk-Reflexive Words," *Semiotica* 121, no. 3–4 (1998): 193–212.

24. Holenstein writes, "The operations of both selection and combination presuppose an antecedent operation, the differentiation of signs, for which contrast functions as the base principle," *Roman Jakobson's Approach to Language*, 151.

25. Burke well illustrates how forms of functional absence characterize our abstract nouns, meaning that such words are more like titles than they are descriptive or pictorial per se. *Language as Symbolic Action*, 361.

26. Both of these lovely expressions come from William Gass's "On Talking to Oneself" from *Habitations of the Word* (New York: Simon and Schuster, 1985).

27. Holenstein, *Roman Jakobson's Approach to Language*, 140.

28. "What matters in the case of information, and produces its distinctive physical consequences, is a relationship to something not there. Information is the archetypical absential concept," in Deacon, *Incomplete Nature*, 373.

29. Corey Anton, "Communication: The Act and Art of Taking For Granted," *ETC: A Review of General Semantics* 75, no. 1–2 (2018): 47–66.

30. Igor Klyukanov, *A Communication Universe: Manifestations of Meaning, Stagings of Significance* (Lanham, MD: Lexington, 2010), 179.

31. Holenstein, *Roman Jakobson's Approach to Language*, 72–73.

32. Holenstein, *Roman Jakobson's Approach to Language*, 172.

33. Holenstein, *Roman Jakobson's Approach to Language*, 172.

34. Holenstein, *Roman Jakobson's Approach to Language*, 71.

35. Maurice Merleau-Ponty, *The Prose of the World*, trans. John O'Neill (Evanston, IL: Northwestern University Press, 1973), 33.

36. See Brian Rotman, *Signifying Nothing: The Semiotics of Zero*. (Stanford, CA: Stanford University Press, 1987).

37. David Crystal, "Un-Finished," Around the Globe 17 (2001): 22–23, accessed March 26, 2019, from http://www.davidcrystal.com/?fileid=-4228.

38. Jeff McQuain and Stan Malless, *Coined by Shakespeare: Words and Meanings First Used by the Bard* (Springfield, MA: Merriam-Webster, 1998).

39. Daniel Boorstin, *The Image: A Guide to Pseudo-Events in America* (New York: Atheneum, 1961), 253–54.

40. Gregory Bateson, "The Message, 'This Is Play'" in *Group Processes*, ed. Bertram Schaffner (New York: Josiah Macy Jr. Foundation, 1956), 150.

41. Anthony Wilden, *System and Structure*, 185. He adds: "'Not' is of a higher logical type than zero or ø, if only because it is the logical prerequisite for zero or ø.... Analog 'negation'... is many valued and does not involve 'not' or zero. Digital negation is two valued and involves 'not' both in the sense of zero and as a rule about zero," in Wilden, *System and Structure*, 186, 188.

42. Anthony Wilden, *The Rules Are No Game: The Strategy of Communication* (New York: Routledge and Kegan Paul, 1987), 252.

43. Corey Anton, "Playing with Bateson: Denotation, Logical Types, and Analog and Digital Communication," *The American Journal of Semiotics* 19, no. 1–4 (2003): 129–54.

44. Bateson "The Message, 'This Is Play,'" 145.

45. Bateson, *Steps to an Ecology of Mind*, 140.

46. Henri Bergson, *Creative Evolution*, trans. Arthur Mitchell (New York: Random House, 1944), 315.

47. Wilden, *The Rules Are No Game*, 180.

48. Burke, *Language as Symbolic Action*, 421.

49. Walter Kauffman, *Without Guilt and Justice* (New York: Delta, 1973), 21.

50. Gregory Bateson, *Mind and Nature: A Necessary Unity* (New York: Bantam, 1979), 105.

51. Bateson, *Mind and Nature*, 105.

52. Also see Corey Anton, "Alphabetic Print-Based Literacy, Hermeneutic Sociality and Philosophic Culture," *The Review of Communication* 17, no. 4 (2017): 257–72.

53. If someone were to shove you, they would bring physical force to your body, and, depending upon relative size, they perhaps could push you down and cause you pain. But words carry no physical force and bear no energy that can physically cause you pain. In fact, unlike causal relations where the cause is said to precede the effect, the relations at stake here concern an overall "definition of a situation." When someone says something to insult you, your response, if anything, is not *caused* by their statement, but you can recontextualize the original statement and change its very meaning. What people say does not "cause" other people's response, but the particular responses of others partly determine the meaning of what people have said.

54. Burke, *Language as Symbolic Action*, 374.

55. Burke, *Language as Symbolic Action*, 376.

56. See Burke's *Language as Symbolic Action* and the chapter by that title.

57. For more on these kinds of metaphor see George Lakoff and Mark Johnson, *Metaphors We Live By* (Chicago: University of Chicago Press, 1980); David H. Freedman, "New Theory

on How the Aggressive Egg Attracts Sperm," *Discover*, June 1992; Jerome Groopman, "The Body Strikes Back," *New York Review of Books* 66, no. 5 (March 21, 2019).

58. Burke, *Language as Symbolic Action*, 379.

59. At first glance, Burke appears to be succumbing to the A-Naturalist Fallacy. He perhaps seems to be suggesting that the verbal order and social-political order are not parts of nature. That is not exactly right, though. He seems, instead, to be trying to fend off an a-historicism in an attempt to show how contingent, varied, and mutable is any given sociopolitical order. Bateson weighs in on this issue: "Language continually asserts by the syntax of subject and predicate that 'things' somehow 'have' qualities and attributes. A more precise way of talking would insist that the 'things' are produced, are seen as separate from other 'things,' and are made 'real' by their internal relations and by their behavior in relationship with other things and with the speaker." *Mind and Nature*, 64.

Words never simply label things or refer to them; they also specify and delimit relations and contexts of involvements. This is what a horizon of meaning is. A word is a kind of "strange attractor," one that carries the meaning of all the contexts in which it has been experienced. Dorothy Lee suggests that words do not "mean" by representing independently existing entities but by carrying the meaning of the situations in which that word has participated. See Dorothy Lee's "Symbolization and Value" in *Freedom and Culture* (Englewood Cliffs, NJ: Prentice Hall, 1959).

60. Sartre, *Being and Nothingness*, 7.

61. Although I cannot locate the video where I saw it, I believe I heard John Searle in a public talk advance this line of argument, or something like it.

62. See Lanigan, *The Human Science of Communicology*; also see Wilden's "Context Theory," in *The Rules Are No Game*, 301–321; Anton, "Lanigan's 'Encyclopedic Dictionary,'" 49–70; and Corey Anton, "On the Nonlinearity of Human Communication: Insatiability, Context, Form," *The Atlantic Journal of Communication* 15, no. 2 (2007): 79–102.

63. Bateson, *Mind and Nature*, 48, 107.

64. Holenstein, *Roman Jakobson's Approach to Language*, 148.

65. Wilden, too, writes, "We communicate both by what we do and what we do not do," in *The Rules Are No Game*, 69.

66. R. D. Laing writes, "The element of negation is in every relationship and every experience of relationship. The distinction between the absence of a relationship, and the experience of every relationship as an absence, is the division between loneliness and a perpetual solitude," in *The Politics of Experience* (New York: Pantheon, 1976), 37.

67. See Paul Watzlawick, Janet H. Beavin, and Don D. Jackson, *Pragmatics of Human Communication* (New York: W. W. Norton and Company, 1967).

68. Erving Goffman, *Interaction Ritual: Essays on Face-to-Face Behavior* (New York: Pantheon, 1967), 43.

69. Goffman, *Interaction Ritual*, 43.

70. Alphonso Lingis, *The Community of Those Who Have Nothing in Common* (Bloomington: Indiana University Press, 1994), 93–94.

71. Laing, *The Politics of Experience*, 40, 44.

72. Obviously, many possibilities of agency have come by way of symbol-use, especially language, but also, perhaps more than some people would suspect, through subsequent communication technologies, especially those made possible through modes of alphabetic print literacy. See Anton, "Alphabetic Print-Based Literacy." These technologies have amplified and extended our sense of agency and self-conscious decision-making. We wake ourselves with alarm clocks, use calendars and schedules to plan and execute multiple-person activities months in advance, travel faster and father in automobile or plane than we ever could make it on foot alone, etc. Ultimately, the oral-noetic economy of consciousness has been transformed through forms of literacy. See Walter Ong, *Orality and Literacy: The Technologizing of the Word* (London: Methuen, 1982). Being literate and living in an alphabetic print–based culture places extra-ordinary demands upon consciousness, demands that shape habits of mind. Deacon writes, "Reading exemplifies the logic of teleodynamic work. A passive source of cognitive constraints is potentially provided by the letterforms on the page. A literate person has structured his or her sensory and cognitive habits to use such letterforms to reorganize the

neural activities constituting thinking. This enables us to do teleodynamic work to shift mental tendencies away from those that are spontaneous (such as daydreaming) to those that are constrained by the text." *Incomplete Nature*, 360.

Deacon's notions of "constraints" and "work" can be used to account for the slow evolutionary transition from "speech," as an emotive form of interpersonal communication to "spoken language" and then to "writing" and to "print" as systems for abstract concept-sharing. Alphabetic print literacy was a necessary form of constraint that enabled the contemporary rise in computing, computational logic, and "artificial intelligence." The ethical, self-aware agent is not, therefore, simply born out of the flurry of the don'ts. This is admittedly true in some ways, but the self-reflective consciousness that we experience today, in the modern world, is not located simply in the brain as if the intelligence and experience of conscious agency were something deep inside the person. And the agency that we experience is not something from a supernatural source. It is the long and fortuitous social-historical folding back upon itself of communication technologies. Writing, clocks, printing press, phone, and computer, these communication technologies have restructured consciousness and made the conscious experience of agency what it is today. Also see Corey Anton, "Diachronic Phenomenology: A Methodological Thread within Media Ecology," *Explorations in Media Ecology: The Journal of the Media Ecology Association* 13, no. 1 (2014): 3–30; Douglas Harding's chapter, "The Middle View," in *The Hierarchy of Heaven and Earth* (London: Shollond Trust, 2011), 67–74; for a broad and more general treatment of technological mediation as the essence of the human condition see Lance Strate, *Media Ecology* (New York: Peter Lang, 2017).

73. Georg Simmel writes, "Neither the father, nor the wife, nor the children had clearly defined individual property rights: the assets remained common property to that particular generation of the family. The various members of the family were not yet individualized in this respect. . . . Everywhere the immovability of property—whether connected with the collectivity or with inheritance—testifies to the obstacle whose removal would permit a corresponding progress in differentiation and personal freedom. Money, as the most mobile of all goods, represents the pinnacle of this tendency. Money really is that form of property that most effectively liberates the individual from the unifying bonds that extend from other objects of possession." *The Philosophy of Money*, trans. David Frisby, Kaethe Mengelberg, and T. B. Bottomore (New York: Routledge, 1990), 354.

74. Dorothy Lee writes of the Navaho, "Wealth may be the result of hard work and skill, but obviously it is also the blatant lack of generosity, lack of responsibilities for one's relatives, perhaps even of malicious witchcraft. No good Navaho becomes and remains 'wealthy' in our terms," in *Valuing the Self: What We Can Learn from Other Cultures* (Englewood Cliffs, NJ: Prentice Hall, 1976), 10–11.

75. Kenneth Burke writes, "Insofar as clothes imply social estrangement or differentiation by status, they are by the same token a kind of 'fall.'" *The Rhetoric of Religion: Studies in Logology* (Berkeley: University of California Press, 1970), 220.

76. Well beyond the scope of the present work would be to address how human sexuality remains qualitatively different than the sexuality of other organisms. All mammals sexually reproduce, but humans talk about their reproduction, and they turn sex into something other than procreation. Moreover, incest taboos, as one clear illustration of "Don't," are primary markers of human life and culture.

77. Burke, *The Rhetoric of Religion*, 292.
78. Burke, *The Rhetoric of Religion*, 292.
79. Simmel, *The Philosophy of Money*, 244.
80. Burke, *The Rhetoric of Religion*, 285.
81. Burke, *The Rhetoric of Religion*, 294–95.
82. Burke states it most explicitly: "The Earth-People will consider themselves so guilt-laden, that only a perfect sacrifice would be great enough to pay off the debt," in *The Rhetoric of Religion*, 295.
83. It is not without a little irony that communism is categorically branded as atheistic, while capitalism aligns with religion, especially with Christianity in the United States. Note, too, that "In God We Trust" is printed on US treasury bills.

84. Marshall McLuhan and Quentin Fiore, *The Medium is the Massage: An Inventory of Effects* (Corte Madera, CA: Ginko, 1967), 147.

85. Alfred Korzybski, *Science and Sanity: An Introduction to Non-Aristotelian Systems and General Semantics*, 5th ed. (Englewood, NJ: The International Non-Aristotelian Library/Institute of General Semantics, 1993), 409.

Chapter Four

Death and the Possibilities of Human Morality

DEATH AS LIFE'S PICTURE FRAME

This study began with a simple yet murky claim: non-being haunts being. I have tried to show in great detail how forms of absence, incompleteness, negation, and non-being pervade human life and language. All life is incomplete, but humans, with their complex nervous systems, sensory, motor, and communicative capacities, are the most incomplete sites of nature, the rangiest in their experience of distances and their sense of possible relations in space and time; they are parts of nature most drenched in negativity, with nothing laminating their lifelong run from womb to tomb.

Of all creatures on the planet, humans are the most open to temporal possibilities; they articulately dwell in the vast expanses of the "no-longer" and the "not-yet," and they feel the weight of what "was," what "will be," and what they think "ought to be." All along, they engage in moral decision-making and often face moral dilemmas that make them question, weigh, and reassess their values. In developing a conscience, that particular kind of time that inherently deals in moral possibilities, adults suffer from knowing the difference between good and evil. They have to make choices and must live with the consequences of those choices. Infants, in contrast, begin in innocence. They have not yet been subject to the gathering of time and deliberation over possible action known as "conscience" and "responsibility." Adults are never fully and wholly innocent if only because they can talk to themselves about moral options. They can plan courses of actions and decide to perform acts that, when all possibilities are considered, amount to choosing a lesser evil rather than doing something recognized by all as an unmitigated good. But decide they must, as time waits for no one, and, hence, by "not making a decision" at a given moment, they end up making a decision by default.

The final and ultimate "not-yet"—that which remains outstanding until the very end—is death. Death is thus a two-tiered phenomenon: the death of the deathbed is the end of all one's possibilities, but "being-toward-death" undergirds existence all the way along; it is the condition of meaning, the organizing principle for prioritizing one's life goals.[1] Knowing that we will die means that we cannot postpone our projects indefinitely. Some will need to be prioritized, and we cannot do everything. Knowledge of death is an essential aspect of existence, one that makes life meaningful. Death, therefore, is not merely an event that will happen to one's body at some future date; it is the continued frame of existence. For those who know of their death, life is inherently significant, even if only in the inverse, negative image: a deep despair regarding the possible meaninglessness of existence. "Meaninglessness" is in fact one of the possibilities of meaning for finite, self-aware beings.

In knowing that they will die, individuals can maximize their openness to nature, to history, to the future, and to others. They can enjoy the splendor of mathematics; can contribute to the world's artistic, athletic, intellectual and scientific accomplishments; and, hopefully, they can love as fully, wholly, and compassionately as possible. Existence offers chances to improve oneself, to exercise courage, justice, prudence, and temperance; to grow to one's fullest spiritual capacities; and to learn how to help others on their quests of self-discovery. Existence is one's sole opportunity for growing wise and communing with the Ultimate. To exist is to gain the lifelong opportunity to enjoy all the possibilities of experience and imagination. People can wonder about the mysterious origin of being, marvel at the mind-stretching immensity of the universe, and contemplate possibilities regarding what, if anything, will happen to them after death.

Incomplete beings with robust imaginations can entertain the possibility that something awaits them after death. As always already haunted by history and by future possibilities (and by absent others, too), the otherworldliness of this world is easily mistaken. Because life is all anyone has ever known and because we experience modes of absence and invariance on countless fronts, people are led to the dubious conclusion that there simply must be something else on the "other side" of life. Imagination basically misconstrues the many modes of absence and incompleteness that make life and mind possible. This also means, said quite otherwise, that if it turns out that there is no afterlife, people will never discover that fact, and moreover, they always will have resources for imagining the possibilities of an afterlife while they are alive. Indeed, speculation about the afterlife may be among the greatest riches produced by the imagination. Afterlife beliefs are artistic creations extraordinaire. They have served as the motivation behind moral deliberation and have helped countless people endure exceptionally difficult circumstances.

Humans around the globe and throughout history have offered different accounts of death and what may come after. Many people believe in some version of reincarnation (e.g., "karma" and "dharma"), and that individual souls are "reborn" as a different kind of organism (or perhaps as another person), all depending upon how virtuously the individuals have acted. Many native peoples have described the afterlife as "happy hunting grounds," where game is abundant and obtained without frustration. The ancient Vikings believed in Valhalla, where souls go to dine with the gods. In some Sufi traditions, death is the beginning of the "wedding night," the union of lover and beloved. Some Islamic traditions believe in eternal erections and ample supplies of voluptuous virgins awaiting the righteous. Most Christians believe in some version of Heaven and Hell, often including depictions of Saint Peter at the Pearly Gates of Heaven, who is "keeper of the keys," and who, more popularly, checks "The Book of Life" to see if the recently deceased is listed.[2] Some people believe that souls must watch their entire life played back before their eyes, recounting and judging all of their decisions and choices, actions and failures to act. In Heaven, according to some, people are released from bondage, bask in blissful unions, and achieve an ultimate "homecoming." Some think of Heaven as an eternal state of looking at the visage of God. Hell, in contrast, places people in endless torment, subjects them to pain, suffering, and eternal despair. Hell is the state of being deprived of any union with God; it is to be subject to the ultimate estrangement: a "weeping and gnashing of teeth in the darkness" while watching the righteous followers of the faith stand closely at the foot of God. It may be, however, that all of these accounts are becoming passé, especially as more and more young people spend so much time online. The more that people live their lives in online environments, the less traditional afterlife notions make sense, for who can imagine a Heaven that has computers and gaming systems? Why would people need computers, or any technology for that matter, in the afterlife? Anyone who wakes up dead and discovers computers in the afterlife has in all likelihood gone to Hell.

A question I always had regarding Heaven came to me in my youth, from my interactions with my grandfather, James E. Plucker. He was born severely disabled: he had one arm that ended just below the elbow, which terminated into a knobby stump with a short thumb (which my brother and I, at my grandfather's request, called "Andy"). Also, both of his legs were deformed, one was cut off above the knee and the other slightly below the knee. He wore wooden legs that were awkward and painful, and, sometimes he wore a scary mechanical hand. (I always preferred Andy.) Perhaps obviously, he was teased as a child, harassed, and had a rough life, although I never heard him complain about it. He became a pretty well-known singer in the church choir. He had an amazing voice, and, all said, he was an inspiring human being; he was an inventor who had patents, a master woodworker, and a postmaster for twenty-five years, among other accomplishments, but he had lived a difficult, painful, and challenging life. I wondered what it would be like for him in Heaven. I would ask priests at church if, when my grandfather dies and goes to Heaven, his body would be repaired and become as a healthy body, or if it would be the same as it was during his life but just not painful and challenging like it was when he was alive. The question was not easily answered. Many priests told me not to worry about such questions, though some priests claimed my grandfather's body would be fully "restored" to a nondisabled body. But for me a nagging question remained: dealing with his disability, accepting it, and learning to live his life despite it was part of what made my grandfather so interesting and remarkable. Why would he, in the afterlife, have a body unlike the one that helped him become who he became? Was he not, at least in God's eyes, perfect as he was? Moreover, if his body were to be "restored" or "corrected" (appear as a healthy, nondisabled body), would that not be a kind of admission, at least on some level, that God had made a mistake with his real body?

Despite the ambiguity and the sheer variety of afterlife accounts, their commonality is that all such stories and lines of thought are playthings of the imagination, ways of thinking for the living, not actual references to possible future events or places. They are nothing but speculation. Moreover, as people will not discover that their afterlife beliefs were wrong, they are always free to speculate over such final possibilities. I, too, must plead guilty to this, for in times of existential weakness and utter despair, I sometimes indulge in such suppositions. I imagine that death is a kind of "crossing the final finish line," a pulling back of the veils of mystery, a rediscovery of something that I have always known but somehow had forgotten and repressed within the whirling busyness of life. It is as if God is at the finish line, confetti is swirling all around me, horns are blowing, and I suddenly remember "the me" who had agreed to be born.[3] I'm stunned, speechless, basking eternally in the radiance of the revelation: my entire life was actually a tiny part of God wearing me, all along, as a mask. But then, in an instant, the imagined house of cards crashes down as my willingness to suspend disbelief fades. I suspect that all of this is just wishful thinking. But then again, what is wrong with a little indulgence in speculation? Could there be possible harm in such imaginative fancy?

A pretty clear fact shows itself here, one disclosed by the wide variety of accounts regarding what possibly happens postmortem, and that fact is that *no one knows for sure*. Moreover, knowing that one doesn't know is an exemplar case of non-being—a stark absence of knowledge—haunting the human world. Wouldn't it be nice to have people candidly admit that they don't know? There are so many different religious faiths, so many different traditions, beliefs, and practices, and so much dogma, but the truth is that anyone who tells you that they know for sure anything about the afterlife is either lying or deluded. *No one knows, and that is the truth.* Now, people might argue that they have all the evidence they require for the existence of God, for life itself is the miracle and that is all they need. Such a Deist position is hard to argue with or is at least defensible enough on its own terms, as life is undoubtedly the one and only miracle, if that word has a referent. But we cannot get from the miraculous fact of life to any particular religious dogma regarding life after death.[4]

In my youth, I so disbelieved in the afterlife that I nearly wanted to kill myself out of raw curiosity; I felt a willingness to die just to know if there was something after. I never gave it an attempt, though, for I fairly quickly concluded that any effort at disclosure would fail. There would no longer be any "I" to see and prove there is nothing after death. I don't want to be dogmatic here. I mean, I do not *know*, but when I am honest with myself I simply cannot believe that there is something still outstanding and to be completed after death. It doesn't make any sense, and it subtly invites a lack of gratitude, exaggerates self-importance, and distorts the transient beauty of existence. Accepting death and the limited time of existence accentuates the world's glory. People and events bristle with intensity and vibrancy; the negative facts of frailty and fragility dialectically generate their own positive forms of care and vigilance.

All of the world's religions cannot be "the One True Faith," meaning none of them is really a "true" faith, all of which points to the obvious: religions are made of stories, narratives, and mythologies.[5] We may find them, as Joseph Campbell would say, "Myths to Live By," offering us truths about ourselves and our relations to others and the world, but none of them are literally, factually, true, certainly not true in their claims to miracles, divine intervention, direct words from God, and the like.[6] Jesus was a real person just as Saint Nicholas was a real person, but there need not be miracles, revelations, angelic visitations, virgin births, life after death, psychic contacts, or other improvable items of faith.[7] The stories of the Bible represent ancient peoples at their times with their own culture's problems attempting to understand themselves and their world. In claiming to know the word or commands of God—to accept covenants made by God because they were purportedly handed down from on high by revelation—people thereby hide from their own freedom and responsibility. They try to flee from the anguish of being both self-aware and finite: the torment comes from having some kinds of agency and power but also suffering vulnerability and exposure to harm. Everything can change at a moment's notice. Homes can be burned to ashes or blown to smithereens. A brain aneurysm, heart attack, stroke, or car accident can be just around the corner. Caught within this tension of agency without ultimate control over outcomes, people commonly succumb to a primal lie rather than accept the ambiguity.[8]

There has never has been a verifiable "Revelation of God" other than the sheer majesty of the cosmos itself, including life and humanity. This world is beautiful, intoxicating, magnificent, mysterious, and beyond any need of human justification. Divine Providence somehow produced all of this, including the possibilities of enabling people to evolve and bear historical conditions as their mode of self-awareness, even if that, unfortunately, entails structurally creating and perpetuating injustices in the name of divine commands.[9]

Much of culture everywhere is superstition and wishful thinking coupled with unrelenting capacities for delusion and self-deception.[10] Self-righteous wars, bigotry, misogyny, racism, sexism, homophobia, xenophobia, and "cleansing" genocides all illustrate the dark side of human imagination, the kinds of horror that come along with self-deceiving, fearful, vulnerable, highly intelligent organisms. Once people misunderstand who they basically are—who they are at the core—they muddle everything up under the flag of "self-interest." People seem willing to believe just about anything that serves what they take to be their self-interests, and they often take on self-serving beliefs and ideologies before they have become fully conscious of their possibilities for self-awareness and self-examination. Ideologies get deep down in the roots of society and become perpetuated throughout social practices, often operating to lessen people's experience of cognitive dissonance. People degrade "others"—those whose views radically differ—in a roundabout attempt to bolster confidence in their own beliefs. Anxiety-prone animals get together to share in the strong and hefty blanket of dogma. That said, beliefs regarding the afterlife, or eschatological beliefs more generally, are perhaps among the greatest hoaxes played upon humanity. Said from the inverse angle, "the afterlife" is very real but it exists only for those who currently are alive.

It is pretty disheartening to think that people's main motivation for helping others is in seeking a good place in the afterlife for themselves or hoping to avoid their own cosmic punishment later. In this regard, versions of modern Christianity have become a farce, as many people give ultimate moral authority to a book they have hardly read, certainly not cover to cover, a book that they don't really understand, nor one that they strictly follow in practice. But that is too simple, as the book cannot be strictly followed without contradiction; it gives so much different advice that people can use it to justify nearly anything. People have used the Bible not just to sanction private property and to exploit scared and gullible people, but also to claim that wealth indicates that some people already have been "chosen," as predestined for entrance into Heaven. This is as disgusting as it is delusional, and it is not so much self-serving as it is perverting a humble and honest sense of self. There are no chosen people; we all die in the end. People need to grow up, sober up, and face this challenging fact, then figure out how to most fittingly respond to it.

Admittedly, we should not throw out the spiritual baby with the phony-baloney bathwater. We must separate all of the good and important work that religious people do in the name of their faith (e.g., caring for the elderly and the sick, social programs for justice and equality, taking care of the poor, consecrating life events, etc.) from all of the dogma and reliance on belief in the afterlife. We also should recognize the human need for meaning, which calls for rituals and practices that consecrate events such as births, weddings, and deaths within the most encompassing of possible contexts. Where and when people commune with the Divine in the attempt to contextualize a situation within the widest possible circumference, or when they seek to release divinity in the details within their artistic accomplishments, they ought to be celebrated. For example, individuals who were attempting to create works worthy of God and God's creation have produced some of the world's most awe-inspiring art and music. Religious truths, for their own part, ought to help people become more compassionate, loving, respectful, and self-disciplined. In contrast, any "religious beliefs" conducive to smug self-righteousness, divisiveness, hatred, bigotry, fear-mongering, or violence need to be interrogated, scrutinized, and discarded as antiquated. Given that religious truths are metaphorical and allegorical, our only rational basis for judging them lies in assessing their consequences.

One can deny all of the religious dogma in the world without self-identifying as an atheist. Many people prefer the term "spiritual" for that reason, because they have a vague but certain sense that life is a sacred divine mystery. I return to the words "spirit" and "soul" at length later in this chapter, but suffice it here to say that life itself is miraculous, and good numbers of scientists are comfortable with nonliteral statements such as "If there were such a thing as angels that could dance on the head of a pin, bacteria would be they."[11] Life is THE miracle, even given all of its dreadfulness and shortcomings, all of its flaws and imperfections, cruelties and injustices. It is miraculous nonetheless. Margulis and Sagan capture some of this sensibility where they write,

> Life is too shoddy a production, both physically and morally, to have been designed by a flawless Master. And yet life is more impressive and less predictable than any "thing" whose nature can be accounted for solely by "forces" acting deterministically. . . . Although something odd may lurk behind and before this cosmos, its existence is impossible to prove. The cosmos, more dazzling than any sect's god, is enough.[12]

If only unknowingly, people already are much more than their wildest dreams imagine, and yet the pervasive tragedy is that so many people spend so much time and energy fretting over the continuance of "themselves." They have come to believe in a shrimpy sense of self, an individual, ego-grounded spirit, and they then cook up shared beliefs regarding what is necessary for its definitive continuance. Put differently, people have come to interpret life itself as being somehow other than what it is: life and the cosmos are not "really real," for all of it is a test, a kind of cosmic trial with "Divine Judgment" awaiting people at the end. In the contemporary world, where self-indulgent ideologies rule the day, some people admittedly have grown skeptical (or tired) of the notion of "Judgment," yet they still adhere to notions of the afterlife. Some contemporary naturalists express belief in the afterlife while remaining agnostic regarding God.[13] What are rational people to make of this? Can they not see how this buries what needs to be uncovered? It simply introduces a whole new realm of questions about "souls" (or something like that) and how they exist outside of the body, and about what life "really is" if there is something other, some kind of "beyond," to which the living go after the death of the body. For example, if souls continue to exist in an afterlife, do they breathe? Age? Eat? Sleep? Have sex? Do they wear clothes and have jobs? Can they get hurt? Is there social inequality there? Overpopulation? Might future scientists find a way to contact souls and perhaps gain control over them? Will there be technologies—computers and such—in the afterlife? Might there be scientist ghosts currently working on developing technologies necessary to become flesh and blood again? Are UFO sightings actually sightings of ghosts working on afterlife-to-life technologies? This short list hopefully suffices to illustrate the dubiousness of any such beliefs. A good deal of chapters 1, 2, and 3 of this book sought to show how each of us is *of* the cosmos not merely organisms *on* the planet; we are places and moments through which the world worlds by protracted bodying: each person is a gravitational center through which aspects of existence show themselves at various distances, always within the throes of finitude. Bodies, while alive, are fundamentally more and less than themselves: to be a body is to be a situation beyond the flesh yet necessarily incomplete and in need; we are multimodal headless caretakers through whom the world makes room for itself. The Earth bodies humans, and humans world.

You already are a part—a vital place and moment—of everything that has ever existed and ever will; you are already a part of life eternal. To clarify, the particular expression "life eternal" is not meant to deny that life on this planet has a history and began at a certain time, nor that the universe has a history too. What the expression "life eternal" recognizes is that the Orderliness of the cosmos, for whatever reason, naturally precipitated life and mind. Life is eternal in that the Orderliness of the cosmos implied human existence as a possibility. To the extent that the emergence of life and mind fundamentally depends upon that Orderliness, they are part of it—that part which has grown back upon itself at countless levels of analysis in what amounts to negations at one level but emergent horizons of possibilities at another. For example, built-in death, ontogeny, means the possibilities of multicellularity and life span; phonemic oppositions become words at a higher level; the "don't," said in infancy, becomes "conscience" across a lifetime, and so on. Moreover, if one assumes that the universe did have a beginning, the so-called Big Bang, then the "odds" of life and self-aware agency emerging from it seem to be "one out of one."

Try it this way: could life, even bacterial life, have not been? Could self-aware consciousness have not occurred? For anyone who answers "yes" to either question, another question remains: on what grounds do you make your claim? If one holds to a hard determinist view, then life did not choose to bring itself into being, and, in that sense, it seems that life could not have not been. It is the natural outcome of whatever actually happened. To think that life might not have emerged is tantamount to denying the reality of the past. Even if life and mind were contingent rather than necessary outcomes, we can be sure that life and mind, as possibilities etched into the cosmos, could not have not been. We, self-aware beings, are not proof of the necessity or inevitability of self-aware consciousness, no; but we are solid evidence that self-aware consciousness must have been at least metaphysically possible. Moreover, interestingly, only living and self-aware beings can imagine the possibility of not being. Finally, we cannot be sure that this is the only Big Bang: could it simply be the most recent Bang in an endless and eternal cycle of Bang to Crunch, Bang to Crunch, and perhaps life (or mind) does not emerge in some cycles? It is sobering that we likely will *never* know the answer to such huge questions. At the least, such mystery epitomizes non-being within existence.

MODERNITY, GOD'S ABSENCE, AND RESPONSIBLE ACTION

John Adams, Thomas Jefferson, and Thomas Paine, among other "founding fathers," were rationalist deists. This means, roughly, that they remained highly skeptical of biblical claims regarding divine revelation, personal verbal commands from God, and the occurrence of miracles more generally. Also, it means that they accepted the moral teachings of Jesus but did not believe in his divinity. Partly because they entered history after the rise of the printing press and mechanical clock,[14] they, like many children of the Enlightenment, came to believe that God, a logically necessary "First Cause" of the universe, got everything "working" at the beginning, as would a master clockmaker, and then left the scene, or, at the least, no longer interferes with the vast Orderliness set in motion.

Paine was particularly aware of the confusions that muddle biblical translations, especially where people fail to differentiate between hearsay, oral reports, written documents, and printed texts.[15] As the scientific method gained increasing foothold and enabled students of astronomy and mechanics to document nature's regularities with greater and greater accuracy, miracles occurred less frequently and were harder to verify. With more and more "laws of nature" established, especially in astronomy and Newtonian mechanics, many Enlightenment thinkers concluded that God governed the world by such eternal rules rather than violated them through active interventions. Their reasoning relied upon a notion of "first cause." Things are not the cause of themselves. They depend upon other things that also, in their own right, were not the cause of themselves, and so on. But God must be the cause of Itself. This means, for Paine, reason can discover the existence of God but falls infinitely short of discovering the whole of God's attributes. All we have is what can be directly witnessed in Nature itself. The "Almighty" is thus revealed only through the "Book of Creation," not through so-called miracles, nor through "revelations" supposedly issued to "chosen" peoples. As Paine, in *The Age of Reason*, states,

> The Creation speaketh an universal language, independently of human speech or human language, multiplied and various they be. It is an ever-existing original, which every man can read. . . . It preaches to all nations and to all worlds; and this word of God reveals to man all that is necessary for man to know of God.[16]

Not surprisingly, one of Paine's more illustrative critiques regards the role of authorial power in those books of the Bible whose authors claim to have had direct revelations from God (e.g., words spoken, commands given, miracles performed, etc.). Unless one had the revelation oneself, the revelation is actually just something someone else said, and we either believe the person or not. "It is a contradiction in terms and ideas," writes Paine, "to call anything a revelation that comes to us at second-hand, either verbally or written. Revelation is necessarily limited to the first communication."[17] Once he establishes this claim, Paine vigilantly shows how books of the Bible have misattributed and unknown authors. Because the authors' credentials are dubious, claims of revelation are fables, not fact. Not only was the Book of Genesis, for example, written well after the death of Noah, but the Gospels of Matthew, Mark, Luke, and John were written (and completed) a great many years after the death of Jesus. In these cases, all claims to revelation or direct words from God are hearsay and depend upon blind faith. In contrast, Paine encourages us to comparatively reflect upon Euclid's *Elements of Geometry*, of which he writes,

> it is a book of self-evident demonstration, entirely independent of its author, and of everything relating to time, place, and circumstance. The matters contained in that book would have the same authority they now have, had they

been written by any other person, or had the work been anonymous . . . for the identical certainty of who the author was, makes no part of our belief of the matters contained in the book. But it is quite otherwise with respect to the books ascribed to Moses, to Joshua, to Samuel, etc.[18]

How, other than by wishful thinking and delusion, can so many people believe in miracles, revelations, and other such fictions? It is hard to deny that many people unfortunately have come to blindly believe what they ought to interrogate with reason and evidence. Paine, for his own part, does not seem to fully follow out his own capacity for reasoning.

Not to deny Paine his prerogative to speculate about afterlife beliefs, but he simply does not follow out his own thinking to the rational conclusion that there is, very likely, no life after death. Paine writes,

> I content myself with believing, even to positive conviction, that the Power that gave me existence is able to continue it, in any form and manner he pleases, either with or without my body; and it appears more probable to me that I shall continue to exist hereafter, than that I should have had existence, as I now have, before that existence began.[19]

Paine returns to these issues at the end of the book, where he first suggests that he cannot believe in the physical resurrection of the body, as that body would likely undergo another cycle to death. But then later, he offers the somewhat famous "a caterpillar transitions into a butterfly" comparison, suggesting that human form could be radically reborn in some natural but elusive way. He writes, "it is not more difficult to believe that we shall exist hereafter in a better state and form than at present, than that a worm should become a butterfly."[20] Relying upon this dubious comparison, Paine fails to notice the direct parallel between his denial of the resurrection of the body and his embrace of the new body of the butterfly. The fact that butterflies die escapes his account. In either case, nature decrees that all living things must eventually come to an end. He comes closest to identifying the underlying source of sympathies for afterlife beliefs where he gives his analysis of the relations between form and content in language. He writes,

> [T]hought when produced, as I now produce the thought I am writing, is capable of becoming immortal. . . . [P]rint and reprint a thought a thousand times over, and that with materials of any kind—carve it in wood, engrave it on stone, the thought is eternally and identically the same in every case. It has the capacity of unimpaired existence, unaffected by change in matter, and is essentially distinct and of a nature different from every thing else that we can know or conceive. . . . That the consciousness of existence is not dependent on the same form or the same matter is demonstrated to our senses in the works of creation.[21]

These thoughts clearly illustrate the nature of information, invariance, and "multiple realizability," but Paine muddles the conclusion. Given his earlier attention to the differences between writing and print with regard to biblical authority, he perhaps should have noticed the differences between the spoken word, *the real word*, which in a living context can resurrect dead letters of the text and all of those dead books left unopened and unread. A text, a kind of undead, does not achieve immortality without the vital life-support of the living; it can be resuscitated and resurrected only as the living breathe new life into it. Texts also amplify the transcendence words afford, partly because they travel autonomously and often outlive their authors. William Gass captures this spirit where he writes, "At this moment, you are reading. I am absent. Still, I shall pretend to talk. Shall you pretend to listen while you read? . . . Our present circumstances—it may be I have no present circumstance—could they be more different?"[22]

Regarding deism more generally, many modern Christians comparatively cast it as too impersonal and indifferent. They not only believe in a *personal* God but they, Evangelicals especially, believe that God both responds to prayers and regularly performs miracles. In other words, God *intervenes*. Reflect upon a most pedestrian example: two sports teams take the field, and each team huddles together in a circle and dispatches a team prayer. In addition, some individual players—and some fans too—make prayers for various occurrences throughout the game. To imagine the possibilities of divine intervention within this sporting event, or any other for that matter, amounts to expanding the negativity within human situations; it is a fantasy, a flight of the imagination, a means of transcendence, but one that brings with it the possibility of covering over the very meaning of responsibility and self-conscious agency. As much as it is a mark of human imagination to indulge in such grand speculative thought, such thinking can lead to distortions in self-understanding.

At this point, it might help to clarify how freedom, agency, moral reasoning, and action relate to non-being. As suggested in chapters 1, 2, and 3, only beings who can entertain possibilities, who can think about *possible* courses of action, can experience their moral agency. A being without horizons of such options is simply a being in "motion." "Action," in contrast, is always infused with negativity. This is not only because the lived body has different sensory capacities, each of which offers different possibilities to the others, but also the verbal "Don't" is the primal source of human conscience. Moreover, language offers the most robust horizon of possibilities, including many moral words that are defined by not-being their opposite: *just* and *unjust*, *right* and *wrong*, *bad* and *good*. With such words at hand, everyday experience becomes bifurcated into countless moral decisions, where the selection of one course of action is, de facto, the denial and disavowal of others. As beings who are moved by natural forces but who also can act, we experience our freedom as responsibility despite not being in control of all that happens. Without assurance over outcomes, we must act nevertheless, and, given the gap between our ability to act and our control over outcomes, a trivialized notion of "God" gets introduced, somewhat as a psychological operation used to fill in the gap. Prayer, too, can become an attempt at leverage for more control in one's life.

Whether they are willing to openly admit it or not, many people privately suspect that God cannot intervene, cannot help one team or another, cannot assist a given player, and cannot answer particular prayers for performance.[23] Any notion of God's intervention in such ways reduces God to a two-bit shill working for people,[24] and, more importantly, it undermines and destabilizes human responsibility. Notions of divine intervention are simply incompatible with personal responsibility, as they introduce and rely upon forever-unverifiable forms of causality. We cannot truly accept our freedom and responsibility but then also believe in a God who would meddle in human affairs. Only as people acknowledge their responsibility and agency, only as they recognize the freedom that they have been sentenced to, are they able to see how notions of intervention—divine or demonic—cannot be anything other than products of the imagination. To suggest that we did what we did because "God instructed us to do so" or to claim that we did what we did because "the devil tricked us into it," is, in either case, to deny freedom and responsibility; it is to place the locus of action outside of human agency.

Over two centuries since the Enlightenment and over a century since the great unmasking and debunking that came with thinkers such as Nietzsche, Darwin, and Freud, it is no surprise that many people gave up what remaining faith they had during the Holocaust. If there ever was a time for God to intervene, people thought to themselves, this was it. Ernest Becker accounts for how many modern individuals, at least since the Enlightenment have been faced with:

> the problem of an absent God. This is a distinctive historical achievement, a luxury of civilized man, this loneliness of the extra-cultural personality yearning for an absent God. It began in the melee of culture in the Mediterranean basin a couple of thousand years ago, where men could so easily compare the obsessiveness of competing cultural ambitions and see into their fictional nature. It has reached its pinnacle in the modern world, where the last comforting religious myth has gone into eclipse.[25]

Although we see it most strikingly today, where increasing numbers of people identify as "atheist," this fact was presaged in the Bible where Christ, dying on the cross, is said to have exclaimed, "My God, My God, why have you forsaken me." In this ancient account, even Jesus himself felt the absence of God.

Humans experience a peculiar mode of loneliness, one arguably unknown by other organisms. It is its own form of non-being. It emerges when we acquire language and as we grow into self-awareness. Once we learn language, we are at one and the same instant rendered utterly alone, and yet aloneness for us is now impossible: we are separated with articulate invisible inward depths but also are stuck with ourselves in modes of self-relation. Other social animals, those without such rich interior lives, likely only feel lonely when away from the collective, and they, accordingly, can remedy their loneliness in a straightforward fashion: stay with the herd. People, in contrast, can develop inner depths that can make them feel lonely in a crowd, as if being with others amounts to neglecting parts of themselves. Becker argues that humans feel this loneliness expand to cosmic proportions, perhaps making humans the only organism on the planet to feel itself as somehow *abandoned*.[26] Exploring the moral possibilities nestled within this impulse, Becker asks:

> What kind of quality of perception of the absence of God can we cultivate, so that individuals may come together without the smugness and righteousness that drives them today, the rigidity of secure and true believers in the idols of money, nationalism, materialistic science? We know that something immense is needed to shock man out of the pathetic yet deadly heroisms to which he has been accustomed. And the first step in this kind of shock is a new openness of perception about the human condition, what it means to have been created on a planet in the sun, why we seem to have been left here to murder and poison ourselves, to wheel and deal in such an idiotic frenzy. With the right intensity and scope of shock, we might even ask ourselves what are we to do with our lives. We might then begin to think of how again to give to people a secure feeling that their lives count, that there is a heroic human contribution to be made to cosmic life in a dialogue with a community of one's fellows.[27]

How are people to best respond to the absence of God? No God will save us from ourselves, and there are no chosen people who will be saved. Moreover, guilt reminds us that we have to live with knowing how we have treated each other. Try to hide from it as we might, we have to live with ourselves, including knowing of our own selfishness, greed, rapaciousness, and lack of compassion.

For millennia, people have spontaneously, for some reason, imagined God, or the gods, or a spiritual realm, and this is a fact of nature that warrants appreciation rather than dismissal. What must the nature of the cosmos be such that transcendental, religious, or psychedelic experiences are even possible? What must the nature of a self be such that it can undergo a transformation in self-understanding? Is it possible to make room for these experiences without subtly smuggling in (or lending legitimacy to) notions of divine intervention or life postmortem? No one needs to hide from the obvious fact of religious experiences, spiritual experiences, experiences of the sublime divinity of nature, art, and imagination. People throughout the ages have wept for humanity,[28] have had life-changing events and moments of self-understanding that set the course for the rest of their lives. Arguably, Jesus embodies an example of the possibilities for compassion that come with spiritual enlightenment. For many other people, too, especially historically and across the globe, spirituality neither originates from nor relies upon some kind of "faith in the unverifiable." On the contrary, many people have had direct personal experiences that have changed their lives, experiences that convinced them that their everyday, common-sense consciousness and sense of self is false. To the extent that religious experiences are personal and cannot be directly communicated to others, they might be taken as a kind of revelation. Admittedly, such experiences basically say more about culture, human brains, and the ability to imagine and self-relate than they do about any possible transcendent realm above and beyond the material world we experience. Prayer, meditation, and psychedelic drugs can induce extra-ordinary mental states, often including powerful emotions and a sense of self-transformation, sometimes even "out of body" experiences. None of these experiences need be denied. It may be that religious and spiritual experiences are among the wildest variety of occasions within nature. To suggest that religious experiences are not part of the natural world is yet another species of the A-Naturalist Fallacy.

Some people have great fear and anxiety in youth: they have a yearning to make something of themselves, a sense of not wanting to be a financial burden upon their family or society, and a desire to be a "success." But the older they get, the less personal wealth is a source of meaning or happiness in their lives. They are not eager to give up what they have, to be sure, but they find it difficult to enjoy their success when they see the unjust suffering of others. Not surprisingly, wealthy people often hide away in gated communities not simply to guard their houses and ward off intruders, but because such separation helps them hide from the pangs of conscience, the guilt of wallowing in abundance while so many people have so little. Along the coasts of the United States, one can find nestled along the shoreline many multimillion-dollar yachts and homes, extravagant palaces—some of which are occupied only part of the year or used occasionally for entertaining. If everyone in the United States had basic health care, including mental health care and substance-abuse counseling, and we had the resources to create affordable housing for low-income families, then, perhaps that would not appear to be a problem. In fact, it might be wonderful, impressive, and awe-inspiring. But such is not the case. All that wealth relates back to the poverty and lack of basic resources throughout the country and world. Demanding that corporations pay a fair share in taxes, taxing the wealthy on their inheritances, and providing healthcare for citizens are not actions of communism or socialism. They are fitting moral responses for a humanity that needs to grow up.

At this point in history, basic healthcare for all is much more important than unending luxury and extravagance for the affluent. Poverty and social inequality persist not because of insufficient resources, but rather because greed, coupled with the belief that God will fix it all later, helps people kick problems down the road; it leaves authentic attempts at long-term solutions eternally deferred. Now, we need to be even more explicit here regarding the subtle ways that people have come to take themselves and others hostage by way of afterlife dogma. When citizens in the United States object to the idea of "healthcare for everyone," they are more likely to make appeals to the unwieldy costs, argue about the impracticality of its implementation, mention their fear of losing a higher quality coverage, and so on. Most people are not inclined to say, "Don't worry about it: God will take care of it all, either here or later in the afterlife." Such a thought may hardly be in the background of their thinking, but it is there nonetheless, repressed and persistent. Chapter 1 of this study addressed the role that anguish, angst, and dread play in everyday life and decision-making. Afterlife beliefs are highly potent anxiety-buffers, and, over many centuries, the moral panic of existence has become quelled, pacified, and enervated by a background belief that there is a God who could save people from themselves and who will ensure that justice is served in the end. If everyone were to give up on that possibility, or at least question that possibility, they might be thrown into an all-encompassing, gut-wrenching dread.[29] Moreover, perhaps such pervasive anguish, itself the result of accepting responsibility for taking better care of each other, is what people most need if they are ever going to wake up and answer the call of conscience.

JESUS AS APOLOGY FROM A GUILTY GOD

If I ever were to make a Hollywood movie, it would be a big-budget production released around Easter time and it would be titled *The New Easter Story*. It would be set a few years in the future, and the main plot would be that, on the eve of Easter, Jesus, the Lord Himself, visits every devout Christian in their dreams. Jesus tells each Christian that He is alive, doing well, and that He has a Revelation, an important message that the faithful need to spread everywhere. Evidently, some important books that should have been included in the Bible were misinterpreted and neglected during the Council of Nicaea. There were some political subterfuges that occurred at the Council as well, but, fortunately, Jesus now has the update and wants it widely disseminated before things get any further confused.

He says there are minor revisions following from this main one, but the chief and most important revision concerns virgin births and the afterlife. Apparently, only virgin births receive life after death. That is how He, Jesus, could be resurrected and also how He was able to enter people's dreams: his was a virgin birth. Everyone else, those who were not born by Immaculate Conception, share the same fate of mortality as all of God's creatures. They eventually die, once again becoming part of the Earth. In the dream, Jesus reminds people, "To dust you shall return." He concludes his Revelation with the following words: "My Father loves you and has provided you with the Reason, the Logos, so that you may have meaningful and purposeful lives. He's displeased that people have not taken better care of each other, and, accordingly, He saw this as the proper time for this Revelation. God also hopes, knowing what you now know, that you can forgive Him for both the earlier confusions from the Council of Nicaea, and, more significantly, for the fact of self-aware mortality." Then, with unseen harps quietly playing, Jesus slowly fades into the background of the dream.

The bulk of the movie would then cover, in excruciating detail, the particular responses of many different people. It would start by showing what people do when they wake up, share their dream, and find that others either had the same dream or already heard about it from others. Obviously, not everyone is a devout Christian, and even some Christians, in the movie that is, would not have received the message, as some were not of strong enough faith, some had been working the late shift, and a few others had unrelenting bouts of insomnia. At first, the story would focus on the many people who are unsure what to believe, especially those who did not have the dream themselves. Some would wonder why Jesus did not come to them, especially given that they often attend Sunday Mass. Most others, those who did have the dream, would initially try to convince themselves that it was just a dream, but that explanation doesn't stick, because too many other people had the exact same dream. A few people claim the dream was actually a temptation of the devil, a malicious deceit meant to seduce people away from their faith on Easter morning. Some suggest it's an alien attack, and others claim it might have been a weapon used by a foreign power. But these are only the initial reactions of a few minor characters.

Most people in *The New Easter Story*, all the main characters, come to believe an authentic Revelation has occurred in modern times and on a mass scale. Christians around the globe are absolutely reeling. Now, in *The New Easter Story*, Jesus gives believers a clear statement that there is no life after this one for mere mortals—not a conjecture, not a speculation that there might not be life after death, not a reasoned inference—but a Divinely revealed certainty.

In some early parts, *The New Easter Story* would revolve around the depression and anxiety that many people initially feel. The characters would be shown struggling with the very purpose of life, asking if it still makes sense or has value. Many would be depicted as besieged by despair and confusion, somehow sensing that life's struggles and hardships are no longer worth it. A portion of the film would also include various "vignette voice-overs" that intimate the belief that once people do not have a threat of eternal damnation or a promise of eternal salvation, they can have no motivation to be good or to be concerned with anyone other than themselves: "People, without the promise of ultimate judgment and justice can become lower than animals, morally worse than fallen angels." As that is said in ominous voice-over, the movie plays visual montages of people becoming more licentious, profligate, and downright evil; riots fill the street. People loot and destroy. They set cars on fire. Some characters in *The New Easter Story* go on berserker killing sprees, raping and pillaging along the way. Shortsighted stab and grab happens in a matter of days in some cities throughout the world. Some people give up their faith, standing before mirrors weeping uncontrollably. Some destroy their crucifixes, icons, and other religious artifacts while shouting that they'd never again pray to a God who cannot guarantee justice at the end of time. Growing numbers of people, especially the very wealthy, try to hide their wealth from others, and many are thrown into profound anguish. Some elderly, dread-ridden, and super-wealthy Calvinists (and some oil company executives, too) form charitable-end-of-life-cults which donate all of their wealth to the poor and to Doctors without Borders, and then, with the help of hospice care, they end their own lives. They write beautiful suicide letters that include heart-felt petitions for forgiveness for all their greed and arrogant misunderstanding about "predestination." Psychics everywhere start closing up shop, and growing numbers of people push for legislation that places term limits on all governmental positions. Congress passes a law that makes voting days national holidays. Suicide rates start to drop significantly, while labor unions of all stripes become reinvigorated, expand, and start taking over churches. No longer sending prayers as their response to school shootings, people take to the streets and protest until the government tightens legislation on guns and gun purchasing. "Prison Reform" becomes a call of the land, and local vigilante groups start to crop up in more and more cities. Funding for longevity and life-extension sciences dramatically increases, but then two billionaires who were leading the way in longevity treatments accidently die in a plane crash, impressing upon everyone the inescapability of death.

Then the storyline of the film significantly changes. People in increasing numbers, especially those who work in health clinics, claim that the message really does not have to mean all that much, and maybe the Revelation is a good thing. A high school principal, speaking at a pep rally, says to the crowd, "We have had no shortage of greed, selfishness, and evil in the world even among those who have claimed to be religious and who said they believe in Heaven and Hell. Perhaps it is time for us accept the new Revelation, and just go back to our lives and try to live basically as we did before. We still have our consciences, our laws, our sense of decency, and our self-respect. Maybe we do need to take better care of each other. Maybe it's time for humanity to grow up a little bit."

One of the most heated parts of the film focuses upon various kinds of forgiveness. At a town hall meeting, one of the main characters, the head of a local bank and father of three (also someone who publicly says he had the dream but really did not), suggests that people cannot just forgive God and move on at this point. He claims that wouldn't make any sense. He says to the people at the meeting, "What is this, some kind of cruel bait and switch? I personally resent having been informed of this 'Revelation' so late in the game, especially now that I know my hard work and moral probity, and my father's work as well, doesn't amount to anything. How can we even be sure this isn't a trick? I resent all the cruelties and hardships of this world. It's just not fair to learn that this is all there is. This is not right, not at all." The banker then suggests that devout people everywhere should try a concerted vigil of prayer to God, getting together as many people around the globe as possible, all telling God that we cannot forgive Him at this point, that He needs to keep the arrangements as Christians have understood them for the last two thousand years. He concludes his speech, "The world is too cruel and we all have built our lives and structured our societies around the belief that there would be ultimate justice, but this just pulls the rug out from under us. I cannot forgive. Either God needs to change things back to what He knew we thought all along, according to earlier Revelations, or, and I hate to say it, that was never really my God. It's not a God I ever would have worshipped to begin with." Many people applaud and exchange knowing, self-assured glances, but many others silently shake their heads, squint their eyes, and vaguely stare into space.

Then a local physician and Christian, someone who admits that he did not personally have the dream, gives his insights into the problems of forgiveness. He provides a couple of stories to help people think about death, forgiveness, and the afterlife. He asks people to consider two children playing. One child suddenly grabs a toy from the other child while also pushing him. The child who was pushed falls to the ground, skins a knee and starts to cry. The aggressor turns, sighs, hands the toy back, and says, "I am sorry." The child with the skinned knee gets up, takes the toy, and says, "That was mean. You are bad." The first child angrily retorts, "I said I am sorry. I gave you your toy back." The second child says, "Oh, all right, I guess I can forgive you." Here, the doctor explains, we find nearly an ideal remedial exchange after a moment of interpersonal violence and injustice. But now imagine this case: some friends, after a night of too many drinks, get in a spirited exchange over some minor issue. Their quarrel gets more and more animated, until one person slightly pushes the other, and then the unspeakable happens. The pushed person loses his balance, slips down a staircase, and, in a freak accident, dies from a head injury. This death, similar to many accidental deaths, generates an overflow of guilt in the person who pushed, and the guilt means an overwhelming need for forgiveness. But in this case, forgiveness cannot be given by the deceased. He also adds that people cannot be enfranchised to simply forgive themselves at will, even for accidental murders, for that would amount to licensing people to become sociopaths. It is partly for these reasons, the doctor goes on, that such persons may seek forgiveness from God or go to a priest if they wish, but more importantly, they need the courage to ask for forgiveness from all those who were affected, and then, as best as they can, "to commit from here on out to beautifying the world and making every single encounter with every person they meet an opportunity for fellowship, camaraderie, and amity."

Toward the end of the film, the message spreads across the globe and starts to sink in. We see Christians and other people taking better care of each other. Near the film's conclusion, set at a nationally televised symposium devoted to discussing the new Revelation, a young girl wheels her wheelchair onto the main stage. She has thick glasses on her face and braces on her teeth, and, speaking softly, she says into the microphone, "I guess I never really felt like I knew for sure one way or the other. At least now we all know, and I want God to know how thankful I am to exist. I am strong enough for this; I am happy to be alive, and I forgive you, Lord, with all of my heart." The crowd goes absolutely crazy. People cheer, tears streaming down their faces. Strangers hug each other, looking each other in the eye and giving weighty sighs. A voiceover announces: "I guess it is all up to us now." As the camera pans out, we see new practices emerging across the culture: more social involvement; increased participation in charity organizations; declining interest in consumerism and fashion; and a rise in religious practices where prayers to God become mainly prayers of acceptance, gratitude, jubilance, and ecstasy. With the credits rolling, we also see in the background various churches holding vigils, trying without success to induce another visitation from Jesus. Then the screen goes black.

We can reconsider *The New Easter Story*, bringing it from an imagined fictional film into everyday life as it were, along the following lines: try to imagine the looks of confusion we'd get if we were to walk up to an average Christian on the street today and ask, "Can you forgive God?" And we'd likely get more than contorted faces and headshakes. We might receive retaliatory responses along the lines of, "Forgive God? It is not people's place to forgive God. God is all good, all loving, and, if anything, you should hope that God forgives you for your sins." The response might be different if and when we were to ask that question to someone of the Jewish faith. Here we are likely to get silent nods and maybe a response along the lines of "Sure.

You really must." The contrast between these two responses shows the contradictions that crop up when Christians think they can boil the Bible down to the New Testament.[30] This is highly problematic. Jesus was a Jew and the only way to make sense of Jesus as the Messiah and Redeemer, the one who will wipe away original sin, is to rely upon accounts in the Old Testament. Indeed, one cannot make sense of the Bible without seeing how the Old Testament and New Testament fit together. The God depicted in the Old Testament, as one example, tries to flood out Noah but then later apologizes, makes a new covenant, and places a rainbow in the sky as a reminder of the covenant. The point is that God is cast as feeling remorse and needing to make some kind of amends. The authors of the Bible stress that God had one and only one Son who He sent down to be sacrificed. Why stress *one and only one* if not to emphasize that God experienced it as a sacrifice?[31] Surely, if God is in fact "all powerful," then, if he so wished, he could have had more than one son. But the story goes that God had only one Son and the Son had to be sacrificed for the "sins of humanity." The various writers of the Bible wanted to stress the significance of God's sacrifice.

The earliest Christians, themselves Jews, understood the world in terms of a guilt-ridden God, a God who felt some remorse over punishing everyone for all of time because of something that Adam and Eve did within a Garden that He had created. In other words, the ancients took God to have some responsibility for the whole situation that people found themselves in, for God had set up everything in the Garden of Eden and placed the forbidden fruit there, and He knew what was going to happen. He "set people up," knew the hardships they would have to endure. The punishment of life, dished up from thereon out, was a heavy weight, as nobody asks to be born. The world overflows with hardships, injustices, pains, losses, and death in the end. It makes sense that God, as the story goes, would feel a bit of moral compunction for having made animals who are both self-aware and finite.

Many people in the Western world have faith that everything will work out fine in the end if only they accept Christ. They put words into an unseen God's mouth, claim to know the wishes and designs of God, call it *Revelation*, and then they believe that if they keep up their end of the deal, God must keep his end of the covenant (one they claim he promised). They take religious stories and dogma literally: they think that God created the world and made covenants with people, they think that God gave people freedom but only as test of human fidelity, and they trust that there will be a kind of judgment of the soul after the death of the body. Many also believe that they will be allowed to ask God questions about why certain things happened in their lives, and that they will finally "understand it all" after they are dead.

Over many years and to many different people, I personally have asked the question: "Could you forgive God if you found out that there were no afterlife?" Many people, more than you would think, told me that they just could not. (Admittedly, a Greek Orthodox priest responded by looking me in the eye and saying that he has many parishioners who spend a fair amount of their devotional prayer time asking God to forgive Satan!) Many people apparently need to believe that there will be justice, that there will be some kind of recompense for this world's many injustices. There is too much suffering, too much sorrow, and far too much luck of the draw. Many people believe that without some kind of ultimate recompense, this world is simply unjustified. But some Christians are quick to point out that God sent his Son to redeem people for all their sins, including original sin. Such a response reveals they do understand the notion of a guilty God—a God who needs forgiveness. Jesus, in fact, is the apology, and when some people say that they accept Jesus into their heart—that they accept the message of Christianity—they are, in a somewhat self-deceiving way, accepting Jesus as a cosmic apology; they are saying to God: "I can accept the gift of life only now that you have included the Apology and Redemption that is your Son."

Historically speaking, Jesus represented a major turning point in Western culture. Substituting the rough "eye-for-an-eye" vengeance system of justice of the Old Testament, we find in its place a "turn the other cheek" philosophy, one of mercy, the "friendly injustices"[32] suggested by the promises of the New Testament. Jesus represents a notion of radical forgiveness, of final forgiveness. And, note, any act of forgiveness occurs as a double negative: it already assumes a wrongdoing and then signifies a removing, an erasing, of that wrongdoing. For those who accept Christ as their personal savior, or even those who want to be like Christ, a critical question emerges: how much can *you*, personally, forgive? Emil Cioran leads in the right direction where he writes,

> God realized in Man all his possibilities for imperfection and corruption. We were made to save divine perfection. . . . Since we carry God's burden, we feel entitled to swear at him. God suspects this, and if he has sent Jesus to relieve us of our pain, he has done so out of remorse, not pity. . . . No terror can be compared to this instant of paradise in which you forgive God and forget yourself![33]

One would think that people who claim to be Christians could, in full turn, forgive God and get over themselves if they learned that there is no life after this one. Would that not be a kind of ultimate human forgiveness? What is one to say of those who would deem God unforgiveable if there is no ultimate judgment and afterlife? Depending upon other beliefs and their overall self-understanding, people may find it more intelligible to give up their religion entirely than to believe in a God who cannot ensure salvation.

In this context, the critical questions become: what ancillary beliefs sufficiently buttress individuals against fear of death and the possible meaninglessness of life? What could people know or understand about themselves to peacefully accept death without fleeing from it by appeals to religious dogma? Which beliefs and practices help make life without an afterlife more tolerable and understandable, and also more morally invigorating?

Obviously, a good number of things would need to be involved. First, people would need an authentic sense of who they are. They would need to recognize themselves as the vacancy that makes room for everything. People are places and moments of the cosmos, sites of transcendence forever caught in the throes of finitude. They would need to realize that they partly are other people, that nothing separates them from others, and that others have helped them and continue to help them actualize possibilities. They must find their common humanity, their common plight in the multicellular world, where death was the price of entrance into this rich buffet of experience. People would need to know that they are delegates of an eternal cause, one that makes its way through the odyssey of time, bearing the contingencies of luck and happenstance as well as the possibilities of Reason as it emerged in humanity. The ability to reason, to think about what is and what is not, to decide over what should be or should not be—is itself an emergent symptom of the Orderliness of the cosmos. Ultimately, people would need to retain the proper respect and gratitude that comes from knowing, at the deepest of levels, that they fundamentally are on loan to themselves.

Perhaps more people need to recognize that existence has, for lack of a better term, what could be called a "gift" character.[34] To speak of gifts is to speak of exchanges, of relations beyond the self. Moreover, life is a gift without the possibility of return, and it is one we don't get to keep. The gift of existence is so big that there is no way to adequately pay for it in kind. At best, one honors existence and appreciatively gives life back, with gratitude, when one's time has come. But let's be even clearer about this: to say life is a gift is not to suggest that you were already "there, existing" and then a gift was given to you, the gift of life. No, the very "you" who "receives" the gift, the you of existence, is already included in the gift of life, which means that you are *free* to love life or to hate it, to treasure it or to trash it. Existence, then, is not the gift that "you" receive. *You, along with your existence, are the gift.*

Those who outwardly claim to "love" God should know that there is no way to repay God directly. The sole course of action is to take care of one another, to love all people, and to realize that everyone needs compassion, care, support, and resources, especially the underprivileged and underserved. Vilém Flusser, celebrating the spirit of Martin Buber, writes,

> The "true image" is any human face. It is the image of the absolute other, the "likeness of God." . . . Therefore each human being is the other for me, and I am the other for all human beings, an image of the "absolute other" (God). Because each person is for me the true image of the absolute other, he is the

only image, the only way I can or should conceive of God. . . . Every single person is my only medium to God, and I can only come to God if I go to Him through the other. . . . The only true love of God is love of another.[35]

Each and every person—an end in themselves and never merely a means—is a partial instantiation of the divine. And, as we are all immeasurably indebted to countless others, the only reasonable or fitting response is to know (and act as if) we are each other's keepers. When interacting with others we need to remember that everyone currently alive is our future, and they all are in the struggle of their lives. And we never really were fully ourselves anyways. Rather, we are the opening of the world. The world that lives on after our death partly is us, even in our absence; it is the "us" whose possibilities remain for-others.

Could it be that afterlife beliefs inadvertently entice people into an inescapable logic of overly narrow and highly deluded "self-interest"? Might such beliefs be an obstacle to doing good for good's sake, out of respect and reverence to the Orderliness of the cosmos, out of a sense of duty to others and out of a sense of self-respect? Once people fully accept their death and the fact that there very likely is no life after this one, they can take care of others and the world without any expectation for "personal" reward. They can see things for what they really are. Actual good, actual care, comes where it is not motivated by ulterior motives. Just as anonymous donations are often the most rewarding and meaningful forms of charity, so, similarly, acts of courage, kindness, and justice done without belief in the afterlife generate more significance and honor than acts performed because one believes in the possibilities of eternal rewards or punishments. To love genuinely and honestly is to bestow without any expectation of reward.

MAKING SENSE OF SOUL AND SPIRIT

Not knowing who they really are, many people simply take themselves to be the sack of skin that others can see, perhaps a fancy sack that can represent the world in sophisticated ways, but a sack of skin all said. Where we find popular resistance to such a view, we most commonly find it in religious dogma, and, in particular, in notions of "soul" or "spirit."

Now there is nothing wrong with "soul food" or "rhythm and soul" or even "soul searching," but people should be fairly skeptical about the existence of "immortal souls." There seems to be no solid evidence for them, so it is hard to believe that they exist.[36] On the other hand, we all directly experience our own non-being—that strange yet pervasive emptiness that makes room for what-is, and, accordingly, it does not require any faith or belief whatsoever. Look for yourself. You are the absence by which features of the world come to presence, the headlessness through which the body, others, and all things show themselves. Before people spend too much time believing in immortal souls, they should try to appreciate the nothing that worlds the world. They might therein discover that they already share in a grandeur and invulnerability, one whose majesty makes talk about souls seem rather trivial and insignificant.

People can question belief in immortal souls without denying the uniqueness of every individual. Each person came from the union of a particular egg and sperm, has distinctive characteristics, qualities, talents, and temperaments, and has had a unique upbringing with a particular set of relatives.[37] Each person is wholly irreplaceable. If the word "soul" means particular constellations and configurations of such relations, well, then, very good; but if it means anything that would be "in addition to" and "separable from" existence, well, then, it sounds like non-sense. To suggest that talk about souls is non-sense is, at the very least, to claim that souls, if there are such entities, remain forever unavailable to anybody's senses.[38]

The word "soul," it should be admitted, has important meaning, even if it remains without a literal referent. The soul, like mind or consciousness, is traditionally set in contrast to the body and accounts for people's intentions and goals as well as their ability to think and reason, even as those remain wholly out of sight. The notion of soul partly conveys a person's character and demeanor. It refers to the special something that makes people who they are. When we speak of loving someone "body and soul," we mean more than attraction to superficial characteristics. We recognize that individuals have an interior life, including unseen depths that can be approached only through hearing what they say and watching what they do in various contexts.

Spirit, too, seems to be widely misunderstood. Spirit is not some kind of inner ghost waiting to be released from the body. It is breath, the fact that we share the air and make ourselves known through speech and language. We are able to manifest ourselves through words and actions. We are spiritual beings in that we do not merely speak about one another but rather we speak to and with one another, transforming ourselves along the way. When the ancients knew themselves as spiritual beings, they were calling attention to the invisible bond between people, the ways that people, as non-surfaces, reveal themselves. The ancient Roman adage, "Speak, that I may see thee," means that people disclose themselves, their background, culture, mood, temperament, and character when they speak. They make themselves known when they voice their views. People, as spirit, live on well past their death, if only in all the things they have said or expressed. Whoever has heard another's word, repeated it, lived by it, well knows the spirit, but at no point is spirit something supernatural.

The early days of the telephone augmented popular belief in spirits and helped to inform today's sentiments regarding such phenomena. People's credulity for such beliefs came from the fact that the telephone gave them direct experiences of disembodied voices.[39] People could, via the telephone, interact with spirits somehow disincarnated yet animated; the person on the other end of the line, reduced to sheer voice, was absent and yet eerily present at the same time. Not surprisingly, around the same time, increasing numbers of psychics and mediums offered to establish lines of communication with the dead.

But belief in the soul is also ancient, and it is partly related to early institutions of ownership and private property. It would be hard to think of oneself as "having" a soul unless one already understood ownership. Possession, private property, marks of "mine" and "not thine"—these are inseparable from the eschatological impulse in humans. The correlation is suggested by the fact that ancient burial sites routinely included personal possessions. And clothing, too, is not only among the very first forms of possession, but, as Cioran risibly writes, "It is because we are dressed that we entertain immortality: how can we die when we wear a necktie?"[40]

Today's inheritance structures amplify this logic and make some people far too big for their own britches. Born into privilege and never knowing poverty and real hardship, these people barely suspect that the cosmos possesses them to the core. As Margulis and Sagan point out:

> The grave is a great leveler, and a good reminder that we are owned by what we own. All of us from street sweeper to billionaire pay our dues. . . . In the restricted economy of human arrogance and fantasy, individuals may amass great wealth and power. But in the solar economy of biological reality each and every one of us is traded away to make room for the next generation. On loan, the carbon, hydrogen, and nitrogen of our bodies must be returned to the biospheric bank.[41]

On loan to ourselves, we are made of ancient materials and have cosmic origins. To be born human is to have hijacked a body with billions of years of survival value in it. We are always already more than what we possibly could possess. How can people legitimately want more than what they are, when they have received everything for nothing? What should be the price tag for knowing that there is such an occasion as Life? We, the existing, have been invited to the greatest banquet ever thrown, literally the banquet of all banquets. What should the bill be? How about death as the final price, with death acceptance as gratuity?

We might compare what could be called the *doctrine of the immortality of the soul* with what could be called the *doctrine of life eternal*. By the "doctrine of the immortality of the soul," I refer to the dubious belief, tracing back to Gnostic traditions, that individuals have some kind of intangible substance subject to the odyssey of time and moral decision-making, all of which make it more or less *pure*. The thought is that, on the one hand, if people make the right moral decisions and act virtuously, the substance remains untarnished, translucent as light, but, on the other hand, if people choose evil, make selfish decisions, and willingly bring harm to others for self-gain, their soul becomes tainted, darkened, and heavy. Pure or tainted, the soul is assumed to be "other-worldly," and at the death of the body it is finally released. If the soul is light it ascends to the heavens, and if it is heavy it descends to hell.

The "doctrine of life eternal," in contrast, refers to the human capacity, as one of cosmos's possibilities, to taste the eternal in the living present. Ludwig Wittgenstein points in the right direction where he writes, "For life in the present there is no death. . . . If by eternity is understood not an infinite temporal duration but non-temporality, then it can be said that a man lives eternally if he lives in the present."[42] We can learn to be fully present to each other and to the world, dwelling in the timelessness of the now. We can know mathematical truths, think through logical principles, and experience the transcendence that comes from dealing in symbols. To use language at all is already to have tasted the timeless. The doctrine of life eternal is about harmonizing with the Orderliness already present in the world, attempting at all points to either add to its beauty and harmony or to bask silently and in rhythm with its glory. Just as one does not dance to get to the end of a song, or listen to a piece of music to get to the final beat, so, too, the meaning of life is not found at the end of life or somehow "after" it, but in the living of it.

Persons too commonly treat themselves as if they do not belong to the earth or are not natural to this world, as if they were placed here, but, ultimately, do not fit except in terms that will make eschatological sense at the end of the world, at some final judgment. Sadly, people routinely make some kind of appeal to an individual "soul," one taken to be intangible, ultimate, real, and removable from worldly existence. They uncritically believe in an individual soul while overlooking the fact that they are *of* the cosmos and not merely *in* it; they mistakenly fail to notice the emptiness that they are—that finite clearing which is the only possible gateway to the Eternal.

BIRTH IS A DEATH SENTENCE

Faith-based "abstinence-only" sex education commonly instructs young people to retain their virginity until marriage and to engage in sex only for procreative purposes. Here we find interesting cases of non-being, for what could be a starker illustration of nothing than what is known as "virginity"? Abstinence, virginity, celibacy, and chastity are taken to be virtues in some religious traditions, but the more important point in this context is that abstinence, virginity, celibacy, and chastity are modes of non-being. The words refer to possible engagements consciously denied, and, in this way, people's self-understanding is enshrouded in what they have *not* done, the fact that they have not had sex or are currently not having sex. Such non-being can show itself as an item of concern only where people experience, and then deny, their sexual possibilities.[43]

Although most people throughout history and across the globe have hardly experienced it as a choice at all, no choice is weightier than the decision of whether or not to have children. To give birth is to issue a death sentence. In his provocative book *The Trouble with Being Born*, E. M. Cioran points out that only the living are burdened with choice and the teetering down toward death, which also means that birth—rather than death—is the real trouble with life, or, as he suggests, "suicide *always* comes too late."[44] Cioran recalls, "In the 'Gospel According to the Egyptians,' Jesus proclaims, 'Men will be the victims of death so long as women give birth.'"[45] Whereas we typically mourn the death of family and friends, we should begin our mourning at someone's birth announcement. "Nothing is better proof of how far humanity has regressed," Cioran writes, "than the impossibility of finding a single nation, a single tribe, among whom birth still provokes mourning and lamentations."[46] Birth is an ominous occasion, one portending many uncertain possibilities while promising hardship, loss, and death. *The Devil's Dictionary*, by Ambrose Bierce, includes an entry for "Birth." It is a noun meaning: "The first and direst of all disasters."[47]

But many pregnancies do not come to term. Miscarriages, which are more common than some people realize, cut a fine line between being and non-being. While some women never discover that a given "late period" was a miscarriage, many couples live with tragedies that are too painful to share with others.[48] A miscarriage can leave people reeling between what occurred, what almost occurred, what is now not occurring, and what might never occur. A loss too large for simple words and easy understandings, some people know the deep hurt of bereavement for an unrealized possibility of possibilities. For months and years, people can quietly dwell in the painful experience of an absent presence, a presence forever absent.

Giving birth to a child launches someone else on an uncertain and precarious journey to death. Despite all the risk, chance, and uncertainty as well as the assurance of death in the end, people regularly choose to bestow this fate. As there is no other way to enter life than to have others bring you into it, this outrageous imposition is also, arguably, a most forgivable act. Birth is a clear exemplar of how deep sociality runs, how others are a necessary condition of our existence. We have been able to experience life and to know that there is such a miraculous occurrence only because someone else brought us into the world. This also means that none of us had the luxury of advanced knowledge regarding what, exactly, would be entailed in "living *a* life." We were not briefed regarding all the possibilities of life—including relevant details such as the epoch we would be born into, where we would be born, our bodily characteristics, the amount of hardship and adversity we would face, and who specifically would be our parents. But, alas, there are some decisions regarding our fate that only others get to make. Nonexistent persons—persons not yet conceived—obviously cannot speak on their own behalf; there is literally no one there. Also, because fetuses cannot speak for themselves, some people take it as their obligation to act on behalf of the fetus, and they do what they believe it would want if it could speak on its own behalf. Acting on behalf of the interests of the unborn, some people will prevent a life while others give life a chance.

Recent backlash of antiabortion sentiment comes, in part, because forms of contraception are more available and more reliable than they were centuries and decades prior. Contraception, it also should be noted, offers yet another exemplar case of preventive measures, tactical means of making sure that something does *not* happen. Because birth control prevents something from happening, there is nothing noticeable "not happening." Our environments have physically present items such as condoms and pills, and these items are observable enough, but the "not conceiving" does not appear directly to everyday public experience. Even the event known as a "late period" is itself a non-event. Outside of those concerned moments, the fact of "not becoming pregnant" can seem like no accomplishment at all. This is undoubtedly why some people who use contraception get sloppy, inconsistent, and lazy. They simply cannot imagine how possible pregnancy is until it happens.

While most people see some moral latitude with regard to abortion decisions (e.g., Was the pregnancy the result of rape? Incest? Is the woman's life or the baby's health in serious danger? etc.), others are more rigid in their stance. Some people are militantly prolife, and their reasoning is almost always grounded in religious belief or dogma. Some people are so extreme that they are willing—and not without obvious contradiction—to take out lives for their "prolife" cause. They believe that laws should protect all fetuses—no matter how they came about and regardless of any risks to the pregnant woman or the fetus. They claim that people not only have a moral duty to procreate but that women should be legally prevented from having abortions, just as doctors should be punished for performing them. We can better contextualize and grab hold of such extreme "prolife" positions by contrasting them with extreme views on the other end of the spectrum.

In recent years, the prolife movement has witnessed the emergence of a diametrically opposed position known as "antinatalism." In his book *Better Never to Have Been*, philosopher David Benatar defends a "proabortion" position. He suggests that much of life is suffering and there is always harm in coming into existence—harm that could have been prevented if only the person had not been—and so Benatar argues that people have a moral obligation to not impose the harm of existence. He writes,

> I shall argue that coming into existence is always bad for those who come into existence. ... [T]here is nothing nonsensical in claiming that nobody is lucky enough never to have come into existence, even though it would have been (playful) nonsense to claim that there are some people who are lucky enough not to come into existence.[49]

His point is that nonexistent people cannot be harmed, not even by being deprived of a possible benefit, whereas those who have come into existence are thereby inevitably harmed. There is always harm in coming into existence. He also acknowledges that "better" can be known only by those in existence; nonexistent persons, as nonexistent, cannot be benefited.

Part of the challenge is that people, mainly philosophers, often ask the question, "What makes life worth living?" This question subtly equivocates between "What makes a life worth starting?" and "What makes a life worth continuing?"[50] One way to help clarify this position is to focus on the former and to identify the specific kinds of disabilities that would incline someone to think that an abortion is the best decision. Imagine possible parents discovering their fetus has clear but early signs of severe, lifelong, and life-debilitating disorders and deformities. Many people have some set of conditions where they will admit someone would have been better never having been. Benatar simply carries that principle over to all of us, suggesting that everyone has some forms of inabilities. Because nonexistent persons cannot be deprived, for "they," as nonexistent, would never have known that "they" could have been, existing people have a moral duty to not procreate.

Benatar impressively advances a series of logical arguments, and his reasoning is quite tight, though, I believe, unpersuasive all said. His position seems to underestimate the irrational within humans and also to invite a hyperrationalistic individualism into thought. Imagine, for example, that the moral imperative to not procreate is accepted and implemented on a global scale. It means the end of parenthood point-blank. Many people simply would not know what to do with themselves. Raising young is an inseparable part of their being, and intergenerational existence is part of what we mean by existence and the human condition. In this context, intergenerationally or evolutionarily speaking, his distinction between "What is a life worth continuing?" and "What is a life worth starting?" shows some of its ambiguity. Benatar also under-represents those who would "reasonably disagree" over whether the costs are worth the questionable possible gains. The situation seems more ambiguous than his arguments suggest. Moreover, some people might argue that "death heals all wounds," and, therefore, the harm of coming into existence is promised as temporary.[51] It is worth noting, too, that his book is dedicated to his parents, "even though" they brought him into existence, and to his brothers, "each of whose existence, although a harm to him, is a great benefit to the rest of us."[52] Here we find an interesting counterdynamic as well as a different criterion for existing: the possible benefits one can bring to others, how one's existence, even if a harm to oneself, can be a benefit to others and can help others in their own possibilities. Many people, undoubtedly harmed by coming into existence, make outstanding and valuable contributions to the lives of others; they make life qualitatively better for many other people and the justification for their coming into being, given that they will die in the end, is to better the conditions for others. This is true not simply of parents who take the time to raise great children, but is a truth concretely lived by artists, builders, cooks, inventors, engineers, scientists, and teachers, among many others.

Although Benatar argues that people have a moral duty to non-procreate, he maintains—in significant contrast to those on the extreme "prolife" side—that people nevertheless should have the legal rights to procreate. Noting that many cultures legally tolerate what many of its members recognize as possibly immoral, he suggests that the harms brought to society by attempting to police non-procreation would be too invasive and a violation of people's personal rights to privacy. In this regard, his position and arguments are more nuanced and helpful than radical "prolife" positions. In fact, he provides an excellent counterargument to religious "prolife" dogma. Antinatalism, even if a bit extreme and counterintuitive, offers useful and important correctives to popular thought about abortion and the right to life. It helps sober up those who get intoxicated on the "thought of babies," and it forces people to recognize that the decision of whether or not to have children is the weightiest of all choices.

People need a radically different notion of "prolife," one that includes informed decision-making over family planning, safe and effective contraception, and resources for abortion when the health of the mother or baby are at stake, and, more fundamentally, people need a broader and deeper concern over the lifespan of *all* individuals. Somewhat splitting the difference between the dogma of the prolife camp and extremes of the antinatalists, Dorothy Lee identifies the difference between giving birth biologically and being responsible for the care and upbringing of individuals for life. In her lecture "To Be or Not to Be," Lee writes, "Which of the people who were so concerned with keeping the child from dying are now concerned with the span of life? There are societies where to save a man from dying means to take on a lifelong responsibility."[53]

Adoption lends conceptual contrast and comparative clarity. Some people, even those who claim to be "prolife," will not adopt children because they want "their own." Many people are not interested in raising "someone else's" child. They want someone who they believe will be similar to them. People want someone who shares in their genetic heritage and who has family resemblance, someone with blood ties. Some people wish to have children, have the means and the love to give, but decide that unless they can have children of "their own," no matter how expensive and cumbersome, they are uninterested in adopting. Unable to procreate and unwilling to adopt, they remain childless. The fate of "other" babies is not their concern. But either you care about life or you don't care. This is why adoption is so important. Those who have come into existence already have been harmed, and those who have been given up for adoption, for whatever reason, face additional uncertainties and ambiguities. Those who understand the common fate of the living, the fact that we are all dying together, realize the bogus notion of "having" children. For good or ill, we are the condition of possibilities for others, and they are the condition of possibilities for us. Individuals do not bring themselves into existence, and, if we are going to bring others into existence, we need to shoulder the weight of the decision and help others as best we can.

DEATH AND HUMAN MORALITY

Life and death are not on par with each other, and they are not opposites: the dead cannot mourn for themselves, and mourning is a task for the living. Life and death therefore form a dependent hierarchy, where the former is the environment for the latter. D. E. Harding accordingly writes, "We must respect the death sentence which the universe passes on itself through us, without forgetting that it is the living universe which pronounces it."[54] Just as non-being is parasitic upon being, so, too, death concerns only those who are alive. E. M. Cioran captures some of this sensibility, where he writes,

> Death is not something from outside, ontologically different from life, because there is no *death* independent of life. . . . The presence of death in life introduces into one's existence an element of nothingness. One cannot conceive of death without nothingness, nor of life without a principle of negativity.[55]

Life only opens to itself from the inside, both at the beginning and at the end: by the time you find yourself, you will find that you always already have begun, and, on the other side, as you are approaching your own death, you will get nearer and nearer to it but never know for sure that it has happened. It will be experienced as: "I'm dying, I'm dying, I'm dying," and so on. One never arrives at: "Now I'm dead." As Cioran writes, "You once told me that death did not exist. Agreed, provided you add that nothing exists."[56] And, along the same theme, Cioran elsewhere writes,

> Each time the fear of death grabs you, look in the mirror. You will then understand why you can never die. Your eyes know everything. For in them there are specks of nothingness. . . . As long as I live I shall not allow myself to forget that I shall die; I am waiting for death so that I can forget about it.[57]

Just as the universe does not have an outside, so, too, life, paradoxically, knows itself only from the inside, by way of negativity.[58] Life is a Möbius strip, a paradoxical knot of self-referential loops, one that remains somehow without an exterior.

As life is all anyone has ever experienced, it is, admittedly, easier to imagine some kind of afterlife, just as, comparatively, it is difficult to imagine what death is for the dead. People only have seen death from the vantage of the living. What would be less an object for thought than the absolute nothingness of our own death? Death, for now-dead individuals, is perhaps best compared with a dreamless sleep from which people never awake, and it would be the end of the world if, *and only if*, all of existence was produced for the benefit of the existing individuals. But such is not the case. The world goes on after one's death.

Because people commonly don't know who they are (because they so routinely think of themselves as other-worldly), they're easily inclined to beliefs in a life after this one. Admittedly, the very mystery pervading this world, coupled with the power of our imaginations, lends some credence to the possibilities of something "beyond" death. And people often need some notion of an afterlife for the deepest of "psychological" reasons, but even calling them "psychological" oversimplifies things quite a bit. The problems here are ontological, partly because part of our being is our being-for-others. We exist in relationships with others, and such relationships are one of the possibilities of the cosmos.

One of the deeply personal and moving parts of Douglas Hofstadter's book *I Am a Strange Loop* is his recounting of the unexpected and painful loss of his wife. Of course Hofstadter grieved over his loss *of her*, but he also grieved *for her loss*: she was now not going to get to watch their children grow up. The pain of the loss was not simply a loss of an other, but a loss felt for the other that the other cannot feel. So deeply do others enter the recesses of consciousness that their unrealized possibilities can remain possibilities for us. We can suffer the loss of their loss of possibilities.

To have experienced sunsets and rainbows, to know the thrill of holding a loved one's hand, to know the ecstasy of love and intimacy, to have shared in robust laughter with friends, to have cried over beautiful pieces of music, to have tasted fresh fruit, to know everything that one has come to know, to have experienced all that one has experienced, how is it even possible to sum these up? We take them for granted but they are amazing once we stop to appreciate them. Understanding how far we have come from nothing and that we will be nothing for ourselves once again, we bring everyday life—others and the larger world—into new dynamic and radiant light. Simple, everyday pleasures can be appreciated at their fullest extreme when compared with the possibility of absolutely nothing after this worldly existence. Also, calls to social actions ring more loudly when one realizes how death curtails one's future opportunity to help others. Only while we are alive can we devote energies to the others who live on after our death. Death is a bell. It calls into action those who understand that time waits for no one. It is the line in the sand that demarcates our last chance for heroism.

As stated in chapter 1, there are significant differences between "never having been" and "no longer existing." Death is loss of all non-being, the loss of our ability to negate. At our own death, we simply are what we are, with no more possibilities for ourselves outstanding. Any possibilities left behind remain exclusively for others. This means that one's own death is not the end of the world. People commonly fear that moral relativism unavoidably accompanies the idea that there is no life after death. This fear is understandable enough. But, all said, it seems wrong-minded the more one thinks about it. It too easily equates one's death with the end of the world. The world will not end along with the individual; no one will even know if they are the last person in existence. Dramatic climate change over the upcoming century may significantly diminish the human population, but there still will be a world that goes on after one's death.

Now if, for the sake argument, we imagine the end of it all (absolutely everything), an explosion that destroys the entire planet or perhaps the eventual end of the universe when it has finally run its course, we are not thereby fated to nihilism. Surely, none of these facts take away from the fact that existing persons, while alive, are always already more than they could possibly achieve within existence. They have been born into a body with billions of years of survival value already built in, and have, as a birthright, inherited a miraculous world that cannot show some of its most beautiful and inspiring features without some of their bodily assistance. While alive and despite being finite, people can taste eternity. As a place and moment of the self-aware cosmos, they thus enjoy a being well beyond any human accomplishment. And, as wonderful and as desirable as it is for people to contribute to the world around them—for them to make their mark by liberating humane possibilities for others—we should never fail to remember that we *are*, in existing at all, much more than we could ever hope to *do* within life.

NOTES

1. This distinction between "death at the end of life" and "being-toward-death all the way along" is nicely captured by Emil Cioran where he gives voice to the dread that many feel regarding death. He writes, "We dread the future only when we are not sure we can kill ourselves when we want to," in *The Trouble With Being Born*, trans. Richard Howard (New York: Viking, 1976), 77. Elsewhere Cioran writes, "The man who has never imagined his own annihilation, who has not anticipated recourse to the rope, the bullet, poison, or the sea, is a degraded galley slave or a worm crawling upon the cosmic carrion," in *A Short History of Decay*, trans. Richard Howard (New York: Arcade, 2012), 37.

2. See Revelation 20:12

3. The great stream, upon flowing over the waterfall that is life, issued one's own particular life-to-death trajectory as a single water droplet momentarily separated from the stream, only to rejoin it at the base of the falls.

4. Lynn Margulis writes, "We need honesty. . . . No evidence exists that we are 'chosen,' the unique species for which all the others were made. . . . One tenacious illusion of special dispensation belies our true status as upright mammalian weeds," in *Symbiotic Planet: A New Look at Evolution* (New York: Basic, 1998), 119.

5. I remain rather sympathetic to Thomas Paine who, in *The Age of Reason*, originally published in 1794, writes, "All national institutions of churches, whether Jewish, Christian, or Turkish, appear to me no other than human inventions. . . . Each of those churches shows a certain book, which they call, *revelation*, or the Word of God. . . . Each of those churches accuses the other of unbelief, and, for my own part, I disbelieve them all." *The Age of Reason* (Lexington, KY: Edward Bulwer-Lytton, 2015 [1794]), 8–9.

Paine, given the resistance to such thinking at the time, lived out the rest of his life ostracized and in isolation. Jefferson, seeing how things stood with Paine, did not have his version of the Bible published until after his death.

6. Once people become dishonest with themselves and others, professing beliefs that they deep down suspect to be false, they and their societies start to rot from the inside out.

7. A good number of Christians, and people more generally, believe that Christianity invented "virgin birth" stories or stories regarding the sacrifice of divine kings. Many contemporary believers remain unaware that by the time of Christ these were already well-known archetypes. This plainly shows how uninterested people are in unmasking their wishful thinking regarding "chosen people." Also see Yuval Noah Harari, *Sapiens: A Brief History of Humankind* (New York: HarperCollins, 2015).

8. For a much more extended treatment of this line of thought see Corey Anton, *Sources of Significance: Worldly Rejuvenation and Neo-Stoic Heroism* (West Lafayette, IN: Purdue University Press, 2010).

9. See Paine's *The Age of Reason*, where he writes: "[T]here is no authority for believing that the inhuman and horrid butcheries of men, women, and children, told of in those books [the books of the Old Testament] were done, as those books say they were, at the command of God. It is the duty incumbent on every true Deist, that he vindicate the moral justice of God against the calumnies of the Bible." *The Age of Reason*, 81.

10. As of 2019, roughly 40 percent of US citizens believe in "psychics," and the "psychic industry" has become a billion dollar enterprise. For some comedic correction, see John Oliver, "Psychics," *Last Week Tonight with John Oliver*, February 25, 2019, https://www.youtube.com/watch?v=WhMGcp9xIhY

11. Lynn Margulis and Dorion Sagan, *What Is Life?* (Berkeley: University of California Press, 2000), 92.

12. Margulis and Sagan, *What Is Life?* 232.

13. My view is nearly the opposite: regarding the origins of the cosmos, I am a mystic or stoic or deist or simple recognizer in Divine Orderliness and Providence. Regarding notions of a deity or a God who is more than the cosmos and outside of it, I am agnostic. Finally, regarding talking snakes, virgin births, divine intervention, "chosen" peoples, and life after death, I am an unbeliever.

14. But the founders did live well before TV, movies, and computers. Today, younger thinkers believe that the cosmos is some kind of giant quantum computer and we are living in some sort of simulation.

15. Paine also contends that the word "prophet" was consistently mistranslated and misunderstood. He says it actually meant "poet."

16. *The Age of Reason*, 31.
17. Paine, *The Age of Reason*, 9.
18. Paine, *The Age of Reason*, 76.
19. Paine, *The Age of Reason*, 67.
20. Paine, *The Age of Reason*, 168.
21. Paine, *The Age of Reason*, 167.
22. William H. Gass, *Habitations of the Word* (New York: Simon and Shuster, 1985), 206.

23. This is not to suggest that superstition has gone away. It seems to be as alive and well as ever.

24. Given the vastness of the universe, such notions inevitably serve to trivialize what is meant by God. Paine, writing in ways that would make SETI proud, suggests that the sheer immensity of space, as disclosed through astronomy, reveals the possibilities of countless other worlds. He writes, "From whence could arise the solitary and strange conceit that the Almighty, who had millions of worlds equally dependent upon his protection, should quit the care of all the rest, and come to die in our world, because, they say, one man and one women had eaten an apple? And, on the other hand, are we to suppose that every world in the boundless creation has an Eve, an apple, a serpent, and a redeemer?" Paine, *The Age of Reason*, 57.

25. Ernest Becker, "The Spectrum of Loneliness," in *The Ernest Becker Reader*, ed. Daniel Liechty (Seattle: University of Washington Press, 2005), 235.

26. The classic Beatles song "Eleanor Rigby" captures the spirit of this profound loneliness quite perfectly.

27. Becker, "The Spectrum of Loneliness," 236.

28. For more on weeping and religious experiences, see Emil Cioran, *Tears and Saints*, trans. Ilinca Zarifopol-Johnson (Chicago: University of Chicago Press, 1995).

29. Heidegger writes, "The only task left to philosophy before the end is to understand death and to bring the totality of anxiety into full individual consciousness thus achieving Existence as Being-in-the-world-of nothingness." In *Existence and Being*, trans. R. F. C. Hull and Alan Crick (Chicago: Henry Regnery Co, 1967), 364.

30. Much of this is an oversimplification, as "The Revelation of Saint John the Divine" is part of the New Testament.

31. Admittedly, there are multiple reasons here, and some of this bears upon the attempt to claim Christianity as the "one" true faith. The Bible authors were trying to distance themselves from the long history of divine sacrifices well known throughout the ancient world.

32. See Kenneth Burke's epilogue in *The Rhetoric of Religion: Studies in Logology* (Berkeley: University of California Press, 1970).

33. Cioran, *Tears and Saints*, 111, 113.

34. Also see Calvin O. Schrag's section titled, "The Gift and the Fitting Response," in his *God as Otherwise Than Being: Toward a Semantics of the Gift* (Evanston, IL: Northwestern University Press, 2002), 125–43.

35. Vilém Flusser, *Into the Universe of Technical Images*, trans. Nancy A. Roth (Minneapolis: University of Minnesota Press, 2011), 156. Also see Vilém Flusser, *Writings*, trans. Eric Eisel (Minneapolis: University of Minnesota Press, 2002), 165–71.

36. Or, if people actually have them, then other animals should have them also. As a child, I distinctly remember asking priests why only humans have souls and go to Heaven and why good dogs do not.

37. Also see Corey Anton, "Beyond Theoretical Ethics: Bakhtinian anti-theoreticism," *Human Studies: A Journal for Philosophy and the Social Sciences* 24, no. 3 (2001b): 211–25.

38. Eric McLuhan argues that the soul is accessible to people, just not through the five well-known senses. See his book *The Sensus Communis, Synesthesia and the Soul* (Toronto: BPS, 2015). For all the reasons given in this book, I respectfully beg to differ. I am more sympathetic to Flusser who writes, "To say that a newborn child has a soul or possesses a spirit is to caricature the rudimentary processes under way in its brain. . . . [T]his . . . is repugnant because it refutes Judeo-Christian anthropology and all the anthropologies that have followed from it. According to these anthropologies, each person has a core and it must be preserved and developed. . . . We now know, however, that this core is a myth and that the anthropologies are untenable. In fact, we know this from completely different disciplines that converge—neurophysiology, depth psychology, informatics, and above all, phenomenological analysis. Eidetic reduction demonstrates that 'I' is an abstract hook on which to hang concrete circumstances and that in the absence of those circumstances, the 'I' reveals itself to be nothing." Flusser, *Into the Universe of Technical Images*, 91–93.

39. See Eric McLuhan, *The Sensus Communis*.

40. Emil Cioran, *A Short History of Decay*, trans. Richard Howard (New York: Arcade, 2012), 172–73.

41. Margulis and Sagan, *What Is Life?* 200–201.
42. Ludwig Wittgenstein, *Notebooks, 1914–1916*, trans. G. E. M. Anscombe (New York: Harper and Row, 1961), 75e. He therein adds, "Fear in the face of death is the best sign of a false, i.e. bad, life," in *Notebooks*, 75e.
43. Additionally, the word "virgin" can be metaphorically applied to countless other horizons of experience. Any time people are about do anything at all for the first time, meaning that they had *not* done it before, they can claim "virginity" with regard to it. Without the horizon of intelligibility that language affords, people would be at a loss for demarcating such facts of non-being.
44. Emil Cioran, *The Trouble with Being Born*, 32.
45. Cioran, *The Trouble with Being Born*, 119. Elsewhere Cioran writes, "The man who managed, by an imagination overflowing with pity, to record all the suffering, to be contemporary with all the pain and all the anguish of any given moment—such a man—supposing he could ever exist—would be a monster of love and the greatest victim in the history of the human heart. But it is futile to imagine such an impossibility. . . . If we could understand and love the infinities of agonies which languish around us, all the lives which are hidden deaths, we should require as many hearts as there are suffering human beings. And if we had a miraculously present memory which sustained the totality of our past pains, we should never succumb beneath such a burden. *Life is possible only by the deficiencies of our imagination and our memory."* Cioran, *A Short History of Decay*, 26.
46. One of the interesting features of the Catholic Church is that although the Bible commands people to be fruitful and multiply, the priests, bishops, cardinals, etc., do *not* marry and do *not* procreate. Cioran, *The Trouble with Being Born*, 4.
47. Ambrose Bierce, *The Devil's Dictionary* (Mineola, NY: Dover, 1993), 12.
48. In chapter 3, I discussed "Contexts Where Nothing Happens" and tried to show how context, often ambiguous and invisible, often temporal rather than merely spatial, relates to non-being (also see Corey Anton, "On the Nonlinearity of Human Communication: Insatiability, Context, Form," *The Atlantic Journal of Communication* 15, no. 2 (2007): 79–102). I here note how this issue can be addressed in terms of "biological periodicity." We can demonstrate the dynamic role that functional absence plays if we consider the biological developments that enable semifixed routines, patterns of growth, and modes of habit formation, noting the need to ensure distances, lags, gaps, and forms of incompleteness within such processes. Periodicity itself illustrates how non-being infects the temporality of the living; it is a kind of orderliness below the level of articulate symbolic thought. Examples of periodicity—strategically built-in absences and lacks—are the amount of time lapsed between meals or how long until one needs more water, the time that must pass between drug dosages, the amount of time until one needs more sleep, the amount of time between monthly menstrual cycles, the recovery period between orgasms, etc. Such built-in intervals, which allow for non-being to be integrated into being, reveal non-being as more than linguistic.
49. David Benatar, *Better Never to Have Been: The Harm of Coming into Existence* (New York: Oxford University Press, 2006), 4–5.
50. See Benatar, *Better Never to Have Been*.
51. Cioran writes, "I think of so many friends who are no more, and I pity them. Yet they are not so much to be pitied, for they have solved every problem, beginning with the problem of death," in *The Trouble with Being Born*, 17.
52. Benatar, *Better Never to Have Been*, v.
53. Dorothy Lee, *Valuing the Self: What We Can Learn from Other Cultures* (Englewood Cliffs, NJ: Prentice Hall, 1976), 82.
54. D. E. Harding, *The Hierarchy of Heaven and Earth* (London: Shollond Trust, 2011), 114.
55. Emil Cioran, *On the Heights of Despair*, trans. Ilinca Zarifopol-Johnson (Chicago: University of Chicago Press, 1992), 23, 26.
56. Cioran, *The Trouble with Being Born*, 149.
57. Cioran, *Tears and Saints*, 87, 105.
58. If one were to claim there is an "outside" to the cosmos, the question becomes: "Well, what is on the outside of that?" Exactly, it's turtles all the way down.

Chapter Five

A Mythological/Mathematical Postscript

SPECULATING ON POSSIBLE ORIGINS

Alan Watts, in various places, spins a story he calls "cosmic Hide-N-Seek." In the proverbial beginning, he suggests, there was One and only One being, and it cried out, "I am lonely." Then, as a response, it divided in two, and then both halves simultaneously exclaimed, "Ugh, now I am bored." Then the one side turned black while the other side turned white. One side then asked, "What is that?" while the other replied just a moment later, "Who said that? What is this? What is going on?" Then the impulse of the division shattered the two into all things: stars, planets, air and sky, all the different plants, animals, humans, everything you can see and touch, everything you can think about. They are all the One, playing a cosmic game of Hide-N-Seek on itself, so that it may avoid being either lonely or bored. Watts's notion of the One dividing itself is a different way of saying that it introduced non-being into itself. This is where I begin recasting Watts's myth.

Before the beginning, the originally undivided paradoxical "ONE," the singular *All-No-Thing*, the Unknowable Mystery, could not even relate to itself. There were no points of distance or reference, no differential gradients. "All" was, paradoxically, without any spatial or temporal dimensions or coordinates. The One could not go anywhere, as there wasn't anywhere to go. The One could not do anything, as there wasn't anything to do. The One could not think about anything because there wasn't anything about which to think. The One could not want anything because there wasn't anything to want, and it could not even be lonely as there was no distance, difference, or otherness. Finally, as the most paradoxical aspect of all, the One was not even definitively "there," could not even Be-as-Itself, because, without a background against which it could disclose itself, it remained absolutely undifferentiated, unable to register any delimitation.

Through unknown and unknowable means,[1] the One somehow infected itself with nothingness and renounced or forfeited its paradoxical nonstatus. Therein it gained some kind of delimitation and definite, even if ambiguous, identity. Because it could not *add* anything to itself, it "divided" itself by part of itself. It all started with an utterly nonsensical, playful, and highly imaginative impulse that took roughly the form of *infinity over infinity divided by one over zero, which also entailed the expression, indeterminate over undefined.*[2] The initial fracture was *as if* the One imagined what it would be like to be delimited and differentiated in different ways; the break in symmetry was, strictly speaking, *a logical possibility always already implied in the One*; *it was not a temporal action per se.* Nonetheless, the initial break resulted in expanding horizons of matter and energy within space-time relations. It was *as if* an imagined forfeiture of absolute self-identity resulted in Möbius structures, donut-like ripples, of "being and non-being," nothing encompassing Being as well as occupying its core. The ripples, too, precipitated out dialectically interwoven movements integrating four imagined fractional relations: "one divided by one," "zero divided by zero," "one divided by zero," "zero divided by one." The movements were (1) a *definite* sense of Oneness,[3] (2) an *undefined* infinity of what exists but remains not unique,[4] (3) an *undefined* expanse of what does not exist,[5] and, finally, (4) a *definite* sense of nothingness.[6]

The matter-energy left in the wake carried possibilities of various physical, chemical, and molecular relations. Those relations eventually led to life, which then bore multicellular bodies, and, finally, opened to the most improbable of possibilities, human existence. The many sights, sounds, scents, and tastes, light and dark, day and night, male and female, microbe, animal, plant, and human existence, all of these and many more, came into the possibilities of being and non-being. In saying "No" to itself, the Paradoxical All-No-Thing, infected itself with room-making negativity, existential temporality, and modes of conditionality and distance that produced the many-leveled empty expanses necessary for life and existence. Thus, at the present moment, you are where you are right now, but all of this could not have begun without the Mysterious Source saying "No" to its unconditional and undifferentiated paradoxical nonstatus. The One thereby inaugurated not an effective means for giving a foundation to Itself as Itself (e.g. "God"), but rather generated modes of dialectical distance, countless forms of contingent and conditional beings, the emergence of possible harvests within morally loaded situations, or ethically charged existential encounters.

E. M. Cioran captures some of the spirit of such profound divine renunciation, where he writes of Jewish mysticism:

> *Tsimtsum.* This silly sounding word designates a major concept for the Cabbala. For the world to exist, God, who was everything and everywhere, consented to shrink, to leave a vacant space not inhabited by Himself: it is in this "hole" that the world occurred. . . . For us to exist, He contracted, He limited His sovereignty. We are the product of His voluntary reduction, of His effacement, of His partial absence.[7]

The cosmos itself, and from it eventually life and then human existence, began with the space-time that became possible with that initial break, the primary fissure. Difference and distance, mystery and becoming, these are routes the All-No-Thing left as residual possibilities. All that was left from the original Act was time and attraction, and, therein, the possibilities for accumulating interactions given geometric tumbling and the coming together of possible relations on various levels of interaction.

During our short existences we can reflect upon the paradoxical origin of our being and the being of the cosmos. People can entertain the possibility that the All-No-Thing logically needed the cosmos, life, and existence, and needed to negate itself, if only to delimit itself and make way for fragmentary visages of Itself now trapped within the contingencies of chance and finitude.

All that is—everything extant, living and existing—directly relates back to the paradoxical Divine Source. But this is not to suggest that each being *is* the eternal source of the cosmos, nor, on the other hand, that there is an actual sentient being, an omnipotent ruler of the universe. It means that we, our sentient life, our capacities to grow hair, digest food, heal wounds, and the "we" who can participate in the perpetuation of the species through procreation, all of these are part of what were left as possibilities in the wake of the original division and shrinking of the One. The position advanced here is neither panpsychism nor pantheism, nor is it scientific reductive materialism. It is a stoic, deistic, Mysticism of Orderliness, one without any miracles other than the miracle of the cosmos itself. One without use for prayers beyond those that approximate meditations drawn upon for strength, forgiveness, compassion, or other struggles with self-relation and social justice, one without need for an afterlife, for it recognizes the mysterious absent Eternal ground in the eyes of all beings, even those without eyes to see.

Strategically ambiguous self-forfeiture—the possible gain that comes from a certain kind of loss—is a key dialectical principle here. Without this miraculous introduction of nothing, the One is void of all delimitation, distances, mystery, and thought. In repeating "No" to its paradoxical Otherwise-Than-Being status, the One thereby opened itself to unforeseen outcomes regarding whatever is and will be, and it left for itself only certain kinds of possibilities, including various kinds of relationships that congealed into the eventual occurrence of awareness, sentience, conscious deliberation over possible outcomes, and the modes of morality implied therein.[8]

How might we best imagine a logical loss that harvests possible gains? Might we be able to find comparably humble examples of how being, by including non-being, can be brought to life and enlivened with otherwise unavailable possibilities? Consider a few of the basic properties of the numerical symbol known as "the cipher" or "zero," represented by the mathematical sign "0."

One of the more interesting books on the subject is Robert Kaplan's *The Nothing That Is*.[9] Historically speaking, human counting and mathematical reasoning did not begin with zero. Whole numbers historically grew out of counting numbers, but the possibilities of zero and negative numbers were already fixed into the possibilities of mathematics, which where themselves tightly stitched into the Orderliness of the cosmos. Hence, although zero was a relatively late discovery, people could learn how to use it, and, because it was etched into nature's tidiness, learning to use it amounted to bringing tighter definition and rigor to numbers and mathematical calculations: instead of counting things that were already there, people could imagine counting past things absent.

Note here that adding 0 to any number amounts to no change in the initial number (zero thus becomes whatever is added to it), just as subtracting 0 from any number yields only the initial number. Within multiplication, any starting number can be retained by multiplying that number by the number 1; any number multiplied by 1 equals itself. Moreover, any number multiplied by 0 equals 0. As we move to division, things get a bit trickier: any number divided by 1 equals itself and any number divided by itself equals 1. The similarities to multiplication might seduce us to assume that (1) any number divided by 0 equals 0 and (2) that 0 divided by 0 equals 1. But what happens when we try to divide by 0? It is commonly suggested that you can't do it or that mathematical errors occur.[10] For example, rigorous yet simple algebraic proofs can be offered to show that dividing by zero leads to fallacious conclusions. But, still, we might want to ask, *why* can we multiply by zero but not divide by it? And also, why was the notion of infinity unable to fully become itself without the defining force of zero? Zero, understood as a verb, means that zero divided by zero approximates an approach toward infinity.

These observations suggest that zero is no mere number; it is a meta-sign, one that reorganizes mathematics itself and makes other numbers more exactly what they are, including how they are not their additive inverse.[11] Dividing by zero remains not technically "impossible" as much as it remains "undefined," and this can be explained rather simply: on the one hand, if we try to divide any number other than zero by zero, we find that no number actually exists such that a quotient multiplied by zero equals that original number. Yet, on the other hand, if we try to divide zero by zero, we find that any and all quotients multiplied by zero equal zero, meaning any quotient would not be unique.

Norbert Weiner, the great cyberneticist, nicely captures the overall thrust of these ambiguities when he addresses the topic of infinity. He writes as if defending negative theology:

> If God surpasseth the human intellect, and cannot be compassed by intellectual forms—and this is at least a defensible position—it is not intellectually honest to stultify the intellect itself by forcing God into intellectual forms which should have a very definite intellectual meaning.[12]

This, he points out, is how we get into those odd sorts of questions such as: if God is omnipotent, can He create a rock so heavy that even He cannot lift it? We get into trouble by reductively thinking of the Infinite now trapped wholly within the finite. He writes,

> It is easy to dispose of this difficulty as a verbal quibble, but it is more. The paradox of this question is one of the many paradoxes that center about the notion of infinity, in its many forms. On the one hand, the least manipulation of the mathematically infinite introduces the notion of zero over zero, or infinity over infinity, or infinity times zero, or infinity minus infinity. These are called *indeterminate forms*, and the difficulty they conceal lies fundamentally in the fact that infinity does not conform to the ordinary conditions of a number or a quantity, so that ∞/∞ only means for the mathematician the limit of x/y, as x and y both tend to infinity. This may be 1 if $y = x$, 0 if $y = x^2$, or ∞ if $y = 1/x$, and so on.[13]

It is for some of these reasons, and many more, that Marshall McLuhan writes,

> Indeed, the mathematical Leibnitz saw in the mystic elegance of the binary system of *zero* and *1* the image of Creation. The unity of the Supreme Being operating in the void by binary function would, he felt, suffice to make all beings from the void.[14]

Today's computer programmers, or those familiar with Boolean logic, likely grasp the rough gist of this sentiment, especially as it pertains to their creation of simulated environments. They routinely deal in modes of orderliness that were made possible by the orderliness of the larger universe.

Mathematical truths represent some of the clearest examples of eternal verities, and we can appreciate that the orderliness that resulted in the cosmos and produced life and humanity also founded the regularities discoverable within the world of mathematics. Warren Sturgis McCulloch asked the question, "What is a number, that a man may know it, and a man, that he may know a number?"[15] We can ask, in parallel fashion: "What is nothing, that people may know of it, and people, that they may know of nothing?" Only those who understand how life and humanity are actually the cosmos itself paradoxically folding back upon itself (i.e., those who comprehend how we are not not the cosmos), can appreciate the significance of such questions.

NOTES

1. D. E. Harding writes, "It is God himself who is the arch-unknower! God (or whatever you call him or her who is No-thingness and Source and Awareness and Being) can't possibly understand how he gave rise to himself, how he pulled himself up by his own bootstraps out of blank non-existence, how he woke himself from that deepest of sleeps, from that long and dreamless night," in *On Having No Head: Zen and the Rediscovery of the Obvious* (Carlsbad, CA: InnerDirections, 2002), 105–106. Henri Bergson has noted, "There is *more*, and not *less*, in the idea of an object conceived as 'not existing' than in the idea of this same object conceived as 'existing.' For the idea of the object 'not existing' is necessarily the idea of the object 'existing' with, in addition, a representation of an exclusion of this object by the actual reality taken in block," in *Creative Evolution*, trans. Arthur Mitchell (New York: Random House, 1944), 311. We might use Bergson's line of reasoning to suggest, speculatively, that God was paradoxically able to "add" something to Itself by somehow imaginatively positing Itself as *Not-Being*: that imaginative positing is the cosmos itself. In this context, we can include a fitting observation by Brian Rotman: "If the Christian ascetic courted heretical nihilism by pursuing a divine union of self with God . . . then Christian mysticism . . . by seeking oneness with God represented, for orthodox theology, the extreme nihilistic heresy of divine usurpation, a hubristic assumption by the mystic of the original nothingness of God himself," in *Signifying Nothing: The Semiotics of Zero* (Stanford: Stanford University Press, 1987), 69.

2. The mythological-mathematical language here, *indeterminate over undefined*, is meant to signify, however vaguely and metaphorically, the need for time and space, respectively. Kenneth Burke, following out negative theology to the end of the line, writes, "[I]nsofar as the 'infinitely inclusive' is the 'all-inclusive,' the 'infinity' of 'everything' is as negative as zero . . . inasmuch as 'God,' the 'most perfect being' . . . would be the most-inclusive term; hence the approach to him would be as the mystic approach to total negation," in *Language as Symbolic Action: Essays on Life, Literature and Method* (Berkeley: University of California Press, 1966), 457.

3. Both "One" and "Infinity" were not rigorously and fully themselves until zero helped to complete their possible modes of relation.

4. Exemplar cases include a variable *as* a variable (e.g., X or Y) pure and simple, and a person *as* a person, (i.e., attending to "personhood" as a possibility in principle rather than attending to the fact of any single, particular existing individual).

5. Whatever actually comes to exist always remains finite and fleeting, meaning haunted by non-being (i.e., its possible nonexistence).

6. Nonexistence preconception is an exemplar, as are one's own dreamless sleep and one's own death.

7. Emil Cioran, *The Trouble With Being Born*, trans. Richard Howard (New York: Viking, 1976), 119. Cioran dispatches a "prayer" of his sentiment regarding this formidable occasion: "Lord . . . Grant me the miracle gathered before the first moment, the peace which You could not tolerate and which incited you to breach the nothingness in order to make way for this carnival of time, and thereby to condemn me to the universe—to humiliation and the shame of Being," in *A Short History of Decay*, trans. Richard Howard (New York: Arcade, 2012), 86–87.

8. See Hans Jonas, "Immortality and the Modern Temper" in his book, *The Phenomenon of Life: Toward a Philosophical Biology* (Chicago: The University of Chicago Press, 1966). Also, Kenneth Burke suggests that "as regards our whole universe, with its constant succession of cosmic cataclysms, the endless turmoil of its belching suns and nebulae, the constant hurrying of its electric particles back and forth across thousands and thousands of light years, conceivably it is a damned creature, a single mighty organism thrashing eternally in distress, and with nowhere to go to escape itself," in *The Rhetoric of Religion: Studies in Logology* (Berkeley: University of California Press, 1970), 267. We might speculatively entertain his rather "impo-

tent" pantheistic depiction by acknowledging that such a universe would be *after* the introduction of nothing.

9. See Robert Kaplan, *The Nothing That Is: A Natural History of Zero* (New York: Oxford University Press, 2000).

10. Consider, too, that any number to the power of 1 equals itself, yet any number, except 0, to the power of 0 equals 1, and, nevertheless, 0 to the power of 0 remains undefined, or perhaps 1 in some cases. In this regard, ambiguities abound whenever 0 is used as a power or as a denominator

11. Brian Rotman, in *Signifying Nothing*, writes, "Zero is to number signs, as the vanishing point is to perspective images, as imaginary money is to money signs. In all three codes, the sign introduced is a sign about signs, a *meta-sign*, whose meaning is to indicate, via a syntax which arrives with it, the absence of certain other signs. . . . One can ask: What is the impact on a written code when a sign for Nothing, or more precisely when a sign for the absence of other signs, enters its lexicon? What can be said through the agency of such a sign that could not be said, was unsayable, without it?" *Signifying Nothing*, 1–2

12. Norbert Weiner, *God and Golem, Inc.* (Cambridge, MA: The MIT Press, 1964), 8.

13. Weiner, *God and Golem, Inc.*, 7.

14. Marshall McLuhan, *Understanding Media: Extensions of Man* (Corte Madera, CA: Gingko, 2003), 155–56.

15. Warren McCulloch, " What Is a Number, That a Man May Know It, and a Man, That He May Know a Number?" *General Semantics Bulletin* 26 and 27 (1961): 7–18.

Bibliography

Abram, David. *The Spell of the Sensuous: Perception and Language in a More-Than-Human World*. New York: Vintage, 1996.
Ackerman, Diane. *A Natural History of the Senses*. New York: Random House, 1990.
Anton, Corey. "About Talk: The Category of Talk-Reflexive Words." *Semiotica* 121, no. 3–4 (1998): 193–212.
———. "Alphabetic Print-Based Literacy, Hermeneutic Sociality and Philosophic Culture." *The Review of Communication* 17, no. 4, (2017): 257–72.
———. "Beyond the Constitutive/Representational Dichotomy: The Phenomenological Notion of Intentionality." *Communication Theory* 9, no. 1 (1999): 26–57.
———. "Beyond Theoretical Ethics: Bakhtinian Anti-theoreticism." *Human Studies: A Journal for Philosophy and the Social Sciences* 24, no. 3 (2001): 211–25.
———. "Communication: The Act and Art of Taking for Granted." *ETC: A Review of General Semantics* 75, no. 1–2 (2018): 47–66.
———. "Diachronic Phenomenology: A Methodological Thread within Media Ecology." *Explorations in Media Ecology: The Journal of the Media Ecology Association* 13, no. 1 (2014): 3–30.
———. "Dialogue with Richard Lang (Who Are We?)." YouTube. https://www.youtube.com/watch?v=hDfd5tZvpIw.
———. "Discourse as Care: A Phenomenological Consideration of Spatiality and Temporality." *Human Studies: A Journal for Philosophy and the Social Sciences* 25, no. 2 (2002): 185–205.
———. "Dreamless Sleep and the Whole of Human Life: An Ontological Exposition." *Human Studies: A Journal for Philosophy and the Social Sciences* 29, no. 2 (2006): 181–202.
———. "Futuralness as Freedom: Moving Toward the Past that Will-Have-Been." In *Media and the Apocalypse*, edited by Kylo-Patrick R. Hart and Annette M. Holba, 189–202. New York: Peter Lang, 2009.
———. "Lanigan's 'Encyclopedic Dictionary': Key Concepts, Insights, and Advances." In *Communicology for the Human Sciences: Lanigan and The Philosophy of Communication*, edited by Andrew R. Smith, Isaac E. Catt, and Igor Klyukanov, 49–70. Pittsburg: Duquesne University Press, 2017.
———. "A Levels Orientation to Abstraction, Logical Typing, and Language More Generally." In *Paradox Lost: A Cross-Contextual Definition of Levels of Abstraction*, edited by Linda Elson. Cresskill, NJ: Hampton, 2010, 183–201.
———. "On the Nonlinearity of Human Communication: Insatiability, Context, Form." *The Atlantic Journal of Communication* 15, no. 2 (2007): 79–102.

———. "Playing with Bateson: Denotation, Logical Types, and Analog and Digital Communication." *The American Journal of Semiotics* 19, no. 1–4 (2003): 129–54.

———. "Presence and Interiority: Walter Ong's Contributions to a Diachronic Phenomenology of Voice." In *Of Ong and Media Ecology: Essays in Communication, Composition, and Literary Studies*, edited by Thomas J. Farrell and Paul Soukup, 71–90. Cresskill, NJ: Hampton, 2012.

———. *Selfhood and Authenticity*. Albany: State University of New York Press, 2001.

———. *Sources of Significance: Worldly Rejuvenation and Neo-Stoic Heroism*. West Lafayette, IN: Purdue University Press, 2010.

———. "Syntagmatic and Paradigmatic Synergism: Notes on Lanigan's 'Encyclopedic Dictionary.'" *The Atlantic Journal of Communication* 25, no. 1, (2017): 48–63.

———. "Technology, Hypocrisy, and Morality: Where, Oh Where, Has All the Hypocrisy Gone?" *Explorations in Media Ecology: The Journal of the Media Ecology Association* 17, no. 2 (2018): 119–35.

Ball, Philip. *Life's Matrix: A Biography of Water*. Berkeley: University of California Press, 2001.

Bakhtin, Mikhail M. *Art and Answerability*. Translated by Vadim Liapunov. Austin: University of Texas Press, 1990.

Bateson, Gregory. "The Message, 'This Is Play.'" In *Group Processes*, edited by Bertram Schaffner. New York: Josiah Macy Jr. Foundation, 1956.

———. *Mind and Nature: A Necessary Unity*. New York: Bantam, 1979.

———. *Steps to an Ecology of Mind*. New York: Ballantine, 1972.

———. "A Theory of Play and Fantasy: A Report on the Theoretical Aspects of the Project for Study of the Role of Paradoxes of Abstraction in Communication." *Approaches to the Study of Human Personality: Psychiatric Research Reports* no 2 (1955).

Becker, Ernest. "An Anti-idealist Statement on Communication." *Communication* 1, no 1 (1974): 121–27.

———. "The Spectrum of Loneliness." In *The Ernest Becker Reader*, edited by Daniel Liechty. Seattle: University of Washington Press, 2005.

Benatar, David. *Better Never to Have Been: The Harm of Coming into Existence*. New York: Oxford University Press, 2006.

Bergson, Henri. *Creative Evolution*. Translated by Arthur Mitchell. New York: Random House, 1944.

Berman, Morris. *Coming to Our Senses: Body and Spirit in the Hidden History of the West*. New York: Bantam, 1989.

Bierce, Ambrose. *The Devil's Dictionary*. Mineola, NY: Dover, 1993.

Bohm, David. *On Dialogue*. New York: Routledge, 2004.

Boorstin, Daniel J. *The Image: A Guide to Pseudo-Events in America*. New York: Atheneum, 1961.

Burke, Kenneth. *A Grammar of Motives and A Rhetoric of Motives*. New York: The World Publishing Co., 1962.

———. *Language as Symbolic Action: Essays on Life, Literature and Method*. Berkeley: University of California Press, 1966.

———. *The Rhetoric of Religion: Studies in Logology*. Berkeley: University of California Press, 1970.

Canetti, Elias. *Crowds and Power*. New York: Farrar, Straus, and Giroux, 1984.

Cioran, Emil M. *On the Heights of Despair*. Translated by Ilinca Zarifopol-Johnson. Chicago: University of Chicago Press, 1992.

———. *A Short History of Decay*. Translated by Richard Howard. New York: Arcade, 2012.

———. *Tears and Saints*. Translated by Ilinca Zarifopol-Johnson. Chicago: University of Chicago Press, 1995.

———. *The Temptation to Exist*. Translated by Richard Howard. New York: Arcade, 2012.

———. *The Trouble with Being Born*. Translated by Richard Howard. New York: Viking Press, 1976.

Crystal, David. "Un-Finished." *Around the Globe* 17 (2001): 22–23.

Deacon, Terrence W. *Incomplete Nature: How Mind Emerged from Matter*. New York: W. W. Norton and Co., 2012.
De Saint-Exupéry, Antoine. *The Wisdom of the Sands*. Translated by Stuart Gilbert. New York: Harcourt, Brace and Company, 1950.
Dunbar, Robin. *Grooming, Gossip, and the Evolution of Language*. Cambridge, MA: Harvard University Press, 1997.
Elson, Linda. *Paradox Lost: A Cross-Contextual Definition of Levels of Abstraction*. Cresskill, NJ: Hampton, 2010.
Flusser, Vilém. *Into the Universe of Technical Images*. Translated by Nancy A. Roth. Minneapolis, MN: University of Minnesota Press, 2011.
———. *Writings*. Translated by Erik Eisel. Minneapolis: University of Minnesota Press, 2002.
Frankfurt, Harry G. *On Bullshit*. Princeton, NJ: Princeton University Press, 2005.
Freedman, David H. "New Theory on How the Aggressive Egg Attracts Sperm." *Discover Magazine*, June 1992.
Gass, William H. *Habitations of the Word*. New York: Simon and Shuster, 1985.
Goffman, Erving. *Interaction Ritual: Essays on Face-to-Face Behavior*. New York: Pantheon Books, 1967.
———. *Strategic Interaction*. Philadelphia: University of Philadelphia Press, 1967.
Gordon, Lewis. *Bad Faith and Anti-Black Racism*. New York: Prometheus, 1999.
Groopman, Jerome. "The Body Strikes Back." *The New York Review of Books* 66, no. 5 (March 21, 2019).
Gusdorf, Georges. *Speaking (La Parole)*. Translated by Paul T. Brockelman. Evanston, IL: Northwestern University Press, 1965.
Harari, Yuval Noah. *Sapiens: A Brief History of Human Kind*. New York: HarperCollins, 2015
Harding, Douglas E. *On Having No Head: Zen and the Rediscovery of the Obvious*. Carlsbad, CA: InnerDirections, 2002.
———. *The Hierarchy of Heaven and Earth*. London: Shollond Trust, 2011.
Heidegger, Martin. *Basic Writings*. Translated by David Farrell Krell. San Francisco: Harper Collins, 1993.
———. *Being and Time*. Translated by Joan Stambaugh. Albany: State University of New York Press, 1997.
———. *The Concept of Time*. Translated by William McNeill. Cambridge, MA: Blackwell, 1992.
———. *Existence and Being*. Translated by R. F. C. Hull and Alan Crick. Chicago: Henry Regnery Co., 1967.
Hofstadter, Douglas R. *I Am a Strange Loop*. New York: Basic, 2008.
Holenstein, Elmar. *Roman Jakobson's Approach to Language: Phenomenological Structuralism*. Translated by Catherine Schelbert and Tarcisius Schelbert. Bloomington: Indiana University Press, 1976.
Jonas, Hans. *The Phenomenon of Life: Toward a Philosophical Biology*. Chicago: The University of Chicago Press, 1966.
Kaplan, Robert. *The Nothing That Is: A Natural History of Zero*. New York: Oxford University Press, 2000.
Kauffman, Walter. *Without Guilt and Justice*. New York: Delta, 1973.
Klyukanov, Igor E. *A Communication Universe: Manifestations of Meaning, Stagings of Significance*. Lanham, MD: Lexington, 2010.
Koestler, Arthur. *The Ghost in the Machine*. London: Pan, 1967.
Konner, Joan. *You Don't Have to Be Buddhist to Know Nothing*. Amherst, NY: Prometheus, 2009.
Korzybski, Alfred. *Science and Sanity: An Introduction to Non-Aristotelian Systems and General Semantics*, 5th ed. Englewood, NJ: The International Non-Aristotelian Library/Institute of General Semantics, 1993.
Laing, Ronald David. *The Politics of Experience*. New York: Pantheon, 1976.
———. *The Voice of Experience*. New York: Pantheon, 1982.
Laing, Ronald David, and David Graham Cooper. *Reason and Violence: A Decade of Sartre's Philosophy, 1950–1960*. New York: Pantheon, 1971.

Laing, Ronald David, Herbert Phillipson, and A. Russell Lee. *Interpersonal Perception: A Theory and a Method of Research*. New York: Springer, 1996.

Lakoff, George, and Mark Johnson. *Metaphors We Live By*. Chicago: University of Chicago Press, 1980.

Langer, Susanne K. *Philosophy in a New Key: A Study in the Symbolism of Reason, Rite and Art*. New York: Mentor, 1942.

Lanigan, Richard. *The Human Science of Communicology: A Phenomenology of Discourse in Foucault and Merleau-Ponty*. Pittsburgh: Duquesne University Press, 1992.

Leder, Drew. *The Absent Body*. Chicago: The University of Chicago Press, 1990.

Lee, Dorothy. *Freedom and Culture*. Englewood Cliffs, NJ: Prentice Hall, 1959.

———. *Valuing the Self: What We Can Learn from Other Cultures*. Englewood Cliffs, NJ: Prentice Hall, 1976.

Lingis, Alphonso. *The Community of Those Who Have Nothing in Common*. Bloomington: Indiana University Press, 1994.

Margulis, Lynn. *Symbiotic Planet: A New Look at Evolution*. New York: Basic, 1998.

Margulis, Lynn, and Dorion Sagan. *Acquiring Genomes: A Theory of the Origins of Species*. New York: Basic Books, 2002.

———. *Microcosmos: Four Billion Years of Microbial Evolution*. Berkeley: University of California Press, 1986.

———. *What Is Life?* Berkeley: University of California Press, 2000.

McCulloch, Warren Sturgis. "What Is a Number, That a Man May Know It, and a Man, That He May Know a Number?" *General Semantics Bulletin* 26 and 27 (1961): 7–18.

McLuhan, Eric. *The Sensus Communis: Synesthesia and the Soul: An Odyssey*. Toronto: BPS, 2015.

McLuhan, Marshall. *Understanding Media: Extensions of Man*. Corte Madera, CA: Gingko, 2003.

McLuhan, Marshall, and Quentin Fiore. *The Medium Is the Massage: An Inventory of Effects*. Corte Madera, CA: Ginko, 1967.

McQuain, Jeff, and Stan Malless. *Coined by Shakespeare: Words and Meanings First Used by the Bard*. Springfield, MA: Merriam-Webster, 1998.

Merleau-Ponty, Maurice. *Phenomenology of Perception*. Translated by Colin Smith. New Jersey: The Humanities Press, 1962.

———. *The Prose of the World*. Translated by John O'Neill. Evanston, IL: Northwestern University Press, 1973.

———. *The Visible and the Invisible*. Translated by Alphonso Lingis. Evanston, IL: Northwestern University Press, 1968.

MinuteEarth. "You Are a Fish." YouTube. https://www.youtube.com/watch?v=yyeDgBm1Du8.

Oliver, John. "Psychics." *Last Week Tonight*. YouTube. https://www.youtube.com/watch?v=WhMGcp9xIhY.

Ong, Walter J. *Interfaces of the Word: Studies in the Evolution of Consciousness and Culture*. Ithaca: Cornell University Press, 1977.

———. *Orality and Literacy: The Technologizing of the Word*. London: Methuen, 1982.

———. *The Presence of the Word: Some Prolegomena for Cultural and Religious History*. Binghamton, NY: Global, 1967.

Paine, Thomas. *The Age of Reason*. Lexington: Edward Bulwer-Lytton, 2015 (1794).

Rotman, Brian. *Signifying Nothing: The Semiotics of Zero*. Stanford, CA: Stanford University Press, 1987.

Sartre, Jean-Paul. *Being and Nothingness*. Translated by Hazel E. Barnes. New Jersey: Gramercy Books, 1956.

———. "Existentialism Is a Humanism." Translated by Philip Mairet. In *The Existential Tradition*, edited by N. Langiulli. New York: Double Day, 1971.

Schrag, Calvin O. *God as Otherwise Than Being: Toward a Semantics of the Gift*. Evanston, IL: Northwestern University Press, 2002.

———. *The Self after Postmodernity*. New Haven, CT: Yale University Press, 1997.

Simmel, Georg. *On Individuality and Social Forms: Selected Writings*, edited by Donald. N. Levine, Chicago: The University of Chicago Press, 1971.
———. *The Philosophy of Money.* Translated by David Frisby, Kaethe Mengelberg, and T. B. Bottomore. New York: Routledge, 1990.
———. *Simmel on Culture.* Edited by David Frisby and Mike Featherstone. Thousand Oaks, CA: Sage, 2000.
Straus, Erwin. *Phenomenological Psychology.* New York: Basic, 1966.
———. *The Primary World of Senses.* New York: Free Press of Glencoe, 1963.
Strate, Lance. *Media Ecology: An Approach to Understanding the Human Condition.* New York: Peter Lang, 2017.
Thayer, Lee. *Pieces: Toward a Revisioning of Communication/Life.* Norwood, NJ: Ablex, 1997.
Watts, Alan. *The Book: On the Taboo against Knowing Who You Are.* New York: Vintage, 1966.
Watzlawick, Paul, Janet H. Beavin, and Don D. Jackson. *Pragmatics of Human Communication.* New York: W. W. Norton and Company, 1967.
Weiner, Norbert. *God and Golem, Inc.* Cambridge, MA: The MIT Press, 1964.
Wilden, Anthony. *Man and Woman, War and Peace: The Strategist's Companion.* New York: Routledge and Kegan Paul, 1987.
———. *The Rules Are No Game: The Strategy of Communication.* New York: Routledge and Kegan Paul, 1987.
———. *System and Structure: Essays in Communication and Exchange.* London: Tavistock, 1972.
Wittgenstein, Ludwig. *Notebooks, 1914–1916.* Translated by G. E. M. Anscombe. New York: Harper and Row, 1961.

Index

a-historicist fallacy, 115
a-naturalist fallacy, 10–12, 14, 18, 21, 27, 30, 32, 35, 41, 53, 56–61, 80n41, 103, 115, 120n59, 136
Abram, David, 56, 79n36
Adams, John, 131
absence, 1, 13, 13–14, 24, 32, 34–35, 37, 40n68, 41, 42, 43, 50, 55–56, 64, 67, 77, 81n52, 83, 92, 106, 108, 109, 117, 120n66, 124, 135, 136, 146, 159n48, 163, 167n11, functional absence, 83, 105, 111, 114, 117n4, 118n25, 159n48. *See also* constraint
abstinence, 149
abstraction, 6, 90, 92, 93, 94, 95, 99, 101–56, 111, 117n4; paradoxes of, 100–101
Ackerman, Diane, 79n26, 79n35
Acquiring Genomes, 45, 78n9
action, ix, 29, 38, 43, 51, 73, 77, 92, 104, 110, 123, 125, 134; contrasted with motion, 26, 29, 134; symbolic action, 27, 111
actuality, 49, 50, 53, 57
aesthetic consummation, 72–73
afterlife, 124–127, 128–129, 129, 133, 138, 146, 150; denial of, ix, 126, 128, 129, 163; sympathies for belief in, 75, 118n10, 129, 133, 155; varieties in afterlife beliefs, 125–126

The Age of Reason, 132, 157n5, 157n9, 157n16–157n21, 158n24
agency, ix, 5, 8, 29, 32–33, 38, 110, 127, 134–135; denial of, ix, 40n63, 134; funded through communication technologies, 29, 120n72, 167n11. *See also* freedom
ancestor worship, 3
anguish, 22, 24–25, 26, 52, 54, 127, 138, 139, 159n45; contrasted with fear, 17, 24–25, 26. *See also* dread
antiques, 8
Anton, Corey, 39n16, 79n23, 79n31, 79n35, 82n68, 117n4, 117n6, 118n17, 118n22–118n23, 119n29, 119n43, 119n52, 120n62, 120n72, 157n8, 158n37, 159n48
athletics, 6, 53, 74

Ball, Philip, 78n8, 80n41
Bad Faith and Anti-Black Racism, 81n64
Bakhtin, Mikhail M., 72
Bateson, Gregory, 89, 90, 92, 93, 99–102, 104–105, 108, 120n59
Beavin, Janet H., 108
Becker, Ernest, 94, 135–136
being, 2, 6, 7, 13, 16, 17, 19, 21, 31, 37, 41, 44, 67, 82n72, 85, 106, 115, 117n5, 156, 161–163, 166n1; extant, 4, 20; live, 20; exist, 20. *See also* existence
being-in-itself, 21, 22, 68

175

being-for-itself, 21, 22, 68, 70, 72, 87
being-for-others, 68, 69, 70, 87, 155
Being and Nothingness, 21, 22
Benatar, David, 151, 152–153
Better Never to Have Been, 151
Bergson, Henri, 13–15, 28, 74, 102, 166n1
Berman, Morris, 81n52, 81n63
Bierce, Ambrose, 90, 150
Bohm, David, 80n42
A Biography of Water, 80n41
Boorstin, Daniel J., 99
The Book, 80n42
Buber, Martin, 145
Burke, Kenneth, 3, 11, 26–32, 39n36, 79n37, 88, 89, 102, 105–106, 111–112, 113–114, 116, 117, 117n4, 117n5, 118n25, 120n59, 121n75, 121n82, 166n2, 166n8

Cage, John, 110
Campbell, Joseph, 41, 127
Canetti, Elias, 75
celibacy, 149
Christianity, 4, 114, 121n83, 128, 143, 157n7, 158n31
Cioran, Emil M., 90, 144, 148, 150, 154, 156n1, 159n45, 159n51, 162–163, 166n7
clothing, 90, 108, 121n75; connected to afterlife beliefs, 90, 148
Coined by Shakespeare, 119n38
Columbo, 109
The Community of Those Who Have Nothing in Common, 2, 109
confiscation, 71
Cooper, David G., 41
conscience, 29, 37, 88, 110–111, 123, 130, 134, 137; call to, 1, 138; connected to money and property rights, 111, 113–114, 115
constraint, 40n68, 63, 83, 88, 110, 113, 120n72. *See also* functional absence
context, 20, 91, 96, 106–109, 120n59, 134, 159n48; choice of context vs. context of choice, 107
cosmic hide-n-seek, 161
cowardice, 26
Crowds and Power, 75
Crystal, David, 119n37

Darwin, Charles, 135; Darwinian evolution, 45, 48
Davis, Miles, 109
Deacon, Terrence W., 32–36, 43, 63, 80n41, 117n4, 118n28, 120n72
death, 1, 2, 20, 44–47, 75, 76, 79n21, 124, 133, 148, 149, 154, 158n29; acceptance of, ix, 38, 127, 144–145, 148; being-toward-death, 1, 2, 25, 124, 155, 156n1; compared to sleep, 75–76, 118n10, 155, 166n6; fear of, 144, 154, 159n42; inescapability of, 78n15, 79n21, 124, 139; of deathbed, 1, 124; programmed death, 44–47, 130. *See also* ontogeny
deception, 90, 94, 95, 128; cues to, 109
destruction, 22, 23
de Saint-Exupéry, Antoine, 80n43
determinism, 22, 26, 33
don't, 26, 28, 29–30, 30, 34, 37, 88, 110, 111, 120n72, 121n76, 130, 134; contrasted with is not, 28, 30, 37, 88, 110
dread, 17, 19, 20, 24, 138, 139, 156n1. *See also* anguish
dreamless sleep, 1, 3, 14, 74–77, 77, 81n59, 118n10, 155, 166n1, 166n6. *See also* nothingness
dreams, 74, 88–90, 94, 138; ghosts appearing in, 90, 138; movies as canned dreams, 94
Dunbar, Robin, 39n19

Eckhart, Meister, 116
Eleanor Rigby, 158n26
Elements of Geometry, 132
Elson, Linda, 118n17, 169
Emerson, Ralph W., 116
eschatology, 128, 148, 149
Euclid, 132
eukaryote, 44–48
existence, 2, 3, 17, 19–20, 54, 80n41, 105, 124, 133, 145, 147, 152, 158n29, 162, 163, 166n5; eventfulness of, 51; as gift, 145. *See also* being

fashion, 7
final causality, 29
Fiore, Quentin, 116
Flusser, Vilém, 39n45, 145–146, 158n38

formal causality, 28
fragility, 23, 69; precipitating care, 127
Frankfurt, Harry G., 118n19
Freedman, David H., 119n57
freedom, 20, 22, 24, 25–26, 39n45, 70, 72, 127, 134–135; condemned to freedom, 22, 26; liberated through communication technologies, 121n73. *See also* agency
Freedom and Culture, 120n59
Freud, Sigmund, 89, 90, 135
Fuller, Buckminster, 116
functional absence. *See* absence; constraint

games, 6–7, 53
Gass, William H., 75, 134
The Ghost in the Machine, 43
Goffman, Erving, 40n64, 109
Gordon, Lewis, 81n64
grammatical mood, 103–104
Groopman, Jerome, 119n57
Gusdorf, Georg, 40n54

Habitations of the Word, 118n26
Harding, Douglas E., 63, 64–68, 74, 81n61, 154, 166n1
headlessness, 64–68, 70, 72, 77, 81n52, 129
Heidegger, Martin, 1, 16–20, 21, 26, 30, 31, 158n29
Hofstadter, Douglas R., 155
Holenstein, Elmar, 95–98, 108, 118n24

I Am a Strange Loop, 155
imagination, 4, 5, 10, 12, 13, 18, 24, 50, 53, 60, 62, 90, 94, 124, 126, 128, 134, 135, 155, 159n45
incomplete, 37, 42, 73, 77, 123, 124
Incomplete Nature, 32
incompleteness, 1, 3, 5, 32, 33, 37, 41, 42, 77; bodily incompleteness, 42–43, 49, 77, 131, 159n48; symbolic incompleteness, 116, 124
infinity, 98, 162, 164, 165, 166n2, 166n3
internal negation. *See* negation
insurance, 8
invariance, 85–86, 98, 124, 134; absent invariance, 96, 124
invariant, 68

Jackson, Don D., 108
Jefferson, Thomas, 131, 157n5
Johnson, Mark, 119n57
Jonas, Hans, 5, 62
justice, 110, 114, 124, 129, 138, 139, 141, 148

Kant, Immanuel, 18
Kaplan, Robert, 164
Kauffman, Walter, 103
Klyukanov, Igor E., 97
Koestler, Arthur, 43
Konner, Joan, 38n7
Korzybski, Alfred, 27, 116

Laing, Ronald David, 6, 41, 42, 46, 109, 120n66
Lakoff, George, 119n57
Langer, Susanne K., 52
language, 3, 9, 28, 31, 33, 40n54, 91, 95, 95–106, 120n59, 136; denotative language, 91, 93, 100; parallels to the body, 83; as self-effacing, 52, 84; as source of non-being, 9, 27, 29, 30, 88, 106, 109; as source of transcendence, 10, 20, 26, 31, 52–53, 53, 54, 84, 86, 87, 103, 111, 114, 120n72, 149; as multileveled, 37, 92, 95, 98, 99–102
Language as Symbolic Action, 27
Lanigan, Richard L., 107
Leder, Drew, 55, 77
Lee, A. Russell, 71–72
Lee, Dorothy, 120n59, 121n74, 153
Life's Matrix, 78n8, 80n41
Lingis, Alphonso, 1, 86, 109
Logology, 31

Malless, Stan, 119n37
Margulis, Lynn, 45, 46, 46–47, 48, 54, 78n11, 78n12, 78n18, 78n20, 79n21, 129, 148, 157n4
McCulloch, Warren Sturgis, 165
McLuhan, Eric, 158n38
McLuhan, Marshall, 39n10, 94, 116, 165
McQuain, Jeff, 119n38
memory, 13–14, 35, 50, 90, 96, 159n45; as metaphysical, 10–12; as Mnemosyne, 11
Metaphors We Live By, 119n57

Merleau-Ponty, Maurice, 85, 98
Microcosmos, 45
miracles, 127, 131, 132, 133, 134, 163, 166n7; life as only miracle, 126, 129, 163
möbius, 155, 162
money, 111–112, 121n73, 136, 167n11; related to Christianity, 113–114, 115; and greed, 114, 115, 136, 138, 139–140
morality, 8, 29, 38, 123–156
morphemes, 98, 99
motion, 26, 29, 134
multiple realizability, 34, 134

negation, 5, 15, 17, 24, 27, 28, 30, 102, 103–105, 117n5, 120n66; analog negation, 119n41; internal negation, 85, 86; of self-identity, 71–72, 73; related to truth, 5; within vision, 55–56
negative theology, 31, 106, 165
negativity, 3, 5, 6, 12, 14, 15, 27, 29, 37, 54, 78n3, 88, 102, 103, 105, 154, 155, 162; related to morality, 28–29, 134; secret sacred sign of, 110–114
New Easter Story, 138–146
Nietzsche, Friedrich, 136
non-being, ix, 2, 3, 4–5, 6, 7–8, 21–22, 22, 23–24, 54, 55, 67, 80n46, 83, 87, 89, 111, 112, 123, 134, 146, 149, 156, 159n48, 161, 162, 164; denial of, 2, 4, 9; inherent in life, 12, 32, 34, 37, 41–42, 44, 46, 47, 123; in language and communication, 95–66; of consciousness, 3, 74–77; related to invariance, 86; related to mystery, 5, 19, 22, 126, 131, 136; related to thought, 6, 8, 18, 36, 37, 89. *See also* dreamless sleep
Notebooks, 159n42
nothing, 2, 3, 3–4, 5, 6, 9, 10, 13, 14, 16, 21, 22, 41, 48, 64, 65, 66, 67, 69, 70, 76, 81n59, 88, 97, 108, 109, 117n5, 118n15, 123, 146, 154, 155, 158n38, 164, 165, 166n8; as idea, 13, 26–27, 83, 88; as metaphysical, 16–19, 20, 21, 30–32, 37, 41, 158n29, 162, 163, 165, 166n1, 166n7, 166n8; contrasted with being, 21, 82n72; implied by perspective, 49, 54, 57–64, 97, 146,

159n48; related to sociality, 69, 71, 73, 81n59, 145
The Nothing That Is, 164
nothingness, 14, 21, 22, 25, 55, 67, 68, 74, 77, 85, 154, 155, 158n29, 162, 166n1, 166n7; related to dreamless sleep, 74–77

On Dialogue, 80n42
Ong, Walter J., 51, 120n72
On Having No Head, 64, 166n1
ontogeny, 130. *See also* programmed death

Paine, Thomas, 131–134, 157n5, 157n9, 157n15, 158n24
panpsychism, 32, 41, 163
paradox, 4, 34, 74, 100–102, 155, 161–163, 165
Parmenides, 4
Plato, 42, 54, 85
play, 90–95, 99, 100, 108, 118n15, 161
Phillipson, Herbert, 81n66
phonemes, 98, 99
Pieces, 118n21
possibilities, ix, 1, 8, 20, 21, 22, 25, 32, 36, 38, 41, 48, 72, 76, 103, 124, 130–131, 144, 145, 146, 149, 150, 155, 162, 164; actualized possibilities, 88, 106, 117; moral possibilities, 114, 115, 123, 136, 146, 163; negating possibilities, 23; related to agency, ix, 5, 22, 26, 35, 50, 77, 87, 120n72, 134, 146, 153, 156, 162; related to thought, 6, 8, 12, 19, 36, 37, 60, 88, 90, 93, 103, 105, 106, 124, 128, 134; spatial possibilities, 37, 43, 47, 49, 50, 53, 57, 65, 77, 87, 110, 163; temporal possibilities, 22, 25, 52, 53, 53–54, 72, 77, 123, 124, 162, 163; unrealized possibilities, 77, 150, 155. *See also* preventive measures
Pragmatics of Human Communication, 108
prayer, 134–135, 136, 143, 163, 166n7
preventive measures, 8, 23, 36, 151
private property, 111, 112–113, 114, 115, 128, 148
psychedelics experiences, 2, 137

questions, 22, 39n36, 103–104

rainbows, 58, 63, 143
redemption, 113, 114, 143
relations, 20, 41, 54, 56, 60, 64, 70, 76, 77, 111, 119n53, 120n59, 147, 162; possible relations, 6, 49, 62, 76, 104, 106, 117, 123; reality of, 41, 57–62, 80n41, 97; self-relation, 20, 21, 25, 26, 70, 95, 136, 163
religious experiences, 136, 158n28
reincarnation, 2, 125
revelation, 127–128, 131–133, 143, 157n5, 158n30; within the *New Easter Story*, 138–139, 139, 142
Rotman, Brian, 119n36, 166n1, 167n11
The Rhetoric of Religion, 27, 31, 113, 121n75, 121n82, 166n8
Roman Jakobson's Approach to Language, 95, 118n24

Sagan, Dorion, 45, 46, 48, 54, 78n20, 79n21, 129, 148
Sartre, Jean-Paul, 1, 21–26, 26, 32, 68, 70, 82n72, 83, 85
self-interest, 70, 128, 146
Schrag, Calvin O., 38n6, 158n34
Selfhood and Authenticity, x
the senses, 50–57; hearing, 4, 50–51, 56; sight, 4, 50–53, 57, 65, 87; smell, 50–51; taste, 50, 79n25; touch, 49, 50, 53, 81n52. *See also* sound; vision
The Sensus Communis, 158n38, 158n39
sex, 42, 149; origin of sex and programmed death, 44–47, 78n11; sexual relations, 111, 121n76
Shakespeare, William, 98
Signifying Nothing, 119n36, 166n1, 167n11
Simmel, Georg, 7, 53, 111, 121n73
social justice, 38, 163
sound, 51–52; of one's native tongue, 83–84

Sources of Significance, x
Steiner, George, 116
Strate, Lance, 120n72
Straus, Erwin, 51, 79n35
sunsets, 63
surplus of seeing, 72
Symposium, 42

Tears and Saints, 158n28
teleology, 34, 40n63
Thayer, Lee, 118n21
A Theory of Play and Fantasy, 90
thou-shalt-nots, 28, 29, 88, 110. *See also* don't
transcendence, 31, 70, 86, 111, 134, 145, 149
transgredience, 72
The Trouble with Being Born, 150, 156n1, 166n7
two-way looking, 66–67, 68, 77, 81n61

undifferentiated, 76, 77, 82n72, 161, 162

virginity, 149, 159n43
vision, 48, 50–51, 52, 53, 54–56, 57, 62, 65, 70, 84. *See also* sight

Watts, Alan, 54, 116, 161
Watzlawick, Paul, 108
Weiner, Norbert, 165
What is Life?, 45, 78n20, 79n21
Wilden, Anthony, 11, 40n68, 92, 99–100, 119n41, 120n65
Wittgenstein, Ludwig, 149, 159n42
work, 62, 63, 88, 120n72; implied by bodily positionality, 60, 61–63

zero, 9, 92, 108, 119n41, 162, 164–165, 165, 166n2, 166n3, 167n11

About the Author

Corey Anton is professor of communication studies at Grand Valley State University and a Fellow of the International Communicology Institute. He is author of *Selfhood and Authenticity*, *Sources of Significance: Worldly Rejuvenation and Neo-Stoic Heroism*, and the collection *Communication Uncovered: General Semantics and Media Ecology*. He is the editor of *Valuation and Media Ecology: Ethics, Morals, and Laws*, the co-editor along with Lance Strate of the collection *Korzybski And . . .* , and co-editor along with Robert K. Logan and Lance Strate of the collection, *Taking Up McLuhan's Cause*. Past editor of the journal *Explorations in Media Ecology* and past president of the Media Ecology Association, Anton currently serves as vice president of the Institute of General Semantics and is on the editorial boards of *The Atlantic Journal of Communication*, *ETC*, and *Explorations in Media Ecology*.

www.ingramcontent.com/pod-product-compliance
Lightning Source LLC
Chambersburg PA
CBHW070640300426
44111CB00013B/2182